SHORTLIST

Edinburgh

WHAT'S NEW | WHAT'S ON | WHAT'S BEST

www.timeout.com/edinburgh

Contents

Balmoral p172

Hotels

In the not so dim and distant past, Edinburgh used to explode into life like a Roman candle during the International Festival and Fringe, before fizzling out just as quickly and allowing the locals to reclaim their city. But the last decade or so has seen the city transformed into a year-round destination, which in turn has created a buoyant demand for accommodation across a range of budgets. Tartan carpets and thistle-patterned wallpaper are becoming things of the past; new investment, particularly from a clutch of ambitious, home-grown hoteliers, has challenged the old-stagers to raise their games.

Almost all places now have Wi-Fi and some top-end hotels have recently opened spas to cater for those after a spot of pampering.

Money matters

If you're planning to visit in the run-up to Hogmanay or during August, or if your stay coincides with a rugby international, you may end up paying a premium for your room; book as early as possible. The flipside is that bargain deals are increasingly commonplace – particularly from October to April, when rates can drop by more than 50 per cent. Significant savings can also sometimes be made if you're prepared to wait until the last minute before booking; most clued-up hoteliers would rather sell their beds at a discount than leave them empty. If you arrive in town without having pre-booked your hotel, it may be worth getting in touch with the Edinburgh &

Royal Scots Club p172

Lothians Tourist Board (pp187-9). Staff can make reservations for hotels across the city direct from its office for a small booking fee.

Many hotels have disabled access and specially adapted rooms; the Edinburgh & Lothians Tourist Board can provide a comprehensive list. Other advice is available from Edinburgh City Council and Grapevine (www.lothiancil.org.uk).

Old Town

Apex International & Apex City

31-35 Grassmarket, EH1 2HS (300 3456/fax 220 5345/www.apexhotels. co.uk). Bus 2, 23, 27, 41, 42. **£££.**
The Apex International's dramatic 2002 transformation from bland mid-market residence to sleek designer spot still holds steady, epitomising mainstream contemporary style. All the rooms are decorated identically. Superior rooms and rooftop restaurant Heights boast stunning views of the castle and there's also a Japanese-inspired Yu Spa.

Bank Hotel

1 South Bridge, EH1 1LL (556 9940/ fax 558 1362/www.festival-inns.co.uk). Nicolson Street–North Bridge buses. **£££.**
The Bank's nine rooms, situated above popular post-work hangout Logie Baird's Bar, are accessed via a hidden doorway at the rear. The mood is determinedly Caledonian, with wood panelling and dark tartan furnishings. Each bedroom is themed around a famous Scottish figure: the James Young Simpson room, named after the pioneer of anaesthetics, contains anatomical sketches, while the Thomas Telford room, in honour of the builder of bridges and aqueducts, is dominated by a black four-poster construction over the bed.

Ibis Edinburgh Centre

6 Hunter Square, EH1 1QW (240 7000/fax 240 7007/www.ibishotel.com). Nicolson Street–North Bridge buses. **£.**
The Ibis chain has a reputation for efficiency and good value, and a tendency towards thoroughly bland anonymity. Its sole Edinburgh operation lives up (and down) to all three characteristics: you know exactly what you're going to

get, even if you won't really remember much about it. Pricing aside, the best bit is the central location, just a few steps away from the Royal Mile.

MacDonald Holyrood Hotel

81 Holyrood Road, EH8 8AU (0870 194 2106/www.macdonaldhotels.co.uk). Bus 35, 36. **£££.**
Located a caber's toss from the new Scottish Parliament, the Holyrood Hotel, perhaps unsurprisingly, was built with the business traveller in mind. The rooms are furnished with maple wood and splashes of Harris tweed, and equipped with heated mirrors to banish the post-shower haze. There's an impressive restaurant, a well-equipped gym and a pool, and, on the Club Floor, a private butler to attend to your every whim.

Paramount Carlton

North Bridge, EH1 1SD (472 3000/ fax 556 2691/www.paramount-hotels.co.uk). Nicolson Street–North Bridge buses. **£££.**
The block-long Carlton offers fine views of the city from every room, something that even its five-star competitors can't match. A dramatic and long-overdue renovation a couple of years back transformed its previously tired appearance, and guests are now greeted by a grand reception with contemporary lighting, pale marble flooring and an imposing staircase. The rooms have also all been revamped, although the style is comfortable rather than cutting-edge.

Radisson SAS Hotel

80 High Street, Royal Mile, EH1 1TH (557 9797/www.radissonsas.com). Bus 35/Nicolson Street–North Bridge buses. **£££.**
Constructed in the late 1980s, the Radisson's faux-Gothic façade was designed to blend with its historic neighbours (judge for yourself whether it succeeds). The interior style is cleancut, sleek and monochromatic, albeit with subtle contemporary Scottish motifs. Just off the main entrance, the

SHORTLIST

Best for foodies
- Balmoral (p172)
- Prestonfield (p181)
- Witchery by the Castle (p172)

Best boutique
- Bonham (p174)
- Borough (p180)
- Glasshouse (p179)
- Rick's (p176)

Budget central
- Frederick House (p174)
- Ibis Edinburgh (170)
- Centre (p170)
- Travelodge (p172)

Something different
- Original Raj (p182)
- Royal Scots Club (p172)
- Salisbury Green (p181)

Here on business
- Apex International (p170)
- MacDonald Holyrood Hotel (p171)
- Point (p181)

Traditional Edinburgh
- George (p175)
- Hilton Caledonian (p175)
- Howard (p175)
- Scotsman (p172)

Latest arrivals
- Hudson (p175)
- Le Monde (p176)
- Tigerlily (p176)

Down at the docks
- Holiday Inn Express (p179)
- Malmaison (p182)

Tucked away
- Channings (p178)
- Royal Terrace (p179)

Party on the doorstep
- Tailors Hall (p172)

Simply enormous
- Radisson SAS (p171)
- Sheraton Grand (p182)

ESSENTIALS

newly opened Itchycoo bar-restaurant has an island bar, stainless steel and black surrounds and huge 3D photographic portraits of 20th-century icons (Warhol, Picasso et al) by Edinburgh actor/artist Bob Kingdom. Another bonus: ample parking space.

Royal Scots Club
29-30 Abercromby Place, EH3 6QE (556 4270/fax 558 3769/www.royal scotsclub.com). Bus 13, 23, 27. **£££.**
A gentlemen's club vibe is still very much in evidence on entering this classic Georgian townhouse, just a short walk from Princes Street. Founded in 1919 as a tribute to those who fell in the Great War, the Royal Scots Club today exudes a strong sense of history and a palpable air of tranquillity. The modernised rooms have been tastefully furnished in a traditional style; some have four-poster beds and fine views towards the Firth of Forth. Classic features abound, most eye-catchingly in the shape of the real fire in the lounge.

Scotsman
20 North Bridge, EH1 1YT (556 5565/www.thescotsmanhotel.co.uk). Nicolson Street–North Bridge buses. **££££.**
The former offices of the *Scotsman* now house the state-of-the-art Escape Health Club, the über-chic Cowshed Spa complete with stainless steel swimming pool, and the Vermilion restaurant, plus individually decorated rooms with estate tweeds and original art, plus a well-stocked wine bar and privacy hatch for delivering room service. The corner turret rooms house giant step-up baths as well.

Tailors Hall
139 Cowgate, EH1 1JS (622 6801/ www.festival-inns.co.uk). Nicolson Street–North Bridge buses. **££.**
Smack in the middle of the Old Town, right on the historic Cowgate, this 17th-century building overlooks the busy courtyard of the Three Sisters bar. Tip: if you plan to get at least some shut-eye, ask for a room in the quieter new wing. The interior is thoroughly modern, and while rooms vary greatly in size and shape, they're uniformly clean and comfortable.

Travelodge
33 St Mary's Street, EH1 1TA (0870 191 1637/fax 557 3681/www. travelodge.co.uk). Bus 35/Nicolson Street–North Bridge buses. **£.**
The review of the Ibis (p170) could virtually double up for the Travelodge, since the same perks (keen value, reliability) and caveats (it looks as if it was designed by a committee somewhere outside Slough) apply here. Once again the location is key: it's in the heart of the Old Town.

Witchery by the Castle
352 Castlehill, EH1 2NF (225 5613/ www.thewitchery.com). Bus 35/ Nicolson Street–North Bridge buses. **££££.**
Taking its name from the witches once burned at the stake nearby, the historic, romantic and charismatic Witchery is not so much a hotel as a restaurant with a few suites attached. Each one is dark, theatrically Gothic: all sumptuous leather and velvet upholstery, claw-foot Victorian baths and grand, carved wooden beds. Often imitated but never bettered, the Witchery is the place to indulge yourself if you have the means.

New Town

Balmoral
1 Princes Street, EH2 2EQ (556 2414/ fax 557 3747/www.thebalmoral hotel.com). Nicolson Street–North Bridge buses or Princes Street buses. **££££.**
A kilted doorman will welcome you to 'Scotland's most famous address', where the trappings are everything you'd expect from a five-star hotel. Exterior rooms offer panoramic views, while the quieter interior rooms overlook the chandeliered Palm Court, where a famous afternoon tea is served in serene splendour before the space morphs into the Bollinger Bar at Palm

Witchery by the Castle

Budget beds

If you're on a tight budget or just up for partying, hostels can be a fun place to stay. All the following places have no curfew but you'll probably need to book ahead, especially during the festival. The Scottish Youth Hostel Association (SYHA/ www.syha.org.uk) runs a number of hostels in Scotland.

Budget Backpackers
37-39 Cowgate, EH1 1JR (476 6351/www.budgetbackpackers.com). Nicolson Street–North Bridge buses. **£.**

Caledonian Backpackers
3 Queensferry Street, EH2 4PA (476 7224/www.caledonian backpackers.net). Princes Street buses. **£.**

Edinburgh Backpackers Hostel
65 Cockburn Street, EH1 1BU (reception 220 1717/reservations 220 2200/www.hoppo.com). Bus 35/Nicolson Street–North Bridge buses. **£.**

Edinburgh Central SYHA Hostel
9 Haddington Place, Calton Hill & Broughton (0870 155 3255/ www.syha.org.uk). Bus 7, 10, 12, 14, 16, 22, 25, 49. **£.**

Edinburgh Metro SYHA Hostel
11 Robertson's Close, Cowgate, EH1 1LY (hostel 0870 004 1115/ central bookings 0870 155 3255/ www.syha.org.uk). Nicolson Street–North Bridge buses. **£.**

Princes Street East Backpackers
5 West Register Street, EH2 2AA (556 6894/www.edinburgh backpackers.com). Nicolson Street–North Bridge buses or Princes Street buses. **£.**

Court. Hadrian's Brasserie does a fair imitation of cosmopolitan Milan, but the real jewel in the crown is the Michelin-starred Number One.

Bonham
35 Drumsheugh Gardens, EH3 7RN (226 6050/reservations 274 7400/ www.thebonham.com). Bus 13, 19, 37, 41, 47. **£££.**
A townhouse exterior gives way to a contemporary blend of comfortable, light and (happily) not very Starck minimalism within. Many of the 48 individually decorated rooms feature original art by local students. The restaurant is another perk, especially with the occasional offer making it far more affordable. Popular with style-conscious visitors.

Edinburgh Residence
7 Rothesay Terrace, EH3 7RY (226 3380/www.theedinburghresidence.com). Bus 13. **£££.**
Like the Howard, its sister property (p175), the Edinburgh Residence is identifiable only by a discreet gold plaque. The three categories of suites (Town House, Grand and Classic) vary in size and facilities, but all have idiosyncrasies: the Town House suites feature bookcases that conceal fold-down beds, while some Classic rooms have separate exits on to Rothesay Terrace. There's no bar or restaurant on site, but meals are served in the suites, and guests can socialise in the Drawing Room, which contains a self-serve honesty bar.

Frederick House
42 Frederick Street, EH2 1EX (226 1999/fax 624 7064/www. townhousehotels.co.uk). Princes Street buses. **££.**
This listed building has been transformed from offices into five floors of bedrooms in patterned greens, golds and reds. The best rooms are situated at the front of the hotel, while the Skyline suite has wonderful views right out across the Firth of Forth. It's run by the same group as the Ailsa Craig and Greenside.

George

19-21 George Street, EH2 2PB (225 1251/www.principal-hotels.com).
Princes Street buses. **£££.**

If the Balmoral and Caledonian are the king and queen of the city's hotels, then the George is the prince. Carvers, the restaurant, remains one of the grandest old-style hotel eateries in the country, and there's also stylish café-bar Tempus for more relaxed dining. All of the 116 rooms in the Contemporary (formerly plain old 'East') Wing have had a complete makeover. The north-facing deluxe doubles on floors five to seven boast eye-popping 180-degree views of the Forth shore and Fife, while those facing west offer views of the castle.

Hilton Caledonian

4 Princes Street, EH1 2AB (222 8888/ www.hilton.com). Princes Street buses. **££££.**

At the west end of Princes Street, the Hilton Caledonian's imposing red sandstone façade has made the hotel an Edinburgh landmark. The Caley steadfastly refuses to follow any current design trends, instead opting to retain a sense of a bygone era throughout: huge arched corridors lead past broad staircases, lit by towering stained glass windows. A high standard of service has made the hotel a favourite with luminaries from Nelson Mandela to Sean Connery, who calls it home whenever he's in town.

Howard

34 Great King Street, EH3 6QH (557 3500/reservations 274 7402/ www.thehoward.com). Bus 13, 23, 27. **£££.**

Built in 1829, the Howard is a perfect example of how to successfully combine Georgian style with modern luxury. The terraced suites in the basement have their own separate entrances and are particularly popular with honeymooning couples. Large bathrooms with state-of-the-art showers and roll-top baths are luxurious bonuses. Service is exemplary; a butler checks in guests in the lavishly decorated drawing room.

Hudson

9-11 Hope Street, EH2 4EL (247 7000/ www.thehudsonhotel.co.uk). Princes Street buses. **£££.**

Howard

The Hudson targets a tech-savvy clientele looking for quality and style without the price tag. A café is unconventionally located in the reception area; there's a bar and a nightclub downstairs (all the male bar staff wear black business kilts). The rooms are all done out in masculine browns, beiges and dark reds, and the beds are generously proportioned, with Egyptian cotton sheets and sumptuous pillows to help your slumber.

Le Monde

16 George Street, EH2 2PF (270 3900/ www.lemondehotel.co.uk). Princes Street buses. **£££**.

Part of a new £12 million entertainment complex in a former office building, Le Monde is quite unlike any other hotel in Edinburgh. The theme, as the name suggests, is the world; 17 of the 18 suites are dedicated to different destinations – Tokyo, New York, Cairo and so on – with the 18th modelled on the waterworld of Atlantis. The fun continues in the bathrooms, with plasma screens and waterproof remotes.

Old Waverley

43 Princes Street, EH2 2BY (556 4648/www.oldwaverley.co.uk). Princes Street buses. **£££**.

Dating back to 1848, the Old Waverley is one of the capital's oldest hotels. A multi-million-pound renovation has recently restored the sparkle and all the rooms have been stylishly refitted. The south-facing rooms boast outstanding views of the castle and Old Town; as do Cranstons restaurant and the Abbotsford Room bar.

Rick's

55a Frederick Street, EH2 1HL (622 7800/www.ricksedinburgh.co.uk). Princes Street buses. **£££**.

Rick's, a bar and restaurant with ten boutique rooms attached, has been one of Edinburgh's trendiest places since its inception in 1998. The New Town location is handy for going out, but you might find it tough to head out at all. The mammoth beds demand

Channings p178

Capital spas

One Spa

The Sheraton Grand (p182) dates back to the mid 1980s and while never the prettiest of hotels, its arrival was an important first step in the regeneration of the area immediately west of Lothian Road. Now the Sheraton has upped its game by adding One Spa in a Terry Farrell-designed building to its rear.

From the outset it was the best facility of its kind in Edinburgh and compared well with urban day spas both in London and internationally. You can come for a swim in the pool, hang around the extensive thermal suite, enjoy the bubbling outdoors hydropool at night, or just pop in for a swift treatment. The menu covers everything from a quick eye lift to a bundled package of exfoliation, shiatsu and head massage that goes on for nearly two hours.

One Spa is not the only recent arrival in the city, though. The Scotsman Hotel (p172) opened the Cowshed, courtesy of the Soho House Group which also runs spas at Babington House in Somerset, Soho House in New York, and elsewhere.

The Cowshed forms part of the Scotsman's Escape fitness centre which features a rather funky stainless steel pool as well as an extensive gym – and the usual array of pamperings. The most extravagant involves a salt scrub, massage, a break for lunch, then a facial and a manicure to finish.

With all this healthy competition around, the Balmoral (p172) decided to get in on the act; general atmosphere and attention to detail has seen it sail into the upper reaches of 'best UK urban day spa' lists. It even does a massage treatment for children with a drink and gift at the end.

The Sheraton Grand, Scotsman and Balmoral may be the city's spa daddies, but the Apex International's (p170) Yu Time leisure facility, with an ozone-cleaned pool and sauna but no treatment rooms, is also worthy of a mention.

Finally, for therapies with no hotel fuss, head for the Renroc Café (p122) where the basement serves as the Nevo Complementary Health Studio.

to be lounged on, while a tempting room service menu could further sabotage your plans.

Roxburghe
38 Charlotte Square, EH2 4HG (240 5500/www.theroxburghe.com). Princes Street buses. **£££.**

The Roxburghe's exterior remains faithful to Robert Adam's Georgian design, but its interior has been transformed into an almost seamless blend of 19th-century elegance and 21st-century style. Some of the bedrooms in the back extension are a little featureless, but views of Edinburgh Castle from the higher floors do much to compensate. There is a swimming pool and a spa too.

Tigerlily
125 George Street, EH2 4JN (225 5005/www.tigerlilyedinburgh.co.uk). Princes Street buses. **£££.**

This sumptuous and ambitious new hotel, restaurant/cocktail bar and nightclub complex is located in a five-storey townhouse building. Each of the 33 bedrooms and suites is decorated differently, but all combine classic and contemporary influences, smooth and textured surfaces and, as the hotel's name suggests, masculine and feminine appeal. In the main stairwell, giant disco balls splash the walls with their sparkle; every window has a row of red pinpoint lights along the ledge, giving the building a soft glow when viewed from outside.

Stockbridge

Channings
15 South Learmonth Gardens, EH4 1EZ (315 2226/reservations 623 9302/www.channings.co.uk). Bus 19, 37, 41, 47. **£££.**

Sir Ernest Shackleton lived here a century ago, and much of Channings' decor is inspired by the polar explorer, including a huge blow-up print of *Endurance*. The bedrooms are crisp and handsome. Downstairs sits the eponymous restaurant.

Inverleith Hotel
5 Inverleith Terrace, EH3 5NS (556 2745/www.inverleithhotel.co.uk). Bus 8, 17, 23, 27. **£.**

This old-fashioned hotel is set in a handsome Victorian townhouse next to the Royal Botanic Garden. Rooms at the rear are compact but exude plenty of warmth, with thick bedspreads and luxurious furnishings. Try to nab the grandest room, which overlooks the Botanics and has a four-poster bed.

Calton Hill & Broughton

Ailsa Craig Hotel
24 Royal Terrace, EH7 5AH (556 1022/www.townhousehotels.co.uk). Playhouse buses. **£.**

Like its sister hotel the Greenside, just along the street at No.9 (557 0022), Ailsa Craig boasts big, clean rooms that have retained their original Georgian features. Though they're a bit on the basic side, some have views towards the Forth, and all enjoy the quiet of this residential crescent, perfect for families.

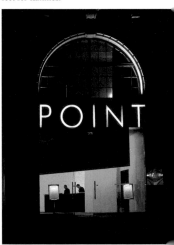

Balfour Guest House

*90-92 Pilrig Street, EH6 5AY (554
2106/www.balfourhousehotel.co.uk). Bus
7, 10, 11, 12, 14, 16, 22, 25, 49.* **£.**
Warm hospitality, a central location
and free parking for those with cars
make this a very popular choice.
There's a decent dining room in the
basement; packed lunches are also
available on request.

Glasshouse

*2 Greenside Place, EH1 3AA (525
8200/www.theetoncollection.com).
Playhouse buses.* **£££.**
The clue is in the name of this hotel,
behind the façade of the former Lady
Glenorchy church at the foot of Calton
Hill. Floor-to-ceiling windows in every
room offer impressive views over the
two-acre lavender-scented roof garden
or the city skyline; even the bathrooms
are glass (with screening, naturally).
The clean, modern lines throughout
make for a stylish boutique hotel, but
it's not been over-designed.

Holiday Inn Express

*Picardy Place, EH1 3JT (558 2300/
www.hieedinburgh.co.uk). Playhouse
buses.* **££.**
As with most hotels in the Holiday Inn
Express chain, this Picardy Place operation offers convenient, good-value
accommodation without too much
character. There are six floors of clean,
uncomplicated rooms (complete with
wireless internet access), plus a popular in-house bar. Continental breakfast
is included in the rates. There are other
branches in Leith.

Parliament House

*15 Calton Hill, EH1 3BJ (478 4000/
www.parliamenthouse-hotel.co.uk).
Playhouse buses.* **£££.**
The hotel was refurbished in 2005,
giving it a more contemporary look
throughout; its rather grandiose name
belies a welcoming residence. Rooms
vary in both size and outlook; some are
cavernous, with views of Arthur's Seat
and the Old Town, while others are of
cosier dimensions, and look out over
Leith and the Firth of Forth. The MPs'
Bistro provides a colourful and roomy
dining space.

Royal Terrace

*18 Royal Terrace, EH7 5AQ (557
3222/www.theroyalterracehotel.co.uk).
Playhouse buses.* **£££.**

Point p181

ESSENTIALS

After a decade of under-investment, the Royal Terrace has benefited from a facelift. The tartan carpets and floral wallpaper have now made way for a more contemporary look, but the Georgian opulence still lives on through the chandeliers, cornices and overall grandeur.

South Edinburgh

Borough

72-80 Causewayside, EH9 1PY (668 2255/fax 667 6622/www.borough hotel.com). Bus 42. **££.**
Considering the location on one of the busiest roads of the city, the rooms at this stylish boutique hotel are surprisingly serene. Beechwood panelling and bold blocks of colour are used to sumptuous effect, and no expense has been spared on the bathrooms. Downstairs sits a spacious, retro-tinged bar and a moderately priced, glowingly reviewed restaurant. A contemporary, snug base, with the city centre a brisk 15-minute walk away.

Links Hotel

4 Alvanley Terrace, EH9 1DU (229 3834/fax 228 9173/www.festival-inns.co.uk). Bus 11, 15, 15A, 16, 17, 23, 45. **£.**
Spread across three adjacent townhouses, the Links' 26 rooms are now bright and modern, thanks to an extensive redecoration. The atmosphere is lively and good-humoured, but peace and quiet are at a premium, particularly in the front-facing bedrooms. Located close to the green expanses of the Meadows and the student-packed suburb of Marchmont, the hotel is a ten-minute bus ride away from the city centre. Rates include a full Scottish breakfast, served in the bar.

Minto Hotel

16-18 Minto Street, EH9 1RQ (668 1234/www.edinburghmintohotel.co.uk). Nicolson Street–North Bridge buses. **£.**
The Minto provides a cheap stopover for groups; there's often a wedding or party taking place in the hotel's function suite. While the establishment falls

Prestonfield

firmly into the basic-but-comfortable category, the warm welcome keeps the regulars flocking back.

Point

34 Bread Street, EH3 9AF (221 5555/ www.point-hotel.co.uk). Bus 1, 2, 10, 11, 15, 15A, 16, 17, 23, 24, 27, 34, 35, 45. **£££.**

The Point completed a light refurbishment a couple of years back of its 140 bedrooms (most of which look out on to the Castle) and softened its formerly minimalist look. The ground floor restaurant serves mainly modish European dishes with a local flavour, while the glass-fronted Monboddo bar is a magnet for the cocktail crowd.

Prestonfield

Priestfield Road, Prestonfield, EH16 5UT (225 7800/fax 668 3976/ www.prestonfield.com). Bus 2, 14, 30. **££££.**

Like its sister, the Witchery (p172), Prestonfield has blossomed under the ownership of restaurateur James Thomson, and to say it's a plush affair

would be a vast understatement. The hotel is set in parkland on the edge of Arthur's Seat and much of the old character remains with rooms decorated in keeping with the sumptuous splendour of the public areas. Outside, don't be surprised to see the odd peacock or Highland cow sauntering past, and the odd guest arriving by chopper; for those who don't do roads, helipad coordinates are on the website.

Salisbury Green

Pollock Halls, 18 Holyrood Park Road, EH16 5AY (651 2000/ www.salisburygreen.co.uk). Bus 2, 14, 30, 33. **££.**

This place has an unusual location in the grounds of a halls of residence complex belonging to the University of Edinburgh. Some rooms have extra features, such as a sunken bath or a reading area tucked snugly into a turret, while others hint at their past with marble fireplaces, beams or carved bookshelves. Guests can use the two bars elsewhere on the site.

West Edinburgh

Dunstane House

4 West Coates, Haymarket, EH12 5JQ (337 6169/www.dunstane-hotel-edinburgh.co.uk). Bus 12, 26, 31, 38. **££.**

Dunstane House dates back to 1852. The traditional decor of the public rooms is complemented by a quaint country feel in the bedrooms, where floral bedspreads and decorative wallpaper in autumnal colours are cosy without straining the eyes. In summer, the patio tables in the front gardens offer excellent views.

Original Raj

6 West Coates, Haymarket, EH12 5JG (346 1333/www.rajempire.com). Bus 12, 26, 31, 38. **££.**

Facilities are a bit basic at this 17-room B&B, but the Indian theme more than compensates. Each room features warm colours, handmade furniture shipped in from Jaipur and a canopy bed – all good for bringing out the inner hippy. There are many other B&B-style hotels in this part of town, but this is the stand-out. Look for the elephant in the garden.

Sheraton Grand

1 Festival Square, Lothian Road, EH3 9SR (229 9131/www.sheraton.com). Bus 1, 2, 10, 11, 15, 15A, 16, 17, 23, 24, 27, 34, 35, 45. **££££.**

The Sheraton Grand's USP is its leisure facilities. Chief among them is the One Spa, one of Europe's best. All rooms are equipped with amazingly comfortable beds. Three restaurants – the Grill Room, the Terrace and Santini – cater to most tastes.

Leith

Malmaison

1 Tower Place, EH6 7DB (468 5000/www.malmaison.com). Bus 1, 10, 16, 22, 35, 36. **£££.**

The first operation in the Malmaison chain set new standards for the city's hotel trade and helped push along the resurgence of Leith. Its Arthur's Suite penthouse has views of Arthur's Seat from the bed and bathtub. Downstairs the candlelit brasserie serves French-influenced food. The adjacent café-bar is a watering hole for local media types and apparatchiks from the Scottish Executive.

Inverleith Hotel p178

Getting Around

Arriving & leaving

By air

Edinburgh Airport
0870 040 0007/
www.edinburghairport.com.
Edinburgh Airport is about
ten miles west of the city centre,
and around 25 minutes' drive
from Princes Street. The airport
is served by all major UK airlines,
among them British Airways
(0844 493 0787, www.ba.com),
BMI (0870 607 0555, www.flybmi.
com) and BMI Baby (0871 224
0224, www.bmibaby.com,
ScotAirways (0870 606 0707),
www.scotairways.co.uk), Easyjet
(0905 821 0905, 65p/min, www.
easyjet.com) and Ryanair (0871
246 0000, www.ryanair.com).
The only direct flights to and from
the US are run by Continental (UK:
0845 607 6760, US: 1-800 231 0856,
www.continental.com), to and from
New York Newark. The airport's
website contains a full list of
airlines and destinations.

The best way to and from the
airport is via the **Airlink 100**
bus service (555 6363, www.lothian
buses.co.uk), which stops at
Maybury, Drum Brae, Edinburgh
Zoo, Murrayfield, the Haymarket,
the West End and Waverley
Bridge. Buses leave the airport
every 20mins from 4.50am to
6.50am (every 30mins between
5am and 8am on Sun), then every
10mins until 9.40pm, then every
15mins until 1.45am, with an
hourly service all night. To the
airport, buses leave Waverley
Bridge every 20mins from 4am
until 6.20am, then every 10mins
until 9pm, then every 15mins until
around 11.45pm, with an hourly

service through the night. The
journey takes around 25mins and
costs £3 for a single or £5 return.

Taxis run from a rank outside
the UK Arrivals hall. The journey
to central Edinburgh usually takes
around 20-25 minutes (more during
peak times) and costs around £20.

By bus/coach

St Andrew Square Bus Station
*Elder Street, New Town. Princes Street
buses.* **Open** 6am-midnight daily.
National Express (0870 580
8080, www.nationalexpress.com)
operates coach services between
Edinburgh and destinations in
England and Wales. Buses run by
Scottish Citylink (0870 550 5050,
www.citylink.co.uk) serve a variety
of towns around Scotland, while
Megabus (www.megabus.com)
runs budget bus services from
Edinburgh to half a dozen
Scottish destinations (including
Glasgow) and a few in England.
All buses and coaches arrive
and depart from St Andrew
Square Bus Station.

By train

Waverley Station
*Waverley Bridge, New Town
(0845 748 4950/www.national
rail.co.uk). Princes Street buses.*
Edinburgh's central station
serves the East Coast main line to
London and Aberdeen. GNER and
Virgin run cross-border services,
while First Scotrail runs trains
to destinations around Scotland,
including a shuttle service (every
15mins) to Glasgow (which also
stops at Haymarket Station).
Local services go to East and
West Lothian and into Fife.

ESSENTIALS

Around town

To fully appreciate the beauty, elegance, charm and contrasts of its city centre and its environs, Edinburgh is best explored on foot. Although the usual caution should be exercised at night, especially around those areas of the city with abundant and rowdy nightlife (Lothian Road and the Cowgate, to name but two), walking around the city is safe and rewarding. Bus travel around the centre of Edinburgh is, on the whole, reasonably fast and reliable, and is certainly a better option than driving. Taxis are numerous, if rather pricey. Cycling is a fast and efficient way of getting around, as long as you don't mind a few cobbled streets and the odd hill.

Public transport

Buses

The city and its surrounding suburbs are very well served by a comprehensive bus network. **Lothian Buses** (555 6363, www.lothianbuses.co.uk) runs the majority of bus services throughout Edinburgh and into Mid and East Lothian; it's these services that we've listed throughout the guide.

Several parts of town are served by a great number of buses. In these cases, rather than list each individual bus number on every occasion, we've instead broken them into groupings. Below are the groupings used throughout the guide, together with a list of bus routes that serve the respective streets or areas.
Nicolson Street–North Bridge buses 3, 3A, 5, 7, 8, 14, 29, 30, 31, 33, 37, 47, 49.
Playhouse buses 1, 4, 5, 7, 8, 10, 11, 12, 14, 15, 15A, 16, 17, 19, 22, 25, 26, 34, 44, 45, 49.

Princes Street buses 1, 3, 3A, 4, 10, 11, 12, 15, 15A, 16, 17, 19, 22, 24, 25, 26, 29, 31, 33, 34, 36, 37, 44, 47.

Night buses, operated by Lothian Buses, run seven days a week on 11 different routes around the city and out into the suburbs. The services operate hourly starting from around midnight. For full information on routes and timetables, see www.night buses.com or visit any of the Lothian Buses Travelshops.

Single journeys within Edinburgh cost £1 for adults and 60p for children aged 5-15, regardless of the distance travelled. Under-5s travel free, up to a maximum of two kids per adult passenger. A single journey on the city's Night Bus network costs £2 (or £1 with a **Ridacard**; see below). Exact change is required for all single fares.

If you're planning on making several journeys during one day, it may be worth buying a **Daysaver** ticket, which allows for unlimited travel on the Lothian Buses network (excluding the Airlink 100 bus, special tour services and Night Buses). Daysavers cost £2.30 (£2 for children aged 5-15), and are available when you board your first bus of the day. Again, exact change is required.

The Ridacard affords the holder unlimited travel on the network (excluding tour services and Night Buses) for longer periods. The card costs £13 for one week (£11 for students aged 16-25, £9 for 5-15s) or £35 for one month (£29 for students aged 16-25, £23 for 5-15s). You can buy a Ridacard from Lothian Buses Travelshops (see below).

Lothian Buses Travelshops

27 Hanover Street, New Town. Princes Street buses. **Open** 8.15am-6pm Mon-Sat.

7 Shandwick Place, New Town. Princes Street buses. **Open** 8.15am-6pm Mon-Sat. *Waverley Bridge, New Town. Princes Street buses.* **Open** 8.30am-6pm Mon-Sat; 9.30am-5pm Sun.

The region's other main bus services are run by the **First Group** (08708 727271, www.first group.co.uk). Its services in East Lothian include a number of routes that run into Edinburgh's city centre. Unfortunately, day tickets are not transferable between First Group and Lothian Buses.

Trains

The majority of rail services in Scotland are run by **First Scotrail**. Details of the firm's various services and fares are available from **National Rail Enquiries** by calling 08457 484950 (lines are open 24 hours daily) or checking www.national rail.co.uk. Specific information on First Scotrail can also be found at www.firstgroup.com/scotrail. The information desk at Waverley station has timetables and details of discount travel, season tickets and international travel.

As well as Waverley and Haymarket stations, the city has several suburban stations including South Gyle, Slateford and Edinburgh Park. For full information on their locations, check National Rail Enquiries.

Black cabs

Most of Edinburgh's taxis are black cabs, which take up to five passengers and have facilities for travellers with disabilities. When a taxi's yellow 'For Hire' light is on, you can hail it in the street. The basic fare, for the pick-up and the first 450 metres, costs £1.45 or £2.20 after 6pm; each subsequent 225 metres travelled

costs 23p (or 24p at night). There's a 20p charge for every additional passenger over two.

Phoning for a taxi is particularly advisable at night or if you're based out of the city centre. To book, contact **Central Taxis** (229 2468, www.taxis-edinburgh.co.uk), **City Cabs** (228 1211, www.citycabs. co.uk) or **Computer Cabs** (272 8000, www.comcab-edinburgh. co.uk). While some taxi firms take credit cards, many others accept only cash; check when you book or get into the cab.

Minicabs

Minicabs (saloon cars) are generally cheaper than black cabs and may be able to carry more passengers; some firms have people-carriers at their disposal, which can accommodate up to eight passengers (always specify when booking). Cars cannot be hailed on the street, and must be booked in advance. Reputable firms include **Bluebird** (621 6666) and **Persevere** (555 3377). It's a good idea to call around first to get the best price.

Cycling

Thanks to some successful lobbying by the local cycle campaign Spokes, Edinburgh is a pretty decent place for cyclists, as long as you get a decent bike lock and are prepared for some hefty hills. The city council has invested in some off-road cycle paths and road-edge cycle lanes.

Driving

If you're planning on staying within Edinburgh during the course of your visit, driving isn't recommended. For one

ESSENTIALS

thing, the town is reasonably small and therefore very accessible either on foot or via the public transport system. And in addition, the city centre is awash with one-way streets and pedestrian-only areas, which can make driving a frustrating experience. Princes Street, in particular, has limited access for private vehicles and is best avoided.

Vehicle hire

Most car rental firms insist that drivers are over 21 years old (at the very least), with a minimum of one year's driving experience and have a current and full driving licence with no serious endorsements. All the firms detailed below have branches at Edinburgh Airport. Prices vary: be sure to shop around for the best rate, and always check the level of insurance included in the price.

Alamo
0870 400 4562/www.alamo.co.uk.

Avis
0844 581 0147/www.avis.co.uk.

Budget
0844 581 2231/www.budget.co.uk.

Europcar
0845 758 5375/www.europcar.co.uk.

Hertz
0870 844 8844/www.hertz.co.uk.

National
0870 400 4581/ www.nationalcar.co.uk.

Car parks

All the car parks detailed below are open 24 hours a day. Rates vary; call for details. There's a full list of city centre car parks, complete with a map, online at www.edinburgh.gov.uk.

Castle Terrace
Old Town (229 2870/ www.ncp.co.uk).

Chalmers Street
South Edinburgh (229 2870/www.ncp.co.uk).

Greenside Place
Calton Hill & Broughton (558 3518/www.ncp.co.uk).

St James Centre
Leith Street, Broughton (556 5066/www.ncp.co.uk).

St John's Hill
Old Town (229 2870/ www.ncp.co.uk).

St Leonard's Street
South Edinburgh (667 5601).

Clamping and fines

Always carefully check street signs to find out the local parking regulations. For the purposes of on-street car parking, the city is divided up into central and peripheral zones. In the central zone, you must pay for parking between 8.30am and 6pm from Monday to Saturday; in the peripheral zone, payment must be made between 8.30am and 5pm. Parking payment should be made either at parking meters or on-street pay-and-display ticket vending machines.

The fine for parking illegally is £60, reduced to £30 if paid within 14 days. If you get towed, a fee of £105 is levied for removal, plus a £12 storage fee for every day the vehicle remains uncollected. These fees are in addition to the cost of the parking ticket. Impounded cars are taken to the Edinburgh Car Compound.

Edinburgh Car Compound
57 Tower Street, Leith (555 1742). Bus 12, 16, 35. **Open** *7am-9pm Mon-Sat; 8.45am-11.30am Sun.*

Resources A-Z

Accident & emergency

In the event of a serious accident, fire or incident, call 999 and specify whether you require an ambulance, the fire service or the police.

Royal Infirmary of Edinburgh
51 Little France Crescent, Old Dalkeith Road, EH16 (536 1000). Bus 8, 18, 24, 32, 33, 38, 49. The city's 24-hour casualty department.

Credit card loss

Report lost or stolen credit cards immediately both to the police and the 24-hour phone lines listed below. Inform your bank by phone and in writing.

American Express
0800 587 6023/ www.americanexpress.com.

Diners Club
0870 190 0011/ www.dinersclub.co.uk.

MasterCard
0800 964767/ www.mastercard.com.

Visa
0800 891725/ www.visa.com.

Customs

Citizens entering the UK from outside the EU must adhere to these duty-free import limits: 200 cigarettes or 100 cigarillos or 50 cigars or 250g of tobacco; 2 litres of still table wine plus either 1 litre of spirits or strong liqueurs (over 22% abv) or 2 litres of fortified wine (under 22% abv), sparkling wine or other liqueurs; 60cc/ml perfume, 250cc/ml toilet water and other goods to the value of no more than £145. For more details, see www.hmce.gov.uk.

Dental emergency

Western General Hospital Dental Clinic
Crewe Road South, Stockbridge (537 1330). Bus 19, 19A, 28, 29, 37, 37A, 38. **Open** 7-9pm Mon-Fri; 10am-noon Sat, Sun.
A walk-in emergency clinic, for tourists and Lothian residents only.

Disabled

Listed buildings aren't allowed to widen their entrances or add ramps, and parts of the Old Town have wheelchair-unfriendly narrow pavements. However, equal opportunity legislation requires new buildings to be fully accessible.

   Lothian Buses' new fleet is accessible to passengers in wheelchairs. Call 555 6363 for details. Newer black taxis are wheelchair-accessible; specify when booking. **Edinburgh City Council** publishes *Transport in Edinburgh: A Guide for Disabled People*. For a free copy, call 469 3891.

Electricity

The UK electricity supply is 220-240 volt, 50-cycle AC rather than the 110-120 volt, 60-cycle AC used in the US. Foreign visitors will need to run appliances via an adaptor.

Embassies & consulates

For a list of consular offices, consult the *Yellow Pages* (118 247/www.yell.com). The majority of embassies and consulates (the US is an exception) do not accept personal callers without an appointment.

Australian Consulate

Euro Business Centre, 21-23 Hill Street, EH2 3JP (226 8161/ www.australia.org.uk).

Canadian Honorary Consulate

Burness, Festival Square, EH3 9WJ (473 6320/www.cic.gc.ca).

Irish Consulate General

16 Randolph Crescent, EH3 7TT (226 7711/ http://foreignaffairs.gov.ie).

US Consulate General

3 Regent Terrace, Calton Hill, EH7 5BW (556 8315/after-hours emergencies 01224 857097/ www.usembassy.org.uk/scotland).

Internet

Public internet access is abundant in Edinburgh. Many cafés and bars offer free Wi-Fi internet access, and chain cafés such as Starbucks offer wireless access via a paid-for subscription. If you're not toting a laptop, a handful of internet cafés also have computers available to rent.

Easy Internet Café

58 Rose Street, EH2 2YQ (226 5971/www.easy.com). Princes Street buses. **Open** 7.30am-9pm daily.

Edinburgh Internet Café

98 West Bow (226 5400/www.edin internetcafe.com). Bus 2, 23, 27, 41, 42. **Open** 10am-11pm daily.

Money

Britain's currency is the pound sterling (£). Three Scottish banks – Bank of Scotland, the Royal Bank of Scotland and the Clydesdale Bank – issue their own paper notes. The colour of the notes varies slightly between the three, but an approximation is as follows: green £1; blue £5; brown £10; purple/pink £20; red or green £50; bold red £100.

Opening hours

In general, business hours are 9.30am-5.30pm Mon-Fri. Most shops are open 9am-5.30pm Mon-Sat and 11am-5pm on Sun. Officially, closing time for pubs is 11pm, but most pubs have licences to sell alcohol until 1am. Many shops, restaurants, pubs and clubs operate longer hours during the August festivals.

Police

If you've been the victim of a crime, look under 'Police' in the phone directory for the nearest police station, or call directory enquiries (118 500/118 800).

Postal services

Post offices are usually open 9am-5.30pm during the week and 9am-noon on Saturdays. For the nearest branch call the Royal Mail on 08457 223344 or check www.royalmail.com.

Smoking

Smoking has been banned in enclosed public spaces across Scotland, including all restaurants and pubs since 2006. Smokers huddled around their cigarettes on street corners is now a common sight around town.

Telephones

The area code for Edinburgh is 0131. International codes are as follows: Australia 00 61; Belgium 00 32; Canada 00 1; France 00 33; Germany 00 49; Ireland 00 353; Italy 00 39; Japan 00 81; Netherlands 00 31; New Zealand 00 64; Spain 00 34; USA 00 1.

Time

Edinburgh operates on Greenwich Mean Time (GMT). Clocks go forward to run on British Summer Time (BST) at 1am on the last Saturday in March, and return to GMT on the last Saturday in October.

Tipping

Tipping 10-15% in taxis, restaurants, hairdressers and some bars (but not pubs) is normal. Some restaurants and bars add service automatically to all bills; always check to avoid paying twice.

Tourist information

The **Edinburgh & Lothians Tourist Board** operates the main tourist office in the city, at the east end of Princes Street. They distribute a wealth of information and can book hotels, event tickets, car hire and coach trips.

Edinburgh & Scotland Information Centre

Above Princes Mall, 3 Princes Street, New Town, EH2 2QP (0845 225 5121/www.edinburgh.org). Princes Street buses. **Open** *call for details.*

Edinburgh Airport Tourist Information Desk

Edinburgh Airport (0870 040 0007/ www.edinburghairport.com). **Open** *Apr-Oct* 6.30am-10.30pm daily. *Nov-Mar* 7am-9pm daily.

Visas & immigration

EU citizens do not require a visa to visit the UK; citizens of the USA, Canada, Australia, South Africa and New Zealand can also enter with only a passport for tourist visits of up to six months, as long as they can show they can support themselves during their visit and plan to return. Use www.ukvisas. gov.uk to check your visa status well before you travel, or contact the British embassy, consulate or high commission in your own country. You can arrange visas online at www.fco.gov.uk.

What's on

The city's most high-profile publication is **The List** (www. list.co.uk). Issued fortnightly on Thursdays (weekly during August), it contains full listings. Scotsgay (www.scotsgay.co.uk) is distributed free each month in gay venues and is available in full online, and gives the rundown on the gay scene.

When to go

There isn't really a best and a worst time to visit Edinburgh, it all depends on what you want from your visit. The slew of cultural festivals means that August is the liveliest and most interesting month of the year, but it's also the busiest. Similarly, the Hogmanay celebrations draw huge crowds, but aren't to everyone's taste. The legendarily changeable Scottish weather further complicates matters. Winters can be quite chilly and summers – May to October – are generally pleasant, but you can never escape the possibility of rain, it is a constant threat all year round.

ESSENTIALS

Index

Sights & areas

Eating & drinking

ESSENTIALS

ESSENTIALS

Time Out
Travel Guides

British Isles

**Written by
local experts**

Edinburgh by Area

Essentials

Published by Time Out Guides Ltd
Universal House
251 Tottenham Court Road
London W1T 7AB
Tel: + 44 (0)20 7813 3000
Fax: + 44 (0)20 7813 6001
Email: guides@timeout.com
www.timeout.com

Managing Director Peter Fiennes
Financial Director Gareth Garner
Editorial Director Ruth Jarvis
Deputy Series Editor Dominic Earle
Editorial Manager Holly Pick
Assistant Management Accountant Ija Krasnikova

Time Out Guides is a wholly owned subsidiary of Time Out Group Ltd.

© **Time Out Group Ltd**
Chairman Tony Elliott
Financial Director Richard Waterlow
Group General Manager/Director Nichola Coulthard
Time Out Magazine Ltd MD Richard Waterlow
Time Out Communications Ltd MD David Pepper
Time Out International MD Cathy Runciman
Production Director Mark Lamond
Group IT Director Simon Chappell

Time Out and the Time Out logo are trademarks of Time Out Group Ltd.

This edition first published in Great Britain in 2008 by Ebury Publishing
A Random House Group Company
Company information can be found on www.randomhouse.co.uk
10 9 8 7 6 5 4 3 2 1

Distributed in US by Publishers Group West
Distributed in Canada by Publishers Group Canada
For further distribution details, see www.timeout.com

ISBN: 978-1-846700-84-2

A CIP catalogue record for this book is available from the British Library

Printed and bound by Firmengruppe APPL, aprinta druck, Wemding, Germany

The Random House Group Limited supports The Forest Stewardship Council (FSC), the
leading international forest certification organisation. All our titles that are printed on
Greenpeace approved FSC certified paper carry the FSC logo. Our paper procurement
policy can be found at www.rbooks.co.uk/environment.

Time Out carbon-offsets all its flights with Trees for Cities (www.treesforcities.org)

Edinburgh Shortlist

The **Time Out Edinburgh Shortlist** is one of a new series of guides that draws on Time Out's background as a magazine publisher to keep you current with what's going on in town. As well as Edinburgh's key sights and the best of its eating, drinking and leisure options, the guide picks out the most exciting venues to have recently opened and gives a full calendar of annual events. It also includes features on the important news, trends and openings, all compiled by locally based editors and writers. Whether you're visiting for the first time, or you're a regular, you'll find the *Time Out Edinburgh Shortlist* contains all you need to know, in a portable and easy-to-use format.

The guide divides central Edinburgh into seven areas, each of which contains listings for Sights & Museums, Eating & Drinking, Shopping, Nightlife and Arts & Leisure, with maps pinpointing all their locations. At the front of the book are chapters rounding up these scenes city-wide, and giving a shortlist of our overall picks in a variety of categories. We include itineraries for days out, plus essentials such as transport information and hotels.

Our listings give phone numbers as dialled from within Edinburgh. To dial them from elsewhere in the UK, preface them with 0131; from abroad, use your country's exit code followed by 44 (the country code for the UK), 131 and the number given.

We have noted price categories by using one to four pound signs (£-££££), representing budget, moderate, expensive and luxury. Major credit cards are accepted unless otherwise stated. We also indicate when a venue is NEW.

All our listings are double-checked, but places do sometimes close or change their hours or prices, so it's a good idea to call a venue before visiting. While every effort has been made to ensure accuracy, the publishers cannot accept responsibility for any errors that this guide may contain.

Venues are marked on the maps using symbols numbered according to their order within the chapter and colour-coded according to the type of venue they represent:

- ❶ Sights & Museums
- ❶ Eating & Drinking
- ❶ Shopping
- ❶ Nightlife
- ❶ Arts & Leisure

Map key		
Major sight or landmark	....	⬛
Railway station	....	⬛
Park or garden	....	⬜
River	....	▨
Motorway	....	═
Main road	....	
Pedestrian road	....	▨
Airport	....	✈
Church	....	✚
Area name	....	LEITH

Time Out Edinburgh Shortlist

EDITORIAL

Editor Keith Davidson
Copy Editor Patrick Welch
Listings Editor Cathy Limb
Listings Researchers Alex Brown,
  Gemma Pritchard
Proofreader Phil Harriss

DESIGN

Art Director Scott Moore
Art Editor Pinelope Kourmouzoglou
Senior Designer Henry Elphick
Graphic Designers Gemma Doyle,
  Kei Ishimaru
Digital Imaging Simon Foster
Advertising Designer Jodi Sher
Picture Editor Jael Marschner
Deputy Picture Editor Katie Morris
Picture Researcher Gemma Walters
Picture Desk Assistant Marzena Zoladz

ADVERTISING

Commercial Director Mark Phillips
Advertising Sales Manager Alison Wallen
Advertising Sales (Edinburgh)
  Christie Dessy
Advertising Assistant Kate Staddon

MARKETING

Head of Marketing Catherine Demajo
Marketing Manager Yvonne Poon
**Sales & Marketing Director, North
  America** Lisa Levinson
Marketing Designers Anthony Huggins,
  Nicola Wilson

PRODUCTION

Production Manager Brendan McKeown
Production Controller Caroline Bradford
Production Coordinator Julie Pallot

CONTRIBUTORS

This guide was researched and written by Keith Davidson and the writers of
Time Out Edinburgh & the Best of Glasgow.

PHOTOGRAPHY

All photography by Olivia Rutherford, except: page 33 Getty Images; 38, 39 Edinburgh
Fringe Festival; 42 Alys Tomlinson; 45, 100, 125 Muir Vidler; 50 Edinburgh
International Book Festival; 109, 113 Royal Botanic Garden Edinburgh; 110, 112
National Galleries of Scotland; 114 Heritage Portfolio; 115 J P Masclet; 116 Angela
Leadbetter; 117 Galerie Mirages; 140 The Royal College of Surgeons of Edinburgh;
142, 143, 145 Douglas Jones; 150 David Axelbank; 152 Jenny Leask; 156 Santini,
Edinburgh; 162 Glasgow Botanic Gardens; 166 Glasgow Science Centre.

The following images were provided by the featured establishments/artists: pages 35,
40, 52, 149, 154, 160, 176, 180, 181

Cover photograph: Olivia Rutherford.

MAPS

JS Graphics (john@jsgraphics.co.uk).

About Time Out

Founded in 1968, Time Out has expanded from humble London beginnings into the
leading resource for those wanting to know what's happening in the world's greatest
cities. As well as our influential what's-on weeklies in London, New York and Chicago,
we publish more than a dozen other listings magazines in cities as varied as Beijing
and Mumbai. The magazines established Time Out's trademark style: sharp writing,
informed reviewing and bang up-to-date inside knowledge of every scene.

Time Out made the natural leap into travel guides in the 1980s with the City Guide
series, which now extends to over 50 destinations around the world. Written and
researched by expert local writers and generously illustrated with original photography,
the full-size guides cover a larger area than our Shortlist guides and include many
more venue reviews, along with additional background features and a full set of maps.

Throughout this rapid growth, the company has remained proudly independent, still
owned by Tony Elliott who started Time Out London as a single
fold-out sheet of A5 paper. This independence extends to the editorial content of all
our publications, this Shortlist included. No establishment has been featured because
it has advertised, and no payment has influenced any of our reviews. And, for our critics,
there's definitely no such thing as a free lunch: all restaurants and bars are visited and
reviewed anonymously, and Time Out always picks up the bill.

For more about the company, see www.timeout.com.

Don't Miss

Edinburgh Castle

Sights & Museums

The United Nations Educational, Scientific and Cultural Organisation, better known by its initials UNESCO, does not bestow prestigious World Heritage status on cultural sites at the drop of a hat. Across the entire planet there are fewer than 700 and at the last count the UK only had 22. These are real headline venues like Stonehenge, the Tower of London or Westminster Abbey.

Edinburgh is a member of this highly select group but in the most all-encompassing way. Here, UNESCO didn't bother with the detail of specific buildings, ancient or otherwise. In 1995, it simply added the entire Old Town plus the Georgian New Town to its World Heritage list. When you emerge from Waverley Station in the city centre, or get off the airport bus on Waverley Bridge adjacent, all you have to do is look around and the sightseeing has begun.

The Castle and the Royal Mile

In terms of prominence, drama, history and sheer popularity the Castle (p55) consistently ranks as Edinburgh's premier visitor magnet with around 1.2 million people a year forking out for a ticket. Far from being a medieval shell, it houses everything from Scotland's crown jewels to a working military garrison, and from the deeply affecting National War Memorial to a revelatory display on prisoners of war. In the late 18th and early 19th centuries, enemy combatants from the American War of Independence, the Napoleonic Wars and other conflicts were kept in its vaults.

The Castle also marks the west end of the Royal Mile. Not a single road as such, it's a catch-all name for four conjoined streets: Castlehill, the Lawnmarket, High Street and Canongate. In the high Middle Ages, they were the backbone of Edinburgh with smaller streets and alleys (known as closes) leading off. This thoroughfare is the heart of what locals have called the Old Town for more than 200 years; before that it simply was Edinburgh. From the end of the 18th century, those who could afford it moved to the airier terraces of the New Town.

Down the Royal Mile, visitors can find some of the city's major attractions along one neatly defined strip. By the Castle itself are the mid 19th-century Camera Obscura (p55) showing an all-round view of the city centre, and the more contemporary Scotch Malt Whisky Heritage Centre (p64) with its comprehensive presentation on Scotland's national drink. Then you go past the headquarters of the Edinburgh International Festival at the Hub (formerly a church, this rather imposing edifice dates to 1844) to find Gladstone's Land and the Writers' Museum (p65) in the Lawnmarket. The former is a showpiece 16th-century tenement now owned by the National Trust for Scotland, the latter dedicated to Scotland's sainted trio of Robert Burns, Sir Walter Scott and Robert Louis Stevenson.

On the High Street sits the slightly dour High Kirk of St Giles (p60) with elements surviving from the 12th century. It was also a key site during the Reformation when

S H O R T L I S T

Super Scottish
- Edinburgh Castle (p55)
- National Museum of Scotland (p60)
- Scottish Parliament (p74)

Best views
- Royal Botanic Gardens (p110)
- Calton Hill (p118)
- Arthur's Seat (p125)

Best royal connections
- Queen's Gallery (p63)
- Palace of Holyroodhouse (p63)
- Royal Yacht Britannia (p128)

Good for kids
- Museum of Childhood (p61)
- Our Dynamic Earth (p62)
- Edinburgh Zoo (p155)
- Gorgie City Farm (p160)

Best for art
- Scottish National Portrait Gallery (p91)
- Royal Scottish Academy (p91)
- National Gallery of Scotland (p91)
- Scottish National Gallery of Modern Art (p112)

Weird and wonderful
- Greyfriars Bobby (p55)
- Writers' Museum (p65)
- Surgeons Hall Museums (p137)

Most iconic churches
- St Margaret's Chapel in Edinburgh Castle (p55)
- The High Kirk of St Giles (p60)

Greenest spaces
- Royal Botanic Gardens (p110)
- Holyrood Park (p125)

Waterside walks
- Water of Leith (p109)
- Union Canal (p154)

DON'T MISS

John Knox was minister. A restored 15th-century building once believed to be his house is further down the High Street, part of the Scottish Storytelling Centre (p64). Just across the road the Museum of Childhood (p60) offers a look at toys through the ages.

Finally it's a short hop via the Canongate, past the People's Story (a social history museum, p63) to the eastern reach of the Royal Mile, book-ended by the Palace of Holyroodhouse (p63) which is the Queen's official Scottish residence, the ruins of Holyrood Abbey (p63) and the enduringly controversial Scottish Parliament which went massively over-budget and over-schedule before it opened in 2004. Also in this neck of the woods is the Queen's Gallery (p63) which arrived in 2002 and showcases art from the royal collection.

To the other side of the Parliament complex, Our Dynamic Earth (p63) on Holyrood Road looks like a mammoth marquee but houses a science museum that covers natural history from the Big Bang to the geological development of our planet and more – teens love the simulated natural disasters.

The Castle and manifest delights of the Royal Mile notwithstanding, the other must-see in the Old Town is the National Museum of Scotland (p60). It comprises the old Royal Museum, completed in 1888 – with its displays on nature, science, culture and the arts – and the adjacent Museum of Scotland added in 1998, a top-class repository for artefacts ancient and modern with an engaging exposition of the country's history. The two are linked so a visit can encompass anything from hoards of Roman silver to Viking brooches, a Formula One racing car to the late (and stuffed) Dolly the Sheep, the world's first cloned mammal.

New Town

The rationale for the New Town was simple. By the 18th century, what is now called the Old Town was grim. 'Let's do the Enlightenment thing and get the hell out,' said the city's great and good. The result was an all-new planned settlement to the north with an intrinsic classical elegance. Unlike the Old Town, it is not quite as packed with tourist attractions, but the assorted crescents, places, rows and streets are plainly gorgeous in themselves. Visitors should simply break out a map and go for a walk. That said, in the more southerly part of the New Town around Princes Street, Queen Street and Charlotte Square sit some of Scotland's most iconic galleries and museums.

The National Galleries of Scotland complex (p91) at the Mound is Edinburgh's second favourite visitor destination after the Castle. The complex comprises two separate buildings by Sir William Playfair, now linked at basement level: the Doric façade of the Royal Scottish Academy (p91) faces directly on to Princes Street, with the Ionic-style National Gallery (p91) directly behind. The former tends to have big summer blockbuster exhibitions; the latter's permanent collection includes Raphael, Titian, Monet and Gauguin among others.

A few hundred yards along the road, is the soaring Gothic spire of the Scott Monument (p91), built as a posthumous tribute to the celebrated writer in 1846; excellent views from the top. A couple of blocks north on Queen Street, the Scottish National Portrait Gallery (p91) has a fine mural in its entrance foyer depicting the big players in Scotland's history. Charlotte Square meanwhile is not

Visit The
Scotch Whisky
Visitor Experience

NEXT TO EDINBURGH CASTLE

COME AND ENJOY AN EXCITING JOURNEY OF DISCOVERY THROUGH THE STORY OF SCOTCH WHISKY

OPEN DAILY
TELEPHONE 0131 220 0441
www.scotchwhiskyexperience.co.uk

only the home of the tented village that hosts the popular annual Edinburgh International Book Festival (p39) but also the Georgian House (p87), an example of how the New Town's well-to-do lived in the 19th century.

One step beyond

Although visitors could spend almost their entire time in the few square miles of the Old and New Towns and never get bored, there are attractions well worth the trip just outside those UNESCO-hallowed spaces.

In the west of the city by Corstorphine Hill, Edinburgh Zoo (p155) has played host to generations of school trips and family days out. It opened just before World War I and is probably best known for its self-sustaining colony of penguins.

Going round the compass to points north, the Royal Botanic Garden at Inverleith (p110) is more flora than fauna, but stands out as one of the UK's most important botanical centres and the ideal place for a peaceful stroll – the views of the Old Town from the gardens are fantastic.

Immediately south-east of the city centre, Holyrood Park is a huge green space incorporating Arthur's Seat (p125). It is said to have been a royal park since the time of Scotland's King David I. Locals and visitors alike tramp up for incomparable views over the city, plus Fife, the Firth of Forth, out to East Lothian, and south to the Pentland Hills. Look directly north, however, and you can see the docks at Leith, just a couple of miles away. Once a separate burgh, Leith became part of Edinburgh's sprawling expansion in 1920. Over the last couple of decades, it has been redeveloped and since 1998

Palace of Holyroodhouse p11

has played host to another of the city's top visitor destinations, the Royal Yacht Britannia (p128). After the Britannia was decommissioned, it became a potent symbol of Leith's regeneration with literally millions of people keen to sample life aboard the Windsor family's rather large boat.

And there's more...

Old Town, New Town and elsewhere, Edinburgh has been around for a long time. Its oldest buildings and ruins date back nearly 900 years. The major sights and museums are worth visiting but the city has much more to offer: walk up Calton Hill just to take in the view, or drop by the macabre Surgeons Hall Museums on Nicolson Street (p137) with their pickled pathology specimens on display. Half the fun of the city is in stumbling across the quirky and unexpected as you're walking from one major venue to another.

Glass & Thompson p17

Eating & Drinking

Edinburgh may not be big but it can be quite clever when it comes to eating out. As a city of just 460,000 souls, it's a mere fraction of the size of the major international food capitals and simply lacks the economic clout to seriously compete with London, although that remains the benchmark rather than Glasgow or the English provinces.

Like many other cities in Britain and Ireland, Edinburgh went through quite a revolution in terms of new restaurants, cafés and bars in the 1990s and, as the millennium approached, start-up fever seemed to get out of hand; there were some notable casualties. A couple from back then to have found a niche are Oloroso (p101) with its bar and terrace, and Forth Floor on top of Harvey Nichols department store (p96). Into the new decade, the city seemed to find an equilibrium with major openings becoming less frequent but more considered.

The latest successes are certainly the Kitchin (p131), which went from a summer 2006 launch to a single Michelin star within a few months. Tony Borthwick then dipped a toe in the water, relocating his acclaimed Plumed Horse restaurant from Dumfriesshire to the city at the end of that year (p134). Into 2007 and Abstract (p140) appeared in the shadow of the Castle, a very cosmopolitan operation in modern French mode. These were all welcome additions at the upper end of the scene, serious competition for a select list of established stagers such as Restaurant Martin Wishart (p134), the Atrium (p140), the Vintners Rooms (p136) and the Balmoral Hotel's flagship diner Number One (p101). A sister Abstract in Inverness and the Atrium's upstairs bar-café Blue (p142) notwithstanding, these are all unique and their head chefs would drop a whisk if anyone mentioned the words 'chain restaurant'. That outrage would also show at another set of important eateries across the city which are not so much chains as clusters, often run by families.

A personal vision

There is nowhere quite like the Witchery (p76). This beautiful room with its candlelight, red leather and wood panelling has almost defined the paradigm of what an Edinburgh restaurant should be since it opened in 1979. Sitting on Castlehill, a few footsteps from the Castle Esplanade, the location could hardly be better. The Witchery is run by restaurateur James Thomson; he added an adjacent dining room with an equally historic feel – the Secret Garden – in 1989. Both restaurants operate from the same Franco-Scottish kitchen. Mr T's next project was the modern European-style Tower (p76) at the Museum of Scotland in 1998 – the plans for the country's national museum had left space for a top-floor restaurant. It took nearly five years before Thomson's follow-up venture got off the ground: the refurbishment of the old Prestonfield House Hotel, relaunched simply as Prestonfield in 2003 (p181) with Rhubarb as its dining room. The hotel was originally a 17th-century mansion and its overhaul saw late-period Stuart meet 21st-century fabrics.

SHORTLIST

Top tables
- Restaurant Martin Wishart (p134)
- Number One at the Balmoral (p101)
- The Kitchin (p131)

With a French accent
- La Garrigue (p73)
- Duck's at Le Marche Noir (p95)

Veg out
- David Bann (p70)
- Kalpna (p145)
- Ann Purna (p140)
- Henderson's (p97)

Rooms with a view
- Forth Floor (p96)
- The Tower (p76)
- Oloroso (p101)

Far East eats
- Kweilin (p98)
- Chop Chop (p156)
- The Jasmine (p145)
- Dusit (p96)

Something fishy
- Creelers (p69)
- Fishers in the City (p96)
- Skippers (p136)

Best breakfasts
- Urban Angel (p103)
- Avoca (p112)

Currying favour
- Roti (p159)
- Suruchi (p146)
- Saffrani (p75)

Cocktail time
- Amicus Apple (p92)
- Dragonfly (p144)
- Rick's (p103)

Best beer
- Cask & Barrel (p121)
- Cloisters (p144)
- Cumberland (p95)
- Guildford (p97)

THE
SHORE
BAR & RESTAURANT

GASTRO FOOD
SERVED ALL DAY

LIVE MUSIC

3 SHORE, LEITH, EDINBURGH EH6 6QW
TEL _0131 553 5080 WWW.THESHORE.BIZ

Also in the hotel business, the Town House Company has a small collection of upmarket stopovers including the Bonham (p174), the Howard (p175), and Channings (p178). Each has a restaurant and is worth visiting in its own way, with the recently relaunched dining room at the Bonham (p92), under chef Michel Bouyer, and the tiny Atholl at the Howard the pick of the three. Much of the Town House Company's success is down to chairman Peter Taylor, another important figure in Edinburgh's food scene.

Meanwhile the chef-proprietor behind Oloroso, Tony Singh, tried an Indian-style restaurant in small premises off Rose Street in 2005 – Roti – checking to see if the public would take to dishes like seared halibut in coconut rather than your traditional bhuna. They did. In fact, Roti was so popular that Singh moved the whole operation to larger premises in Morrison Street in 2007 (p159), allowing him to offer a tiffin bar menu (small metal pots of tapas-size dishes) as well as à la carte and tiffin in the main dining area.

One of the most celebrated foodie names in the city is Valvona & Crolla, an Italian delicatessen dating to 1934 and run by the Contini family. The success of the deli saw them add a Caffè Bar (p104) to the rear of the premises, then a separate VinCaffè (p104) in Multrees Walk off St Andrew Square. However, the two Valvona & Crolla outlets are not the only Contini family businesses in Edinburgh. In the same year the VinCaffè opened, Victor and Carina Contini decided to go it alone, leaving the family brand behind and opening Centotre on George Street (p92). Modern, Italian, informal, this does everything from coffee and cake during the day to three-course

meals in the evening – again with that sumptuous Contini flair for well-sourced ingredients. The couple opened another eaterie in 2007 on the fringes of the New Town and Stockbridge. Bright and colourful, Zanzero (p116) is a 21st-century caffè with a great attitude to food.

And there's more…

There are great Indian restaurants, a decent choice for vegetarians, good bistros and outstanding cafés like Glass & Thompson (p96), not to mention Italian places like Santini (p159), Domenico's (p130) or La Bruschetta (p158) and specialist French restaurants – the list goes on. There are even a few specifically Scottish eateries such as Stac Polly (p103) and Dubh Prais (p70), and a handy aggregation of choices within easy walking distance of each other in Leith (home to two of the city's very best, as well as one contender, well-established seafood bistros, and a few great gastropubs). For the best at a glance, check out the Shortlist box on page 15.

Drinking through the ages

As with much else of life in Edinburgh, elements of its pub scene are defined by the longevity of some classic premises. The Café Royal dates from 1862 (p92) while the Guildford next door (p97) was built even earlier but only became a bar in the 1890s. Bennet's at Tollcross is another Victorian survivor but the King's Wark in Leith (p131) takes the cake. A 15th-century building once occupied the site but was destroyed in an English invasion in 1544. It was rebuilt in the time of James I & VI and still stands today. It does fairly decent food too.

Pubs like these have appealed for years although there has been a great deal of development with café-bars and style bars since the 1980s, crossing the food-drink boundary. The pioneer was Negociants (p75) with its French decor, while another pace-setter was the City Café (p69) with its retro-Americana feel. A more self-conscious commitment to design marked the opening of the Basement in 1994 (p120) and many others took that as their cue.

Into the new decade, however, and everything was dark wood and clean lines. At the populist end of the market Assembly (p67) and the Human Be-In (p144) show evidence of this approach, although it works far better at Rick's (p103) or the Opal Lounge (p101). But what next? Hotel-restaurant-bar venues in the George Street area applied the principle 'more is more' so Tigerlily (p178), Le Monde (p176) and EH2 Tempus at the George Hotel (p96) piled on the ostentation when they opened in 2006.

The Kitchin p14

As an alternative, there has also been a growth in what might be called anti-style bars that hung on to the original interiors and freshened them up, relying on attitude rather than big money refurbishments to carry them forward. This is especially evident in the small Leith-centred group that started with Boda in 2003 and grew to include Sofi's, the Victoria, and Pearce's (for more on these bars, see p133). In the same vein, but with different owners, the gay-friendly Regent (p126) manages cask ale, friendly bar staff and bargain food. For cocktail and cask ale recommendations, see the Shortlist box on p15.

Whisky galore

You could come to Edinburgh and spend your time drinking industrial lager in a soulless style bar, but since you're in the Scottish capital, why not try the national drink? Although all pubs will have some selection of whiskies, some are better than others. Bennet's (p142) has more than 100 varieties on its grand Victorian gantry – try sampling some one sunny afternoon when the sun filters through the front window. The Canny Man's in Morningside (p143) is a much more upmarket venue and also has an amazing choice with some rare bottlings. The selection at Kay's (p98) is more limited but the cosiness of this New Town bar gels neatly with whisky-drinking. For rare single cask bottlings you will have to join the Scotch Malt Whisky Society (p134) with its members' bars in Leith (traditional, clubbish) and Queen Street (modern, stylish), but if you just want to walk into a traditional Old Town pub and be blown away by some of the premium whiskies on offer, the Bow Bar (p67) remains at the top of the list.

Organic Pleasures p22

WHAT'S BEST
Shopping

Catch Edinburgh in February when Scotland are playing a home game in the Six Nations rugby union tournament and it's almost certain that the odd posse of French or Italian fans will be seen sporting lamentable 'hey jimmy' hats, an appalling tartan bonnet and fake ginger hair. The occasional fun-loving tourist during the summer also seizes on these allegedly hilarious souvenirs.

The hats look suitably stupid, but who is more risible, the person who bought one or the shopkeeper who sold it? Scottish tat is a major part of the Edinburgh retail experience: those hats, cheap impulse-purchase kilts, mediocre shortbread, tea towels and Loch Ness monster T-shirts. Fortunately

for the country's international standing the upmarket version of Scottishness does a roaring trade with single malt whiskies, properly tailored Highland dress and vacuum packs of smoked salmon or venison also selling well.

This is such a major tourist centre that it's no surprise that Caledonia good and bad forms one half of the city's shopping proposition. However, the other half involves an increasing number of independent fashion boutiques, design shops and quirky little stores offering locals and visitors rather more appealing wares.

Princely purchases

The best-known shopping drag remains Princes Street. On its south

side, in the shadow of the castle, lie expansive and immaculately maintained gardens, while retail outlets line the north side of the road. Edinburgh's famous department store Jenners is here, with its soaring grand hall, but even this venerable old stager was bought by House of Fraser in 2005, bringing to an end an independent tradition that dated to 1838. These days Princes Street is generally home to the names that you'll find in any other British city centre: Marks & Spencer, Debenhams, Topshop… you'll find everything you need here, but not much that really inspires or surprises.

Much the same can be said about the malls at the east end of Princes Street, the Princes Mall above Waverley Station or the nearby St James Centre which houses a major branch of John Lewis. Thankfully, you don't have to go far to find something a little more interesting.

In recent years, the grand old banks and offices of George Street have been converted into boutiques, bars and restaurants. The result is an upmarket alternative to Princes Street, with fashion brands such as Whistles, Coast and Hobbs sitting alongside renowned jewellers Hamilton & Inches and diamond specialists Lime Blue. The arrival of Harvey Nichols on St Andrew Square in 2002, at the street's eastern end, was another boost; next door, Multrees Walk has become the city's version of London's Bond Street, home to Emporio Armani, Louis Vuitton and Kurt Geiger among others.

Boutique bonanza

To find Edinburgh's most interesting shops you have to venture a little off the beaten track. In the West End, William Street is home to a range of engaging

SHORTLIST

Fine for wine
- Demijohn (p78)
- Cornelius (p122)
- Villeneuve (p122)
- Peter Green (p151)

Foodie heaven
- I J Mellis (p78)
- Herbie of Edinburgh (p117)
- Valvona & Crolla (p122)
- Crombie's (p122)

Whisky central
- Cadenhead's (p77)
- Royal Mile Whiskies (p81)

Up your kilt
- Geoffrey (Tailor) (p78)
- Kinloch Anderson (p136)

Outdoor action
- Tiso (p106)
- Boardwise (p148)
- Freeze (p149)
- Edinburgh Bike Co-op (p149)

Something for the ladies
- Boudiche (p104)
- Organic Pleasures (p122)

Street style
- Armstrongs (p77)
- Oddities (p81)
- Focus (p149)

Label chic
- Corniche (p78)
- Jane Davidson (p106)
- Sam Thomas (p106)

Jewels in the crown
- Arkangel (p104)
- Hamilton & Inches (p105)
- Joseph Bonnar (p106)
- Gallerie Mirages (p116)

Book bonanza
- Beyond Words (p77)
- Word Power (p151)
- Armchair books (p148)

Best record shops
- Ripping Music (p81)
- Underground Solu'shn (p82)

Boudiche

boutiques, from Helen Bateman's exclusive shoes to Arkangel's show-stopping jewellery. Head to the buzzing Grassmarket for a less well-heeled but livelier shopping experience. Vintage clothes emporium Armstrong's (p77) and a good selection of antique shops create a raffish vibe.

At the corner with Cowgatehead, Transreal Fiction is the sci-fi bookshop that caters to the inner fanboy, and Wind Things does a nice line in kites. Nearby sit Oddities (p81) on Victoria Street and Swish (p82) on West Port, both offering fashionable togs.

In Broughton Street, off the top of Leith Walk, you will find Joey D (p122) with unique fashionwear reconstituted from older garments, and bargain shoes too. And as of 2007 Organic Pleasures (p122), an erotic emporium run by women, has been providing non-toxic and hypo-allergenic sex toys among other items.

Staying with the ladies, Boudiche (p104) stocks decadent lingerie. If it's Independent music shops you're after, Underground Solu'shn (p82) on Cockburn street offers an alternative to the high street megastores, as does Ripping Music (p81) on South Bridge. Beyond Words (p77), again on Cockburn Street, is the kind of specialist photography bookshop where you could lose hours just browsing.

The twisting street leads up to the Royal Mile, which caters to your every Scottish-themed need (and then some). Treat yourself to a sugary box of Edinburgh rock and a tartan scarf by all means, but don't miss out on the interesting bottles of whisky at Cadenhead's (p77) or Royal Mile Whiskies (p81), Ness Scotland's (p81) vibrant knitwear or the accessories and 21st-century kilts on sale at Geoffrey (Tailor) (p78). Also on the Royal Mile, opposite the High Kirk of St Giles, the International

Newsagents has a decent selection of magazines but excels with its range of papers, selling everything from *USA Today* to *Le Monde*.

Another string to the city's bow is the way it caters to sports and outdoors enthusiasts. Tiso (p106) is one of the UK's leading stores for walkers and climbers with outlets in Rose Street and Leith; Freeze (p149) on Bruntsfield Place is brilliant for ski and snowboard equipment; the Edinburgh Bike Co-op (p149) on Bruntsfield Links is a two-wheeled nirvana, and there is nothing that Focus (p149) on Grassmarket doesn't know about the Scottish skateboarding scene.

Edible Edinburgh

One often unheralded feature of Edinburgh's shopping landscape is its preponderance of great food shops. Valvona & Crolla (p122) is the most famous of several delis around the city – and wins awards for its Italian wine range – but there are also a number of terrific speciality shops. Try the gourmet sausages from Crombie's (p122) on Broughton Street or Iain Mellis's (p78) famous cheese shop on Victoria Street – you'll smell it before you see it. The property price inflation of recent years has also gentrified a number of old tenemental neighbourhoods, so venture down Easter Road – en route to Leith – and you'll find a great wine shop called Cornelius (p122). Other wine specialists well worth seeking out are Villeneuve (122) on Broughton Street and Peter Green (p151) up in Marchmont.

Mall of the same

In contrast, anyone looking for a functional mall with hectares of car parking space will head for Cameron Toll in the south of the city or the Gyle Centre at its

Cadenhead's

western edge, while Fort Kinnaird on the city's eastern rim almost stands as a zoned shopping village. Standing head and shoulders above them all, though, is Ocean Terminal (p127) in Leith. A central feature of Edinburgh's waterfront regeneration programme, this mall was designed by Sir Terence Conran and opened in 2001. Sitting bang on the Western Harbour, Ocean Terminal is home to the Britannia Experience, which allows access to the decommissioned royal yacht (p128), and also has a cinema complex and various bars and restaurants. Many of the shops fall into the 'usual suspects' category (Waterstone's, the Body Shop, Gap, Bhs), although not all. The iconic Scottish food store Baxters might be of interest to tourists and cock-a-leekie soup aficionados, while Ligne Roset is one of the best places in Edinburgh to blow serious money on designer armchairs, sideboards, beds and other household accessories.

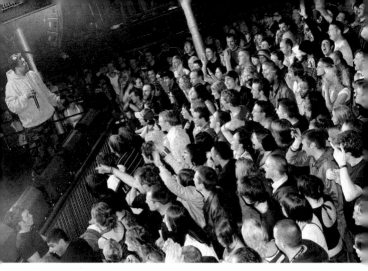

Nightlife

The first thing anyone ever says about nightlife in Edinburgh is, 'It's not as good as Glasgow'. But with better licensing hours, some seriously good club nights and a live music scene that spans everything from indie pub bands to enormous gigs in sports stadia, Edinburgh is not exactly lacking for entertainment. It may not be as vibrant as its West of Scotland cousin but it has its moments. For up to date information on all nightlife venues and events, check the local fortnightly listings magazine *The List*.

Clubs

If you want to wave your hands in the air like you just don't care, spend your evening dancing with students taking advantage of drinks promotions, or even boogie with the Friday night post-work posse burning off a week's worth of wage-slave frustration, then Edinburgh offers it all. Fortunately, for the more discerning clubber there is also a range of pre-club bars and nightclubs where the music is more interesting than chart cheese.

Almost every corner of the compact city centre seems to hold a style bar and among those that make a perfect base from which to embark on an evening's clubbing are the City Café (p69) and Dragonfly (p144). Assembly (p67) and the Human Be-In (p144) have a DJ-focused appeal while The Street (p126) adds a touch of colour to the east end, run by DJ Trendy Wendy. The beer garden at the nearby Outhouse (p121) is well used by smokers during the summer.

A number of Edinburgh drinking dens open until 3am, or even 5am

Liquid Room

during the Festival and the week leading up to Hogmanay. Most offer free admission; those that don't will levy only a minimal door charge. Pivo (p122) is the most renowned, its loose Czech theme adding little to what is an already bustling bar. House and techno DJs play seven nights a week. Cosy basement lounge Medina (p73) is also enlivened by a dynamic mix of house and funk. And if cocktails in sleek surroundings are your thing, don't miss Opal Lounge (p101) where the weekly programme of events includes Tuesday's excellent Motherfunk.

As for the clubs themselves, several operate dual existences as venues for live music as well as DJs. Chief among them is Cabaret Voltaire (p83) with a range of nights including Ultragroove, the Sugarbeat Club (an offshoot of the original Leeds Sugarbeat created by the Utah Saints), and the highly rated Optimo (an 'annexe' of the Glasgow original).

The Liquid Room (p85) and the Bongo Club (p83) also mix live

SHORTLIST

The late late bars
- Favorit (p70)
- Negociants (p75)
- Opal Lounge (p101)
- Pivo (p122)

Pub rockers
- Bannermans (p86)
- Whistlebinkies (p76)

Best pre-club places
- Assembly (p67)
- City Café (p69)
- Human Be-In (p144)
- The Outhouse (p121)

Great for gigs
- Cabaret Voltaire (p83)
- Liquid Room (p85)
- Usher Hall (p83)
- Wee Red Bar (p137)

You're having a laugh
- Jongleurs (p126)
- The Stand (p107)

Best gay venues
- CC Bloom's (p124)
- Regent (p126)
- Street (p126)
- Vibe at Ego (p126)

Just drinkin' and dancin'
- Ego (p126)
- Espionage (p85)
- Massa (p73)

Most laid-back
- Forest (p85)
- Medina (p73)
- Jazz Bar (p85)
- Out of the Bedroom (p85)

Best for brilliant DJs
- Bongo Club (p83)
- Cabaret Voltaire (p83)
- Touch at Ego (p126)
- Voodoo Rooms (p104)

Best for goths and metalheads
- Studio 24 (p126)

bands with DJ sets. The former continues to thrive on a repertoire of well-established nights, foremost of which is the long-running and indie Evol. The latter boasts the eclectic Headspin, the dub-heavy Messenger Sound System and drum'n'bass Xplicit.

Goths and metalheads should investigate Studio 24 (p126), though it always seems under threat of closure due to complaints from neighbours. No such problem at Ego (p126) on Picardy Place which is home to a range of acclaimed clubs, straight and gay.

Without a permanent home, Vegas! is Scotland's peripatetic orgy of swinging music and Rat Pack fabulousness (www.vegas scotland.co.uk) and crops up at various places including the Voodoo Rooms (p104), a bar-club-restaurant in a classic Victorian space that opened in late 2007.

Music

In Scotland's post punk and new wave scene, a talented Edinburgh band called TV21 recorded an album, built a decent following, and secured a prestigious support slot when the Rolling Stones played the city's Playhouse Theatre back in spring 1982. Some said they should have been as successful as Simple Minds or Echo and the Bunnymen, but after the engagement with Mick and the boys TV21 promptly split up and vanished until they got together again in autumn 2005 for a commemorative John Peel Day gig.

This could almost be a paradigm for local rock'n'roll. Aside from a few notable breakthrough names (the Bay City Rollers, the Rezillos, Shirley Manson with Garbage), Edinburgh has often been bridesmaid where Glasgow got to wear the big white dress. In 2004, for example, when the world-conquering Franz Ferdinand played a homecoming gig at Glasgow's SECC, they asked the Fire Engines to reform as the support act. Never famous but fairly influential, they were another early 1980s ensemble from the Scottish capital.

Thanks to the fluid nature of Edinburgh's young population (tourists, travellers and students) new bands and music scenes can still find it hard to anchor themselves here. The more fragmented nature of the contemporary music business doesn't help either. All the same, you can find live music virtually every night of the week in pubs like Whistlebinkies (p76) or Bannermans (p83); the Wee Red Bar at Edinburgh College of Art (p137) has a regular new bands showcase, while the Bongo Club (p83) stages everything from up and coming local electro rockers to Polish hip hop.

Edinburgh has also exploited its fairly civilised licensing hours to blend clubbing with live music in a way that Glasgow, hampered by relatively draconian alcohol laws, has been unable to do. Many venues in the city start out the evening as live music spots before morphing, in some cases seamlessly, into a nightclub around 10.30pm or 11pm.

As for well-known bands and major venues, the really enormous gigs are held in stadia like Murrayfield (p160), Meadowbank or Easter Road – even Edinburgh Castle Esplanade. The Playhouse Theatre (p126) attracts big names like Neil Young and the Beach Boys, or what remains of them. Those Old Town club-crossover venues, Cabaret Voltaire (p83) and the Liquid Room (p85), may be smaller but they tend to have a better atmosphere. In addition, a couple of the city's concert halls stage regular rock and pop shows: the Queen's Hall (p153) has hosted gigs from cultured acts such as Richard Thompson and Eddi Reader, while the Usher Hall (p153) has seen everyone from Björk to the Flaming Lips.

Check out the Triptych Festival (www.triptychfestival.com), a jumble of alternative acts in the run-up to the May Day bank holiday at many venues. The Edge festival (1-26 August 2008) replaces what used to be T on the Fringe, which has brought everyone from Arcade Fire to Nancy Sinatra to town.

Gay and lesbian

For a town with so many students and transient young people in general it's surprising that Edinburgh's gay scene has yet to divesify beyond the standard scene clichés of Kylie, vests and plucked eyebrows. But for what its gay scene lacks in variety it makes up for in friendliness. You won't get any of the snottiness you get with fashionable queer clubs in London, and no one's going to turn you away for not being cool enough, or not gay enough for that matter. Come one, come all.

Centred on an area known as the Pink Triangle (p124), bounded on two sides by Broughton Street and Leith Walk, Edinburgh's gay scene thrives on drinking and late-night hedonism. For years CC Blooms (p124) was the only permanent gay club and while the balance has been tipped by heaps of homo venues opening in the area, CC's still squashes them in. And there's a fair amount of gay nights at other 'straight' venues too, especially at Ego. The quality and quantity of LGBT bars also keeps things in healthy shape.

Unsurprisingly things get an awful lot gayer during August with an invasion of razor-tongued drama queens from all over the world. For a more specifically Scottish night out the Lothian Gay & Lesbian Switchboard (www.lgls.co.uk) organises a ceilidh every spring and autumn where you can reel away until the wee small hours.

Comedy

Edinburgh is the feast or famine capital of comedy. During the Fringe in August fans get to gorge themselves and the number of comedians in the city isn't even funny. New performers are desperate to get noticed by award judges while talent-spotters from London are just as desperate to find the next big thing. Sometimes you want to laugh, sometimes the whole process is as chortlesome as a job interview. The real comedy superstars now tend to either avoid the city in August or parachute in for short runs in major venues.

For the other 11 months of the year, the dearth of consistent top-notch comedy is no joke. Comedy nights launched by local promoters and frustrated comedians come and go with alarming regularity, making it virtually impossible to predict which will still be around a few months hence. The only guarantee is that Jongleurs (p126) and the Stand (p108) are here to stay, and that's often your lot. At the former, one of the 16 Jongleurs clubs across Britain, you always know what you're going to get – fairly mainstream giggles – which is the chain's greatest strength and biggest weakness. At the Stand the surroundings are a lot more grungey and the material can have a little more edge but less consistency. Both venues mix local talent with occasional luminaries from the UK scene.

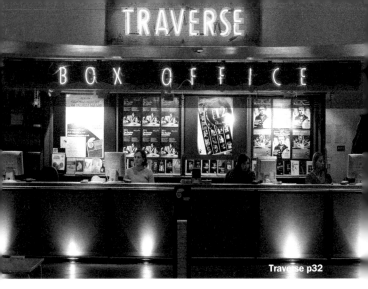

Traverse p32

Arts & Leisure

August here is both hectic and unique, a few weeks when Edinburgh becomes the world centre for the arts. The other 11 months of the year cannot quite match the intensity of the International Festival and Fringe, but that doesn't mean that the city is bereft of creativity. There are some major sporting events too.

Classical music

Classical music in Edinburgh took off in the 18th century when the Edinburgh Musical Society moved into St Cecilia's Hall on the Cowgate. Named for the patron saint of music and musicians, and completed in 1763, it was the first purpose-built concert hall in Scotland and hosts concerts to this day (Niddry Street, Cowgate, Old Town, 650 2805). Fast-forward to the 21st century and classical music is still thriving, although perhaps not to the extent of a guaranteed full house at every one of the city's events.

Edinburgh's leading venue is the Usher Hall (p153), closed for a lengthy period in 2007-8 for refurbishment and the addition of a new, modern wing, although it should be open again in time for the 2008 Edinburgh International Festival. Meanwhile the two most notable ensembles playing regularly in the city are the Royal Scottish National Orchestra (www.rsno.org.uk) and the Scottish Chamber Orchestra (www.sco.org.uk). The RSNO has been staging a lively programme of concerts at the Festival Theatre (p152) while the Usher Hall is indisposed. When not touring, the SCO mainly divides its time between the Usher Hall and the Queen's Hall (p153).

A few other native groups play frequently in the city, led by the BBC Scottish Symphony Orchestra (www.bbc.co.uk/scotland/bbcsso). The Scottish Ensemble (www.scottishensemble.co.uk) specialises in less celebrated works that may not otherwise see the light of day, while Mr McFall's Chamber (www.mcfalls.co.uk) is an ingenious experimental project that unites SCO players and other talented, broadminded musicians who are equally at home tackling Zappa as they are Liszt. Edinburgh University's Reid Concert Hall (p86) has a programme covering everything from student composers and new experimental music to more established ensembles playing the likes of Haydn or Bach. While the city has no dedicated opera house, Glasgow-based Scottish Opera (www.scottishopera.org.uk) stages productions at the Festival Theatre (p152).

Dance

Since 2001 Edinburgh's Grassmarket has been home to Dance Base (p86), Scotland's national centre for dance. This is more a custom-built space for classes and workshops rather than major performances, but it is a focus for the city's dance community and caters to professionals as well as enthusiasts who might just want to learn to salsa. If you want to see something happening on stage, the Festival Theatre (p152) hosts performances all year round, notably by the Scottish Dance Theatre (www.scottishdancetheatre.com), Scottish Ballet (www.scottishballet.co.uk) and visiting groups from near and far.

SHORTLIST

The big ones
- Edinburgh International Festival (p37)
- Edinburgh Festival Fringe (p37)

August's best of the rest
- Edinburgh Jazz & Blues Festival (p37)
- Edinburgh International Book Festival (p38)
- Edinburgh Tattoo (p38)

Best for cineastes
- Scotsman Screening Room (p86)
- Filmhouse (p152)
- Cameo (p152)

Alternative drama
- Royal Lyceum (p57)
- Bedlam Theatre (p85)
- Traverse (p153)
- Theatre Workshop (p117)

Best for classical music
- Reid Concert Hall (p86)
- Usher Hall (p153)
- Queen's Hall (p153)

Best for musical theatre and dance
- Playhouse (p126)
- Festival Theatre (p152)
- King's (p153)

Specialised subjects
- Scottish Storytelling Centre (p64)
- Dance Base (p86)

Sporting emotions
- Scotland in the Six Nations at Murrayfield (p160)
- The local football derby at Hearts (p160)

Don't miss festivals
- Edinburgh Science Festival (p35)
- Edinburgh International Film Festival (p37)
- Hogmanay (p40)

DON'T MISS

Recently both the Northern Ballet Theatre and La La La Human Steps have graced the stage. Both the Festival Theatre and the Playhouse (p126) go in for the odd classical blockbuster like *Mary Poppins* or *Swan Lake*, while the Traverse (p153) may be better known for its innovative theatre shows but also has more intimate contemporary dance gigs from time to time.

Film

For a relatively small city, Edinburgh packs a cinematic punch. Its most famous son, Sean Connery, is still the most celebrated James Bond, and were it not for JK Rowling chewing her pen in the town's cafés (p115) there would be no Harry Potter.

Given the history of the place, it has been an ideal setting for film makers looking to adapt costume drama classics. At the other end of the spectrum you've got *Trainspotting* and *Shallow Grave* which put some cool grit back into the town's film scene (p100). And then there's always *The Prime of Miss Jean Brodie,* which was shot in the city, or the *Da Vinci Code*, filmed at nearby Rosslyn Chapel.

When it comes to movie-going, Edinburgh is fairly typical in that enormous multiplexes dominate the local market. On the other hand, the celebrated Filmhouse (p152) has served as an outpost of arthouse and foreign cinema since 1979, as well as the nerve centre of the annual Edinburgh International Film Festival (p37). Established in 1947, this is the second longest-running film festival on the planet. The Cameo (p152), just up the road, also shows international cinema and arthouse films, leavened with more mainstream programming and late-night horror flicks.

Sport & leisure

With a professional rugby union side, the national rugby stadium, two top-flight football teams and even international games of cricket – Scotland's cricket team (www.cricketscotland.com) now plays in the International Cricket Council Intercontinental Cup against the likes of Kenya or Namibia – Edinburgh is good for spectator sports. Murrayfield (p160) is arguably Scotland's best sports stadium and hosts Edinburgh's rugby union games in the Magners League and Heineken Cup (www.edinburghrugby.org). Attendances tend to be only a few thousand in a 67,500 capacity arena, so the atmosphere is better when the national side plays sell-out home games here in the Six Nations (www.scottishrugby.org).

Scotland have never won the Six Nations, but that's hardly surprising given that they only managed outright victory in the Five Nations on three occasions in the postwar era. It's a similar story with football, with local clubs Heart of Midlothian (p160) and Hibernian (www.hibs.co.uk) being rather overshadowed by Celtic and Rangers in neighbouring Glasgow. Although they have managed the odd domestic cup in the last couple of decades, no Edinburgh side has been Scottish champion since 1960.

It's clear then that the city does not lack sporting spectacle, just sustained success among its various teams. There are also any number of golf courses in Edinburgh and nearby, most famously Muirfield in East Lothian (www.muirfield.org.uk). SportScotland(www.sportscotland. org.uk) has more information about local events, clubs and governing sports bodies.

Theatre

Edinburgh's two main producing houses are the modern Traverse (p153) for new and untried theatre and the Victorian-era Royal Lyceum for the more established (p153). The roots of the Traverse go back to the 1960s although it moved to its current purpose-built premises within the Saltire Court building on Cambridge Street in 1992. There are two performance spaces, both fairly small, but they are the best places in the city to see fresh, innovative writing. The Royal Lyceum is a far larger, traditional venue where you can see classics both ancient and modern (Shakespeare, Tennessee Williams), adaptations like *Vanity Fair*, as well as contemporary drama. The two theatres sit back to back beside the Usher Hall in the 'arts quarter' off Lothian Road.

The King's up by Tollcross (p153) and the Festival Theatre over on Nicolson Street (p152) are run by the same management and you can find a range of material at either. The former puts on everything from pantomime to Gilbert and Sullivan or Peter Shaffer plays; the latter can have short runs of populist shows like *Half a Sixpence* or *Doctor Dolittle*, but also *The Mighty Boosh* on tour.

For large-scale mainstream entertainment, though, you need to head for Edinburgh's largest theatre, the Playhouse (p126). This is where you will catch major music-theatre extravaganzas like *High School Musical*, *Fiddler on the Roof*, or *Seven Brides for Seven Brothers*.

There are stars treading the boards in Edinburgh on a regular basis, and non-stop during August, but the city's theatre scene is hardly driven by celebrity or glamour. Audiences tend to be attracted by the standard of the ensemble or the promise of new work from a promising playwright, or a more established name. Some names to keep an eye on are Liz Lochhead, David Harrower, John Clifford, Henry Adam, Douglas Maxwell, Gregory Burke and David Greig, whose play *Black Watch* was the critically acclaimed success of the 2006 festival, followed by *Damascus* in 2007.

Cameo p31

Calendar

Six Nations

The following is a pick of the annual events that happen in Edinburgh. Further information and exact dates can be found nearer the time from the local listings magazine, *The List* (fortnightly), and also from the local tourist information centre (p189). Dates in **bold** are public holidays.

January

1 **New Year's Day Triathlon**
Holyrood Park
www.edinburghtri.org
A relatively short course to burn off Hogmanay hangovers.

25 **Burns Night**
Various venues
www.burns.visitscotland.com
Celebrating Scotland's national bard.

February

Early Feb-mid Mar **Six Nations**
Murrayfield
www.scottishrugby.org
Scotland's home games in the annual rugby union tournament.

Early Feb-mid Mar **Scottish Snowdrop Festival**
Royal Botanic Garden
http://white.visitscotland.com
Winter flora at its most cute.

March

Ongoing **Six Nations, Scottish Snowdrop Festival**

Late Mar **Ceilidh Culture Festival**
Various venues
www.ceilidhculture.co.uk
A celebration of Scottish song, dance, music and storytelling.

Late Mar **Edinburgh International Science Festival**
Various venues
www.sciencefestival.co.uk
A fortnight that puts the fun back into science with more than 130 events.

April

Late Apr **Triptych**
Various venues
www.triptychfestival.com
Five days of gigs and cinema centred on the inventive end of popular music.

30 **Beltane**
Calton Hill
www.beltane.org
Modern pagans welcome the spring with dance, costume and fire.

May

Early May **BUPA Great Edinburgh Run**
City centre
www.greatrun.org
Enduringly popular 10km race with over 10,000 runners.

Late May-early June **Leith Festival**
Various venues, Leith
www.leithfestival.com
Leith does a scaled-down version of the Edinburgh Fringe over ten days.

Late May **Bank of Scotland Imaginate Festival**
Various venues
www.imaginate.org.uk
A theatre extravaganza for children with a week of international artists and shows.

Late May **Taste of Edinburgh**
The Meadows
www.channel4.com
Four days celebrating Scottish food – foodie heaven in a tented village.

June

Ongoing Leith Festival

Mid June **Royal Highland Show**
Ingliston
www.royalhighlandshow.org
One of the UK's top agricultural shows with over 5,000 animals, competitions, crafts and food.

Edinburgh international Science Festival

The best guides to enjoying London life

(but don't just take our word for it)

'Get the inside track on the capital's neighbourhoods'

Independent on Sunday

'I'm always asked how I keep up to date with shopping and services in a city as big as London. This guide is the answer'

Red Magazine

'A treasure trove of treats that lists the best the capital has to offer'

The People

Rated 'Best Restaurant Guide'

Sunday Times

Available at all good bookshops and timeout.com/shop from £8.99

100% Independent

Mid June Seven Hills of Edinburgh Race & Challenge
Edinburgh's seven hills
www.seven-hills.org.uk
A popular 14-mile race around Edinburgh's hills starting and finishing on Calton Hill in the city centre.

Mid June Scottish Traditional Beer Festival
Assembly Rooms
www.camra.org.uk
Three days with stalls, food, and more than 120 rare cask ales on tap.

Mid June Pride Scotia
City centre
www.pride-scotia.org
Biennial gay pride march and rally, alternates with Glasgow; to be held in Edinburgh in 2009 and 2011.

Mid-late June Edinburgh International Film Festival
Filmhouse & other venues
www.edfilmfest.org.uk
Major event on the global film festival calendar: two weeks of premieres, retrospectives and more.

July

Early July Holyrood Week
Palace of Holyroodhouse
www.royal.gov.uk
The Queen is in residence and hosts her annual Scottish garden party; invitation only of course.

Late July Edinburgh Jazz & Blues Festival
Various venues
www.edinburghjazzfestival.co.uk
Ten days of jazz and blues from the longest-running festival of its kind in the UK.

August

Early-late Aug Edinburgh International Festival
Various venues
www.eif.co.uk
World famous arts shindig over more than three weeks.

Early-late Aug Edinburgh Fringe
Various venues
www.edfringe.com

Beltane p35

Edinburgh Fringe p37

Enormous, diverse, vibrant: 31,000 performances of more than 2,000 shows in just over three weeks.

Early-late Aug **Edinburgh Military Tattoo**
Edinburgh Castle Esplanade
www.edintattoo.co.uk
Music, dance and military display with a dramatic castle backdrop.

Early-late Aug **Edinburgh Art Festival**
Various venues
www.edinburghartfestival.org
An all-encompassing showcase for the visual arts.

2nd Sun of Fringe **Fringe Sunday**
The Meadows
www.edfringe.com
A massive outdoor carnival of live performance with a crowd estimated at 250,000.

Mid Aug **Edinburgh International Book Festival**
Charlotte Square Gardens
www.edbookfest.co.uk

Famous authors and more than 700 events over more than two weeks, all in a tented village in a New Town square.

Aug bank holiday weekend **Edinburgh International Television Festival**
EICC
www.mgeitf.co.uk
Media Guardian-sponsored three-day knees-up for the television industry.

Late Aug **Festival of Politics**
Scottish Parliament
www.festivalofpolitics.org.uk
Three days of events at Holyrood bringing together politics, media and the arts.

Late Aug **Edinburgh Mela**
Venue to be confirmed
www.edinburgh-mela.co.uk
The city's annual South Asian festival with three days of music, dance, poetry, puppetry and more.

Last Sun of Festival **Festival Fireworks Concert**
Princes Street Gardens
www.eif.co.uk

Festival fever

For most of the year, Edinburgh is a relaxed, reasonably sedate city, revelling in the benefits of its capital status while enjoying the calm that comes with a population of less than half a million. Come August, it's all change. The population doubles, the atmosphere becomes almost continental, and the grey stone façades burst into colour. It's the largest arts celebration in the world, drawing performers from Uppsala to Uluru and all points in between.

The Edinburgh International Festival started the fun in 1947, aiming to bring the best available drama, music and visual arts to postwar Scotland. The Fringe also started in 1947 as an unofficial, offbeat riposte, but grew to dwarf its big brother. August also sees assorted other festivals, all administratively

separate, like the Edinburgh Military Tattoo or the Edinburgh International Book Festival. The schedule has become so crowded that the Edinburgh Jazz & Blues Festival now kicks off in late July and the Edinburgh International Film Festival has moved wholesale to June.

In the busy weeks of August, however, not everyone is enamoured with the dramatic shift in the city's character. Some locals jump ship and rent out their properties to visitors for massive fees; meanwhile others simply stay and grumble, but they're in the minority: for most, the festivals together comprise the highlight of the city's cultural calendar. Unique is an overused word, but it absolutely applies here, taking in everything from high-budget opera to low-concept DJ nights, and from literary discussions in the New Town to tightrope walkers on the High Street.

Legions of internationally renowned writers, artists and performers descend on the city, and the usually busy London comedy circuit virtually closes for a month. But Edinburgh also fills with rank amateurs on a wing and a prayer, making a tilt at fame and fortune before the money runs out. You may have to queue for three hours to get into the latest hot-ticket show, or you may be the only person in the audience. You might be moved to tears by dramatic theatre and sent into paroxysms of laughter by the routine of a stand-up comic. Or, of course, vice versa.

Climactic end to the Edinburgh International Festival with a huge crowd gathering in the city centre to witness music and an amazing pyrotechnics display.

September

Late Sept **Doors Open Day**
Various venues
www.cockburnassociation.org.uk
The Cockburn Association persuades the owners of many of Edinburgh's finest private buildings, from sewage works to stately homes, to allow the public a free peek behind their doors for one day each year.

October

Late Oct **Scottish International Storytelling Festival**
Scottish Storytelling Centre
www.scottishstorytellingcentre.co.uk
Scotland's annual celebration of its oral tradition with ten days of tales delivered with a certain artistry and panache.

November

Mid Nov **Edinburgh Art Fair**
The Corn Exchange
www.artedinburgh.com
Affordable prints to £50,000 paintings at Scotland's biggest art fair.

30 **St Andrew's Day**
No specific venue
Have a drink and celebrate Scotland's patron saint.

December

Early-late Dec **Edinburgh's Christmas**
Princes Street Gardens
www.edinburghchristmas.com
Ferris wheel, German market, Winter Wonderland skating rink and more.

29-31 Dec **Edinburgh's Hogmanay**
Various venues
www.edinburghshogmanay.org
Torchlight procession, street theatre, massive street party and a major rock concert to bring in the New Year.

Hogmanay

Itineraries

Edinburgh Castle

Millennium Mile

Where does Edinburgh's history start? Volcanic eruptions from hundreds of millions of years ago that shaped Arthur's Seat? Mesolithic hunter-gatherers who ranged across the Lothians after the last Ice Age? Or from hints of holy men and warlords during the Dark Ages?

They are all beginnings of a kind but the solid soap opera of place and people dates to King Malcolm III, giving the city a story to tell that spans a millennium, from the 11th century to the 21st.

Although the Castle Rock had been fortified for many years, it was Malcolm who built the first known Castle. He also fell in love with, and married, Princess Margaret of England, who had fled to Scotland with members of her family in the years after the Norman invasion of 1066. Before Malcolm and Margaret, Scotland would have been unrecognisable to anyone from the modern era. Afterwards it began to take shape.

Margaret herself built a priory in Dunfermline and started a ferry service across the Forth from a village still called Queensferry. Their son, King David I, established religious foundations throughout Scotland and was also responsible for **St Margaret's Chapel** (p55) in the grounds of the Castle in the early years of the 12th century. This is the place to begin a walk through Edinburgh's millennium narrative.

You could spend a whole day following our itinerary, taking in some sights or stopping for lunch, say. Or cut it short after half a day and pick it up again whenever you find yourself on the Royal Mile – the choice is yours.

Witches' Memorial

High Kirk of St Giles

Although you have to pay to get into **Edinburgh Castle** (p55), given the attractions the ticket is worth the price. Within its confines, you find David's simple and unpretentious memorial to his mother. At nearly 900 years old, this Norman-style structure is the oldest building still in use in the city; tourism aside, it hosts small weddings. Elsewhere you can find a display on Scotland's crown jewels and another on the prisoners who were kept here during the American War of Independence and the Napoleonic Wars.

Perhaps the most affecting building of all is the **Scottish National War Memorial**. Once a barracks, it was substantially refurbished in the 1920s to commemorate Scots who perished in World War I. The original honour roll sits in a casket standing on a platform built into the very Castle Rock. Given the regional regimental nature of the British Army, it's not hard for Scots to browse the pages of the memorial books sitting by individual regimental monuments and find the names of old family members.

When you leave the Castle, and head across the Esplanade to Castlehill, you'll find yourself at the top of the **Royal Mile** and the strip of adjoining streets (Castlehill, Lawnmarket, High Street, Canongate) that formed the backbone of late-medieval Edinburgh. Look out for the **Witches' Memorial** where over 300 women were burned as witches between 1479 and 1722. The imposing former church at the Lawnmarket corner, now called the **Hub** and home to the Edinburgh International Festival, dates to 1844 and was co designed by Scottish architect J Gillespie Graham and the celebrated Augustus Pugin, who was also responsible for the Houses of Parliament in London.

Heading down to the High Street, there is a vast wealth of historical buildings, principally the

High Kirk of St Giles (p60).
Parts of the Kirk survive from the
12th century, although much of the
modern fabric dates to the 19th.
It played a key role in the Scottish
Reformation in the 16th century
and was the location of a famous
incident in the summer of 1637.
Local woman Jenny Geddes was
said to have thrown her stool at
the minister who was trying to use
a new book of common prayer
promoted by King Charles I and the
Archbishop of Canterbury; this was
all too Popish for Ms Geddes – and
many other locals – who famously
berated the minister with a cry of,
'Daur ye say mass in my lug?'
('Dare you say mass in my ear?').
The following year, Scots flocked to
sign the National Covenant at the
nearby **Greyfriars Church** (p55),
a political and religious statement
in opposition to the Anglicanism
of Charles, and another example
of the tumult all over the British
Isles during those years.

Walk behind St Giles to
Parliament Square and you find
a statue of King Charles II astride a
horse, dating to 1685 and believed
to be the oldest statue in the city.
Adjacent Parliament House was
home to Scotland's parliament in
the 17th century and now to the
Supreme Courts of Scotland. On
the other side of the road, the **City
Chambers** is the headquarters for
Edinburgh's local authority but
was originally built as the Royal
Exchange in 1761 over earlier
streets and buildings.

This is hard to imagine until
you drop down one of the steep
closes from the High Street to
Cockburn Street, view the City
Chambers from the rear or north
side, and see how extensive the
structure really is. A local company
runs regular tours (p84) of the
abandoned subterranean Old Town
underneath, while others will let
you see the spooky vaults under
South Bridge nearby.

Edinburgh makes great capital
of such history but the unfortunate
fact is that the further back you go,
the fewer actual structures survive,
especially the more ordinary
examples rather than castles or
palaces. The city was fortunate
then to hang on to **John Knox's
House** down on the lower reaches
of the High Street, now adjacent to
the **Scottish Storytelling
Centre** (p64). Not only was this

ITINERARIES

Edinburgh Castle p43

thought to be the home of a major figure from the country's past, but is one of the few remaining 15th-century tenements. As it turns out, it probably belonged to a goldsmith called Mossman rather than Knox. But hey, it's at least 500 years old.

Keep walking down into the Canongate and you can go from a 'who lived where' debate of the 15th century to a controversy of the 21st in a short stretch. The £300 million Caltongate development (www.caltongate.com) is seeking to create a large new stretch of homes, commercial premises and arts facilities in the land fronting on to the Canongate, down New Street to the north and over to Calton Road. This has been described as the biggest alteration to the Old Town since the 12th century, but after many objections was given the go-ahead by the local council in early 2008. Its path to completion will doubtless provoke more opposition.

In part this may come from people's experience of the **Scottish Parliament** less than half a kilometre further down the road (p74), a building that was delivered severely over-budget and three years late. An innate conservatism in certain aspects of Edinburgh life was always going to struggle with Catalan architect Enric Miralles' vision for the country's new democratic chamber, regardless of the budget and deadline disasters. Whatever anyone thinks of the design, though – best viewed from Salisbury Crags to get a sense of the complex as a whole – its execution was a textbook case of project management failure which caused much soul searching in Edinburgh and throughout Scotland both before and after the building's official opening in 2004.

Not all modern buildings cause gnashing of teeth however. Small contemporary premises that sneak quietly into odd corners here and there soon inspire affection – the **Scottish Poetry Library** appeared in Crichton's Close off the Canongate in 2000 without any fuss. Edinburgh now only seems to have a problem with the big and bold, which was presumably not the case when David completed **Holyrood Abbey** (p63) in 1128, or when Kings James IV and James V constructed the adjacent **Palace of Holyroodhouse** in the 16th century (p63).

These buildings provide the eastern terminus for the Royal Mile. The abbey ruins take visitors back to the late medieval period, but the palace jumps forward again in time. Still the Queen's official residence in Scotland – she hosts a garden party here every summer – the various rooms and apartments give a whistlestop tour of the last 400 years and more of Scottish history. One of the strangest display items anywhere in the palace is simply a humble set of cufflinks. They appear to be made of simple glass with some brownish cloth behind them. The cloth is a fraction of handkerchief and the colouring is said to be the blood of Charles I, which the handkerchief was dipped into at his London execution in early 1649 – less than 12 years after Jenny Geddes threw her stool in protest at the High Kirk of St Giles. Not a case of cause and effect, but certainly part of the same whirlwind.

From the Scotland of Malcolm and Margaret to the developments and architectural crises of the 21st century via religious strife and regicide, Edinburgh covers an entire millennium along the Royal Mile. The rest of the city adds further flesh to the bones.

Ocean Terminal p49

Coastal City

Even today, some first-time visitors to Edinburgh express surprise that it lies on the Firth of Forth. 'I never knew it was beside the sea!' they exclaim. The Old Town of Edinburgh never was, of course; it sits about 2 miles inland. But as the Scottish capital grew and sprawled, it started to incorporate waterfront real estate from **Cramond** in the west to **Portobello** in the east – just under 9 miles of coastline encompassing river mouths, small harbours, major docks and beach. Investigating Edinburgh's coast on foot reveals a completely different side to the city.

To start this exploration – a good, long day out, give or take a pub lunch – you can take a taxi or a Lothian bus from the city centre (No.24 or No.41, www.lothian buses.net) to Cramond, an almost self-contained village way out on Edinburgh's western edge.

Cramond is actually the earliest known settlement in the Lothians and the site where the River Almond meets the Firth of Forth. Waste has been found here from the camps of Mesolithic people who occupied the area from as long ago as 8500 BC, while the Romans turned up around 140 AD; the local church grounds have the remains of their fort and in 1997 a Roman sandstone statue – depicting a lioness eating a man – was hauled out of the river mud. The artefact is now at the **National Museum of Scotland** (p60); more local history is available from the **Cramond Heritage Trust** (www.cramond heritagetrust.org.uk).

The Old Cramond Bridge, just a few minutes from the bus stop at the southern end of Whitehouse Road, is the best place to start, the beginning of a leafy and attractive riverside walkway, not even two miles long. This goes past the ruins

Newhaven harbour

of 18th-century mills and ends at the mouth of the River Almond, itself a popular spot for berthing small yachts and dinghies.

Standing at the river mouth, on the Forth, you can see **Cramond Island** a kilometre offshore. This is tidal and can be reached by causeway but visitors need to pay strict attention to high and low tide times, usually on a noticeboard on the esplanade – otherwise you risk being cut off. The island's old gun emplacements and abandoned buildings date to World War II.

Back on the foreshore there is a seriously scenic walk to the east: two miles of big skies and panoramas out over the Forth to Fife before you leave the greenery behind and hit the old industrial reaches of **Granton** at Shore Road. The first kilometre or so along Shore Road is not exactly picture postcard territory, but that's all been changing in recent years due to a massive redevelopment plan known as **Edinburgh Forthside** (www.edinburghforthside.co.uk). Further on you hit historical

interest at the Victorian harbour. One of the lighthouse-building Stevenson family, which also spawned Robert Louis Stevenson, had a hand in its construction.

Keep heading east along Lower Granton Road and within minutes you pass the **Old Chain Pier** (32 Trinity Crescent, 0131 552 1233). Perched right above the water, it's a handy stopover for a beer and pub lunch. In the 19th century there was an actual chain pier here, extending way out into the Forth but it was destroyed by a storm in autumn 1898. The pub used to be its booking office; in winter the spume from the Forth still speckles the windows while on a quiet day you might spot a solitary heron.

Leaving the pub and continuing east along Starbank Road, it takes no time to reach **Newhaven**. Founded by Scotland's King James IV around the turn of the 16th century, this was originally a dockyard where foreign shipwrights flocked to build a new Scottish navy. They married local women and their descendants clustered around the neighbourhood, which nearby Edinburghers viewed as insular.

Until the first half of the 20th century Newhaven was a prosperous fishing village, well known for its colourful fishwives who would sport Flemish bonnets, bright skirts and waistcoats. When they carried their creels of fresh fish up to Edinburgh every morning to sell, it looked like an incursion from the Low Countries rather than the coast. The **Newhaven Heritage Museum** explains all this and more (24 Pier Place, www.cac.org.uk). As in many other parts of the British Isles, however, the fishing industry faded away, though you can still sample Scottish produce at the Loch Fyne Restaurant right by the harbour (p132).

It's a scant kilometre from Newhaven to the western edge of **Leith**. It's not the most picturesque stretch of road, relieved only by the soaring white tower of Chancelot Mill, the second largest flour mill in Europe. Several Lothian buses pass along here, though, so hop on if you want to save yourself the walk (the No.16 runs from Granton Square to the heart of Leith then back to the city centre).

This end of Leith is home to the expansive Western Harbour where passing cruise liners call, the Ocean Terminal shopping mall and the **Royal Yacht Britannia** (p128). The old docks area has nowadays been reclaimed as a site for retail, tourism, leisure and even government; the Scottish Executive building just a few hundred metres east of Ocean Terminal at Victoria Quay was a major step in the rehabilitation of Leith back in 1995. Follow Ocean Drive round the north side of the Scottish Executive and there sit ships and boats great and small, cranes and

quays in Scotland's largest enclosed deepwater port.

It doesn't take long to swing back into the historic centre of Leith where the **Water of Leith** meets the coast. This locale is known now for its bars, bistros and restaurants but was also a fishing settlement from the early 12th century. Leith grew as a centre for international trade, got caught up in wars with England and existed as a burgh in its own right from 1833-1920, before being swallowed up by Edinburgh. All the same Leith would still rather be thought of as its very own people's republic rather than just another suburb.

Dedicated walkers can get from Leith to **Portobello** without too much urban dereliction by going via Leith Links, but much simpler is to catch a Lothian bus No.12 from Leith to King's Road in Portobello, or just treat Portobello as a destination in its own right and get a No.26 bus straight there from the city centre.

This coastal suburb has all the hallmarks of the traditional British seaside: arcades, fish and chips, and over a mile of proper beach. Another small town that was once outside Edinburgh, Portobello can trace its roots to 1739 when retired sailor George Hamilton built a house here called Portobello, named after an action against the Spanish at Puerto Bello in Panama. The neighbourhood developed as a renowned Victorian holiday resort, referred to with no sense of irony as the 'Brighton of the North'. Its 19th-century grandeur may be faded today, but if you want a walk on the sands, or even a swim – the Scottish Environmental Protection Agency (www.sepa.org.uk) rates the water quality at Portobello as 'good' – it's a just over three miles from the end of Princes Street.

ITINERARIES

Edinburgh International Book Festival

Literary City

Edinburgh has its annual **International Book Festival** in Charlotte Square (p38) and offers walking tours that celebrate everything from the works of Irvine Welsh (p100) and Ian Rankin to the role of pubs in its literary heritage. In 2004, UNESCO even designated Edinburgh as its first City of Literature (www.cityofliterature.com; the website also has details of all the walking tours).

That the Scottish capital has a nose for books is hardly in doubt – but long before Renton or Rebus, and certainly before UNESCO got in on the act, the old **Writers' Museum** in Lady Stair's House off the Lawnmarket (p65) served as a focus for three true giants of Scottish letters: **Robert Burns**, **Sir Walter Scott** and **Robert Louis Stevenson**. It houses assorted memorabilia great and small like the printing press that produced Scott's *Waverley* novels, pictures of Stevenson in the South Seas, and works by all three writers to browse. It also serves as an ideal starting point for a day's informal exploration of these key figures and their relationship with the city.

Robert Burns

Burns was from Ayrshire but he lived right across the close from Lady Stair's House in 1786 when he first came to Edinburgh, as acknowledged by a plaque above the entrance passageway off the main street. He was a regular visitor to the capital over the next five years but there are a couple of specific locations within walking distance of the Writers' Museum where his presence is more keenly felt than elsewhere.

Head back out on to the Lawnmarket and turn left, down the hill to the High Street then on to the Canongate, a stroll of less than a mile. Outside the handsome, late 17th-century Canongate Kirk stands a statue of a poet named Robert Fergusson, the man Burns described as 'by far my elder brother in the muses'. Born in the Old Town in 1750, Fergusson killed himself when he was just 24 during a spell in the city's insane asylum and was then buried in a pauper's grave in the Canongate churchyard.

In his short life, he built up a body of work that was a huge influence on the young Burns; *Auld Reekie*, a lyrical and observant day in the life of the city, is seen as his masterpiece. You can find a copy via the **Scottish Poetry Library** (5 Crighton's Close, 557 2876, www.spl.org.uk) off the south side of the Canongate, a few seconds' walk from Fergusson's statue. Burns rated his fellow writer so highly that he commissioned a headstone for his grave in 1789. Later in the 19th century Robert Louis Stevenson saw to its upkeep but it took until 2004 for the statue to be unveiled and Fergusson to receive wider public acclaim.

If the Lawnmarket was where Burns first stayed in Edinburgh, and local poet Fergusson had a major impact, then a pub in the Grassmarket formed the other bookend to his jaunts. Passing the Scottish Poetry Library on Crichton's Close, keep going to Holyrood Road then turn right and walk for around a mile via the Cowgate to the Grassmarket. On its north side, there are several bars and restaurants including the White Hart Inn at No.34 (0131 226 2806) which dates to the 18th century. Burns stayed here on his last visit to the capital in 1791 and wrote the bittersweet love poem *Ae Fond Kiss* here, so it's an ideal place to raise a glass in memory of Scotland's national bard.

In a historical footnote, the White Hart later provided lodging for William and Dorothy Wordsworth on their travels in romantic Caledon. Centuries later a phone box in the Grassmarket itself played its part in the grisly endgame of Iain Banks' *Complicity*, the last few pages of which are almost like a self-contained tour of Edinburgh and environs.

Sir Walter Scott

Burns died in 1796, at which point his fellow Writers' Museum scribe Sir Walter Scott was still living in his childhood home at 25 George Square. Although not open to the public, and these days better known as a University of Edinburgh campus, George Square is not far from the White Hart Inn. Leave the Grassmarket by its east end, head up Candlemaker Row then along Bristo Place to Bristo Square. George Square is immediately to the south.

After Scott married in 1797, he and his wife Charlotte lived in the New Town, initially in **George Street** (p93). This is about a mile north of George Square across the Old Town, down the Mound, then across Princes Street and up Hanover Street to the next corner. The couple lodged briefly at No.50, significant for its proximity to the **Assembly Rooms** (p67), which were the site of set piece events when King George IV came to the city in 1822. Scott was a leading public figure by then, thanks to the success of his writing, and orchestrated the landmark visit, helping set a fashion for all things tartan, romantic and Highland that persists to this day. His effect on the national myths of modern Scotland cannot be underestimated.

The Scotts' next residence was 10 Castle Street, less than half a mile to the west, between George

ITINERARIES

Street and Princes Street. The family only stayed there for three years or so before an even shorter hop to a rather splendid townhouse at 39 North Castle Street, just the other side of George Street. This is now home to a firm of solicitors but look closely at the glass above the door and you can spot a small replica statue of Scott, a discreet homage to the former owner. The larger original sits grandly under the **Scott Monument** (p91), half a mile or so back towards the east end of Princes Street. Completed in 1846, and offering a fabulous perspective from the top, the monument resembles a Gothic Thunderbird 3, ready for takeoff from Princes Street Gardens.

Robert Louis Stevenson

Like Scott, the third member of the sainted triumvirate, Robert Louis Stevenson, drew on images of dashing clansmen in his work – particularly in adventure stories like *Kidnapped* (1886) and *Catriona* (1893). He also cast his eyes further afield, not least with his travel writing and books like *Treasure Island* (1883). Stevenson lived for just 44 years and spent many of those away from Edinburgh, dying on one of the Samoan Islands in 1894. Despite such itchy feet, the city always exercised an influence.

He grew up at Heriot Row in the New Town, which can be the final leg of the day's literary explorations. From the Scott Monument work your way north over to Queen Street and follow along until you reach Queen Street Gardens East. Head downhill here then immediately left into Heriot Row. This is an elegant terrace of New Town houses, facing on to Queen Street Gardens, and a few minutes' more walking will bring you to No.17 where the young Stevenson grew up. This may be a private residence but it's good to get a flavour of this polite, ordered neighbourhood as it stands in marked contrast to the saltier closes and wynds of the Old Town. Stevenson's youth spanned both: family life in the former, drinking with friends in the latter. This is most apparent in the Janus-faced dynamic of his 1886 classic *Strange Case of Dr Jekyll and Mr Hyde*. To follow in the footsteps of the carousing Stevenson that came out after dark, head to the Old Town or Lothian Road and pick any pub.

Burns was an enthusiastic visitor, Scott an Edinburgh-born native who helped write modern Scotland into existence. But for final evidence of the enduring pull that the city had on Stevenson, cast your eyes down at the pavement outside the Writers' Museum. Chiselled into the stone are various quotes from important figures in Scottish literature, from the 14th century to the 20th. Stevenson's reads: 'There are no stars so lovely as Edinburgh street-lamps.' Amen.

Writers' Museum p50

Edinburgh by Area

Mercat Cross p60

Old Town

EDINBURGH BY AREA

Viewed from the air – or, more easily, on any one of the copies of 17th- and 18th-century maps you can buy around town – the Old Town resembles some ancient leviathan, running from the castle down to Holyrood. The **Royal Mile** is its undulating spine, while the ribs of the beast splay out to the north and south, taking in both major thoroughfares and tiny passageways.

On the ground, this translates into a compact, sloping walk that takes in more historic attractions and key sites than any other pocket of land in Scotland. Politics, religions, lives and loves were forged, betrayed and destroyed in among the closes, pends, wynds, tunnels and vennels of the Old Town. With much of the commerce centred around the tourist industry

it's hardly surprising that the Old Town is like a huge open-air museum, with around 900 years of architecture on show.

If you're not from Scotland, or even if you are, signposting in the Old Town can seem bizarre. Bear in mind that a close is a narrow alleyway that usually opens up into a courtyard of some sort (check out Trunk Close or Lady Stair's Close, and read the Scottish poetry extracts carved into the flagstones); a wynd is a narrow winding lane leading off the main thoroughfare (go into the Tron and you can see Marlin's Wynd, a roadway that was lost to the city years ago); a pend is a narrow, covered entryway to the backcourt of a block of houses; and a vennel is simply a narrow alley.

54 **Time Out** Shortlist | Edinburgh

Narrow is the key word when it comes to the Old Town. The older buildings are easy to spot from the way they are crammed together; Edinburgh's citizenry of old built upwards, not outwards. The population lived in teetering tenements, the poor eking out an existence in the basements and attics while the more genteel classes lived in comfort on the mid-level floors. At one point in the city's history, the poverty-stricken and socially excluded existed in dank dwellings in the dark vaults and caverns found below South Bridge.

Running from the edge of the castle grounds to the **Palace of Holyroodhouse**, the Royal Mile often changes its identity. At various points, the street is called Castlehill, Lawnmarket, the High Street and the Canongate, although the latter two predominate along much of its length: just over a modern mile. Kings and queens have ridden and driven from the castle to the palace and back, battles have been fought up and down its length, and men have been hanged and women burned upon it. It's more sedate these days, at least for 11 months of the year.

At the western end of the Royal Mile, high on the forbidding **Castle Rock**, you'll find St Margaret's Chapel, the oldest extant building in Edinburgh. Across the castle's Esplanade, on the corner of Lawnmarket, is the Hub, built in 1844 by Augustus Pugin who designed the Houses of Parliament in London.

To the south you can make out **Greyfriars Church** which was reduced to ruin in 1718 after the local council's gunpowder store exploded. Nowadays it's an impressive if a little sparse space to pop your head into. Back up towards the Royal Mile stands one of the city's more curious attractions: the statue of a dog named **Greyfriars Bobby**. When a man named John Gray was buried in the kirk's graveyard, so the story goes, his loyal Skye terrier Bobby kept constant watch over his grave for 14 years until his own death in 1872. It's not uncommon to see passers-by kiss the doggy statue. Back on the Royal Mile at it's eastern extremity, at the foot of the Canongate and next to the imposing Palace of Holyroodhouse, sits the hugely controversial **Scottish Parliament** building, completed in 2004 – the original estimate of £40 million turned out to be roughly £400 million short.

Sights & museums

Camera Obscura & the World of Illusion

Castlehill (226 3709/www.camera-obscura.co.uk). Bus 23, 27, 41, 42, 45. **Open** *July, Aug* 9.30am-7.30pm daily. *Apr-Jun, Sept, Oct* 9.30am-6pm daily. *Nov-Mar* 10am-5pm daily. **Admission** £7.95; £5.50-£6.50 reductions. **Map** p56 B3 ①

The Camera Obscura is a system of mirrors that projects a periscope image of the city on to a white disc in the centre of a small darkened room. Major landmarks are pointed out by the guides as they pan the lens across the city. While it's certainly no longer as thrilling as it must have been in Victorian times, the camera is an authentic working example of an historic visitor attraction. The Camera is preceeded by three floors of exhibits including holographs and morphing machines. Also impressive is the set of powerful telescopes housed up on the roof, which offer superb views across the city.

Edinburgh Castle

Castlehill (enquiries 668 8800/ticket office 225 9846/www.historic-scotland.gov.uk). Bus 23, 27, 41, 42,

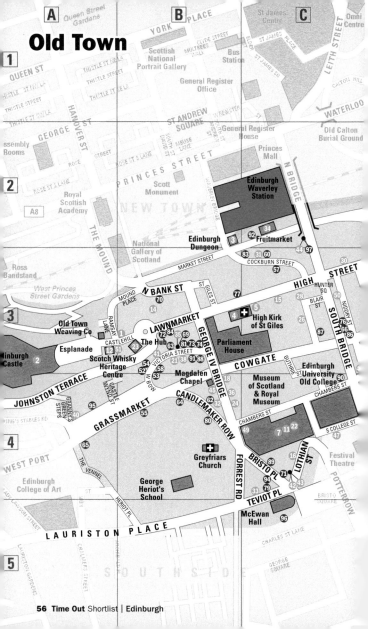

Old Town

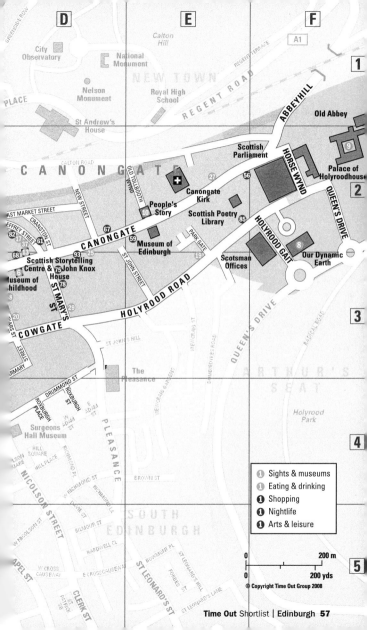

timeout.com

Over 50 of the world's greatest
cities reviewed in one site.

45. Open (last entry 45 mins before closing) *Apr-Sept* 9.30am-6pm daily. *Oct-Mar* 9.30am-5pm daily. **Admission** £11; £5.50-£9 reductions. **Map** p56 A3 ❷

Military barracks, prison, royal residence, murder scene, birthplace of kings and queens... Edinburgh Castle has served a variety of purposes during the centuries it has stood high above the city. While its lofty position was employed to military advantage in years gone by, it's now extremely useful as a navigational guide if you get lost in the surrounding warren of streets and closes. However, most visitors chiefly use it as the city's main tourist attraction.

The buildings are the main attractions at the castle, but it's also worth keeping your eyes peeled for more ephemeral bits and pieces: the Dog Cemetery on the Upper Ward, the graffiti scrawled by Napoleonic and American POWs (and their banknote forgery equipment), the 'Laird's Lug' spying device in the Great Hall, and Mons Meg, the huge six-ton cannon that stands next to St Margaret's Chapel. Representing the height of technological advancement in her time, Meg was presented to James II in 1457 and last fired in 1681, when her barrel burst. While you're enjoying the views or scaring yourself with a peep over the sheer drops, spare a quick thought for Sir Thomas Randolph and his men, who bravely scaled the northern precipice in 1314 in order to wrest the castle from the English.

The most illuminating way of exploring the castle is with one of the audio guides (available in six languages; £3 adults, £1-£2 reductions). There's a café and a restaurant within the castle, as well as plenty of toilets. The gift shop's offerings cover all bases, from standard tartan tat and pocket-money treats to toys, T-shirts and full-size replica weaponry. Disabled visitors should note that a wheelchair-accessible courtesy vehicle runs from the Esplanade to the upper reaches of the castle.

Boom time

The Fringe may have the upper hand when it comes to highbrow comedy, but for sheer slapstick nothing beats being within within decent earshot of Edinburgh Castle at 1pm. The closer the better – Princes Street Gardens are the perfect spot. Sit and wait and soon enough: Bang! Watch an international bunch of previously contented tourists jump clean out of their skins.

Contrary to popular belief, the gunfire that emanates from Edinburgh Castle each lunchtime (except for Sundays) isn't a tribute to its military history. It's a tradition that arose in the 19th century as an aid to sailors in Leith Harbour, and an echo of the time ball atop Nelson's Monument on Calton Hill. Starting in 1861, the ball was raised and then dropped at 1pm to allow seamen to check their chronometers were set correctly. Unfortunately, the ball was often shrouded in fog, and it was decided that a cannon should be fired as well. That way, if sailors couldn't see the signal, they could at least hear it.

Navigational technology has moved on a little since then, but a burst of shellfire still blasts from a 105mm field gun on the castle walls. Since the death in 2005 of local hero Tom McKay, who performed the task for 27 years, the work has been shared by various bombardiers. McKay's long service was commemorated with the 2006 arrival of a memorial bench close to the gun; if you think your eardrums can take the noise, it affords a good close-up view of the action.

Edinburgh Dungeon

*31 Market Street (240 1000/www.
thedungeons.com). Princes Street
buses.* **Open** *15 Mar-27 June* 10am-
5pm daily; *28 June-31 Aug* 10am-7pm
daily; *1 Sept-2 Nov* 11am-5pm daily;
3 Nov-20 Mar 11am-4pm Mon-Fri,
10.30am-4.30pm Sat, Sun. **Admission**
£12.95; £9.50-£11.95 reductions.
Map p56 B2 ❸

If you like your history packed with
facts, this might not be for you.
However, if raw flesh, disease, murder,
exaggerated pantomime mayhem and
the pornography of violence are more
your bag, then a trip to the Edinburgh
Dungeon – run by the folks behind the
similar operation in London – is an
entertaining way to find out about
Scotland's murky past.

High Kirk of St Giles

*High Street (225 4363/visitor services
225 9442/www.stgilescathedral.org.uk).
Bus 23, 27, 35, 41, 42, 45/Nicolson
Street–North Bridge buses.* **Open** *Apr-
Sept* 9am-7pm Mon-Sat. *Oct-Mar* 9am-
5pm Mon-Sat. Call for service times.
Admission free; donations welcome.
Map p56 B3 ❹

There has been a church on the site of
St Giles since 854. Nothing remains of
the earliest structures, but the four pil-
lars that surround the Holy Table in
the centre have stood firm since around
1120, surviving the desecration of
marauding armies during the
Reformation in the 16th century.
Numerous memorials and statues pay
tribute to the likes of Knox, Robert
Louis Stevenson and even Jenny
Geddes, but perhaps the most notable
feature of the interior is its magnificent
stained glass windows.

Outside there's plenty to divert visitors too. The Heart of Midlothian, a
heart shape set into the cobblestones of
the street, marks the spot where
Edinburgh's Tolbooth prison stood.
The long-held habit of spitting on the
Heart of Midlothian, begun by the
criminal fraternity when the land
was still held the Tolbooth, is still
upheld by locals. To the east of the kirk
you'll find the Mercat Cross (literally,

'market cross'), identifiable by the
white unicorn holding a Saltire flag at
the top of its turret.

Loch Ness Discovery Centre

*1 Parliament Square, Royal Mile
(225 2290/www.3dlochness.com).
Bus 23, 27, 35, 41, 42, 45/Nicolson
Street–North Bridge buses.* **Open**
Apr-June, Sept 9.30am-6pm daily;
July, Aug 9.30am-8pm daily; *Oct-
Mar* 10am-5pm daily. **Admission**
£5.95; £3.95-£4.50 reductions.
Map p56 C3 ❺

No, Loch Ness hasn't been piped down
to Edinburgh in order that tourists
needn't bother making the long
journey north. Based on the work of
Loch Ness expert Adrian Shine, the
Discovery Centre houses a multilingual
exploration of the facts and myths that
surround this most infamous body of
water. Enjoy the 3D displays and
decide for yourself whether Nessie
really could exist.

Museum of Childhood

*42 High Street (529 4142/www.
cac.org.uk). Bus 35, 36/Nicolson
Street–North Bridge buses.* **Open**
10am-5pm Mon-Sat. **Admission**
free. **Map** p57 D3 ❻

The extensive collection of toys and
childhood mementos stretches back
decades, to when lead soldiers and
china-headed dolls were state-of-the-art
toys, but also runs through to the era
of Barbie and Ken. In truth, while grins
of recognition are usually spread wide
across the faces of kids-at-heart of
all ages, older generations may enjoy
their trip down memory lane far more
than pre-teens.

National Museum of Scotland

*Chambers Street (247 4422/www.nms.
ac.uk). Bus 2, 23, 27, 41, 42, 45.*
Open 10am-5pm daily. **Admission**
free. **Map** p56 C4 ❼

The museum, previously known as
the Museum of Scotland before merg-
ing with the Royal Museum, was
judged to be the Scottish Building

National Museum of Scotland

'SEE YOU JIMMY' HATS ONLY £3.99

Royal Mile p54

of the Year after its opening in 1998. Thousands of artefacts are on display, from small everyday objects to a steam locomotive. Grim relics of the darker side of Edinburgh's past are also on show, among them the Maiden of Edinburgh guillotine and an iron gaud which was used to restrain prisoners on the old Tolbooth. Be sure to check out the ramped entrance with its lovely frieze by the late Ian Hamilton Finlay.

Our Dynamic Earth

112 Holyrood Road (550 7800/www. dynamicearth.co.uk). Bus 35, 36. **Open** *Apr-June, Sept, Oct* 10am-5pm daily. *July, Aug* 10am-6pm daily. *Nov-Mar* 10am-5pm Wed-Sun. Last entry 70 mins before closing. **Admission** £9.50 adult; £5.95-£7.50 reductions. **Map** p57 F2 ❽

Our Dynamic Earth is located near the former home of Edinburgh-born James Hutton, the so-called 'Father of Geology'. It's anyone's guess what he'd make of its ultra-modern, tent-like exterior, but he'd surely approve of its educational aims: to take visitors back to the creation of the universe nearly 14 billion years ago, then bring them forward to the present day. Tilted primarily at school-age children, it's a science museum that combines natural history with simulated natural disasters, and attempts to make geology fun.

Palace of Holyroodhouse

Holyrood Road (524 1120/www. royalresidences.com). Bus 35, 36. **Open** *Apr-Oct* 9.30am-6pm daily (last entry 5pm). *Nov-Mar* 9.30am-4.30pm daily (last entry 3.30pm). Closed 15 May-3 June, 27 June-8 July, 7 Nov & during royal visits. **Admission** £9.80; free-£8.80 reductions. **Map** p57 F2 ❾

The Palace of Holyroodhouse has its origins in the Abbey of Holyrood (now picturesque ruins), established in 1128 by David I. When Edinburgh was confirmed as the nation's capital city, royal quarters were built adjacent to the abbey and have been gradually upgraded and renovated over the years. It's still used by the Queen as an official residence. When she's elsewhere, parts of the building are open to the public, as an audio tour details the history of a series of plush bedrooms, galleries and dining rooms.

The intricate and ornate entrance to the Queen's Gallery leads most visitors to expect a rather grand, ornate and old-fashioned room; in fact, the interior is surprisingly contemporary. Made up of a series of flexible spaces, the gallery hosts a changing programme of exhibitions from the Royal Collection, with a focus on works from the Royal Library at Windsor Castle. There's also computer access to an e-Gallery, with interactive online exhibition catalogues and details of other works from the collection.

People's Story

Canongate Tolbooth, 163 Canongate (529 4057/www.cac.org.uk). Bus 35. **Open** *Aug* 10am-5pm Mon-Sat; noon-5pm Sun. *Sept-July* 10am-5pm Mon-Sat. **Admission** free. **Map** p57 E2 ❿

With Edinburgh's Tolbooth long since consigned to the annals of history, the Canongate Tolbooth is one of the most emotionally resonant buildings in the Old Town. It's where justice was meted out and prisoners awaited their fate, whether hanging, beheading, branding, burning, transportation or any of the other official punishments of the day. These days it houses the People's Story museum, but visitors are reminded of its history by the tableau of three of the city's less illustrious citizens. The museum also affords a glimpse into the grinding poverty that some of Edinburgh's citizens endured long into the 20th century, and continue to endure to this day in run-down estates. Take the time to read their testimonials, and a very different side to the city is revealed.

Royal Museum

Chambers Street (247 4422/www. nms.ac.uk). Bus 2, 23, 27, 41, 42, 45. **Open** 10am-5pm daily. **Admission** free. **Map** p56 C4 ⓫

Heart of Midlothian p60

The Royal Museum is in the throes of a Herculean reinvention (due to finish in 2011) and now forms part of the National Museum of Scotland. The beautifully airy main hall, with its wrought-iron 'birdcage' construction, is worth the trip alone. Although many more exhibits will be on show by the time the work is complete, there are still thousands to enjoy in the meantime. There are currently three floors of displays, and while some are rather dated – the stuffed tigers look particularly sad – they have a peculiar charm. The Connect Room is more up-to-date, housing a rocket, Dolly the sheep, interactive robots and energy transfer machines. It gets very busy, so be prepared to queue.

Scotch Whisky Heritage Centre

354 Castlehill (220 0441/www.whisky-heritage.co.uk). Bus 23, 27, 41, 42, 45. **Open** *Apr-Sept* 10am-7pm daily. *Oct-Mar* 10am-6.30pm daily. Last tour 1hr 30mins before closing.

Admission £9.50; £4.95-£7.25 reductions. **Map** p56 C4 ⑫

The shop alone makes this tourist-orientated whisky centre worth a visit. The huge selection of blends and malts, some popular and some obscure, includes one of only 83 bottles of 50-year-old Balvenie Cask 191 ever produced. The catch? It costs six grand. However, the hour-long tour remains the main attraction.

Scottish Storytelling Centre & John Knox House

43-45 High Street (556 9579/www. scottishstorytellingcentre.co.uk). Bus 35, 36/Nicolson Street–North Bridge buses. **Open** *July, Aug, Sept* 10am-6pm Mon-Sat; noon-6pm Sun. *Oct-June* 10am-6pm Mon-Sat. **Admission** *Scotland's Stories* free. *John Knox House: Inside History* £3.50; £1-£2.75 reductions. **Map** p57 D3 ⑬

Through the unassuming doorway and past a bright café selling organic and homemade food, a light, airy space

Greyfriars Church p55

holds a free permanent exhibition entitled 'Scotland's Stories'. It's full of mini tableaux behind doors, and touchy-feely boxes for the little ones; there's also a sound and vision display on Robert Louis Stevenson. There are myriad treasures in the rooms, leading off a turnpike stair complete with a trip-step – a 17th-century burglar alarm – and doors with false locks to foil intruders. Look out for the Tower of Destiny, with its gruesomely jolly representations of the final moments of Knox, Mossman, Mary, Queen of Scots and Sir William Kirkcaldy of Grange, who defended Edinburgh Castle against the enemies of Mary.

Writers' Museum

Lady Stair's House, Makars' Court, Lawnmarket (529 4901/www.cac. org.uk). Bus 23, 27, 41, 42, 45. **Open** 10am-5pm Mon-Sat. **Admission** free. **Map** p56 B3 ⑭

The only original dwelling of Lady Stair's Close still standing, Lady Stair's House is remarkable for its sharp turnpike staircases and maze-like layout containing curiosities and memorabilia relating to three of Scotland's most celebrated writers: Sir Walter Scott, Robert Burns and Robert Louis Stevenson. Also on display is a selection of personal effects, including a chessboard and a large ornate pipe once belonging to Scott and one of Burns' snuffboxes. A small corner of the building contains a selection of the authors' works and comfy chairs in which to curl up and read them.

Eating & drinking

Always Sunday

170 High Street (622 0667/www. alwayssunday.co.uk). Bus 35/Nicolson Street–North Bridge buses. **Open** 8am-6pm Mon-Fri; 9am-6pm Sat, Sun. **Café**. **Map** p56 C3 ⑮

Thanks to its prime site, bang on the Royal Mile, this contemporary café can get terribly crowded in August. But it's well worth trying for a table; the quality of food on offer (soups, salads,

decent bread and daily specials) means it's a great place to have lunch, an afternoon snack or even a leisurely Sunday breakfast. No frills, but quite a gem.

Assembly

*41 Lothian Street (220 4288/www.
assemblybar.co.uk). Nicolson Street–
North Bridge buses.* **Open** noon-1am daily. *Food served* noon-8.45pm daily.
Bar. **Map** p56 C4 ⑯

If you're in an upbeat mood, with company, and looking for nachos and lager or wine, Assembly is a good option. Hit it on the wrong day or come on your own, though, and the uninterested (or should that be overstretched?) service can grate as much as the student-heavy clientele. There are outdoor tables, and Sunday barbecues in summer.

Barioja

*19 Jeffrey Street (557 3622). Bus
35/Nicolson Street–North Bridge buses.*
Open 11am-late Mon-Sat; noon-10pm Sun. **£**. **Tapas**. **Map** p57 D2 ⑰

Sister venture to Igg's next door, Barioja is a smart tapas bar. All of the old favourites are here (tortilla, gambas a la plancha, queso manchego); the lunchtime special offers four tapas for a set price. You could just come here to sit and drink wine, but you'll crack and order some food eventually.

Bar Kohl

*54-55 George IV Bridge (225 6936).
Bus 23, 27, 42, 45.* **Open** 4pm-1am daily. **Bar**. **Map** p56 B4 ⑱

Bar Kohl has provided Edinburgh's vodka connoisseurs with a second home since its launch in 1993. There are innumerable imported varieties of vodka, including many flavoured versions; staff can even knock up a vodka milkshake. The room itself has a contemporary look (bare stone walls, stone floor), and gets louder and livelier as the night wears on.

Beanscene

*67 Holyrood Road (557 6549/www.
beanscene.co.uk). Bus 35, 36.* **Open** 7.30am-10pm Mon-Sat; 9am-10pm Sun. **Café**. **Map** p57 E3 ⑲

There are other outlets in Ayr, Glasgow, St Andrews and Stirling along with four here in Edinburgh (this one is the most convivial), but Beanscene is very much a home-grown Scottish affair rather than some pan-global retail assault. It's hardly elaborate, but simple pleasures such as the toasted cinnamon and raisin bagel with cream cheese are not to be scorned. The chain hosts regular in-store gigs and even has its own record label, Luna; check online for more.

Black Bo's

*57-61 Blackfriars Street (557 6136).
Nicolson Street–North Bridge buses.* **Open** noon-1am daily. *Food served* noon-10.30pm daily. **Pub**.
Map p57 D3 ⑳

This relaxed and bohemian little howf, with no style bar flourishes in sight, is a two-part operation. The pub is a winning little spot that even boasts a basement pool room (albeit one without much elbow room); next door is an often adventurous vegetarian restaurant. Handy place if you want to escape the overkill of the Royal Mile.

Bow Bar

*80 West Bow (226 7667). Bus 2, 23,
27, 41, 42.* **Open** noon-11.30pm Mon-Sat; 12.30-11pm Sun. *Food served* noon-2.30pm Mon-Sat. **Pub**. **Map** p56 B4 ㉑

This small and simple one-room pub has one of the largest and most interesting ranges of single malt scotch in the city. The Port Ellen distillery on Islay, for instance, was mothballed in 1983, but the Bow may still have three different bottlings on offer. There's also a good choice of ales, along with some interesting Nicaraguan rums.

Café DeLos

*Royal Museum of Scotland, Chambers
Street (274 4114/www.nms.ac.uk/
royal). Bus 23, 27, 42, 45.* **Open** 10am-4.30pm daily. **Café**. **Map** p56 C4 ㉒

Completed in 1888 and built by Captain Francis Fowke, also responsible for the Royal Albert Hall in London, the Royal Museum is a Victorian marvel, and its spectacular, soaring atrium is one of

EDINBURGH BY AREA

Always Sunday p65

the most impressive places in Edinburgh to sit and have a cup of coffee and a slice of cake. The more peckish may prefer one of the stromboli, or a choice of sandwiches, soups and other platters.

Café Hub

Castlehill (473 2067/www.eif.co.uk/thehub). Bus 2, 23, 27, 41, 42. **Open** 10am-6pm daily. **Café**. **Map** p56 B3 ㉓

The catering wing of the Edinburgh International Festival HQ, Café Hub sits in a building dating to 1845, originally an assembly hall and offices for the Church of Scotland. The daytime menu is flexible, with more ambitious food (halibut, maize-fed chicken) served in the evenings, but the Hub is also a great place to simply have an al fresco beer on a sunny day. It gets stupidly busy in August, of course, both on the inside (with soaring ceilings) and out on the terrace.

Caffè Lucano

37-39 George IV Bridge (225 6690/www.caffelucano.co.uk). Bus 23, 27, 42, 45. **Open** 7am-10pm Mon-Fri; 8am-10pm Sat. **£**. **Italian**. **Map** p56 B4 ㉔

A simple Italian establishment with a relaxed and friendly atmosphere, Caffè Lucano offers breakfast (scrambled egg and smoked salmon on toast), filled ciabattas and focaccias, cakes, coffees and even full-on plates of fettucine, steak or chicken washed down with a glass or two of house wine. The good-natured staff and lack of whimsy or pretension make it a welcome find.

Canons' Gait

232 Canongate (556 4481). Bus 35, 36. **Open** noon-11pm Mon-Thur; noon-12.30am Fri, Sat; 12.30-11pm Sun. *Food served* noon-3pm Mon-Sat. **Pub**. **Map** p57 D2 ㉕

Roomy and comfortable, with a pub-grub lunch menu and music on some evenings, the Canons' Gait offers a modern take on what a Royal Mile bar should be. Despite its location smack bang in the middle of tourist country,

the place still attracts its share of locals. After all, any pub featuring a wall-mounted display about the cost over-runs on the nearby Scottish Parliament has to be worth a look.

City Café

19 Blair Street (220 0125). Nicolson Street–North Bridge buses. **Open** 11am-1am daily. *Food served* 11am-9pm Mon-Thur; 11am-10pm Fri-Sun. **Café-bar**. **Map** p57 C3 ㉖

The City Café was one of the first modern café-bars on the scene; these days it feels as much a part of Edinburgh as the castle. The ground floor features a pool table and fill-you-up meals, to be devoured in the booths at the back or the more open seating up the front. Downstairs is more club-like, with DJs spinning. It's packed with pre-clubbers at weekends; the late mornings bring a clientele in search of a serious breakfast (carnivore or veggie versions). And still the famous spelling error behind the bar endures.

Clarinda's

69 Canongate (557 1888). Bus 35, 36. **Open** 9am-4.45pm Mon-Sat; 9.30am-4.45pm Sun. **Café**. No credit cards. **Map** p56 E2 ㉗

Hanging baskets of flowers outside, politesse inside: nothing changes at Clarinda's, a traditional tea room par excellence. Along with your pot of tea, sample a chocolate crispy, sherry trifle or melting moment. It's all very Scottish and home-made, with cakes and biscuits your grandmother might have baked, but it also runs to breakfasts, sandwiches and lunches.

Creelers

3 Hunter Square (220 4447/www.creelers.co.uk). Bus 35/Nicolson Street–North Bridge buses. **Open** *June-Sept* noon-2.30pm, 5.30-10.30pm Mon-Thur, Sun; noon-2.30pm, 5.30-11pm Fri; noon-3pm, 5.30-11pm Sat; 1-3pm, 6-10.30pm Sun. *Oct-May* noon-2.30pm, 5.30-10pm Mon-Thur; noon-2.30pm, 5.30-11pm Fri, Sat; 1-3pm, 6-10pm Sun. **£££**. **Seafood**. **Map** p56 C3 ㉘

Owners Tim and Fran James opened this smart seafood restaurant, a sister establishment to the Arran original, in 1994. The formula is simple: good produce sourced from Scotland's crinkly west coast. Food may arrive unadorned (a signature seafood platter) or with more elaborate preparation (king scallops with sweetcorn risotto). The menu always includes one or two meat and vegetarian options for those not fishily inclined.

David Bann

56-58 St Mary's Street (556 5888/ www.davidbann.com). Bus 35/Nicolson Street–North Bridge buses. **Open** 11am-10pm Mon-Thur, Sun; 11am-11pm Sat, Sun. **££. Vegetarian. Map** p57 D3 ㉙
There are Indian vegetarian venues in Edinburgh, and Michelin-starred establishments with meat-free menus. But when it comes to modern, European-style and completely vegetarian eateries, David Bann is the market leader. The approach is flexible; it's fine for a quick coffee and a light snack, but also for a full lunch or dinner. Try parmesan and basil polenta to start, followed by spinach and smoked cheese strudel. The wine list is short and affordable.

Dubh Prais

123b High Street (557 5732/www. dubhpraisrestaurant.com). Bus 35/Nicolson Street–North Bridge buses. **Open** 5-10.30pm Tue-Sat. **££. Scottish. Map** p56 C3 ㉚
This small, discreet cellar doesn't exactly trumpet its presence among the tourist delights of the Royal Mile. Scottish ingredients served with little fuss define the menu: Aberdeen Angus steak on Arran mustard sauce, chicken breast stuffed with ham from Argyll and cheese from Mull. It's tiny, so book well ahead.

Ecco Vino

19 Cockburn Street (225 1441/www. eccovinoedinburgh.com). Bus 35/ Nicolson Street–North Bridge buses. **Open** noon-midnight Mon-Thur; noon-1am Fri, Sat; 12.30pm-12.30am Sun. *Food served* noon-9.45pm Mon-Thur; noon-10.45pm Fri, Sat; 12.30-9.45pm Sun. **££. Italian. Map** p56 C3 ㉛
The formula at this perennial Old Town favourite has a simplicity bordering on genius. Create a basic Italian menu (antipasti, risotto, focaccia, pasta) and throw in the odd special. Devise an Italian-slanted wine list. Store the bottles of wine along one wall as a design feature, run the bar along the other side of the room, light some candles and abracadabra: watch eager drinkers and diners flock in. A good spot for a relaxed tête-à-tête.

Elephant House

21 George IV Bridge (220 5355/ www.elephant-house.co.uk). Bus 23, 27, 42, 45. **Open** 8am-11pm Mon-Fri; 9am-11pm Sat, Sun. **Café. Map** p56 B4 ㉜
This popular café draws everyone from juice-sipping students to grannies out with the grandchildren. Some of the teas and coffees are first-rate (and organic), but there's also a short and affordable wine list. The food menu runs to salads, baguettes and savouries, and the main room at the back has fantastic views out over the Old Town. Elephants & Bagels, the sister operation, is located on Marshall Street.

Favorit

19-20 Teviot Place (220 6880). Bus 2, 41, 42. **Open** noon-3am Mon-Fri. **Café-bar. Map** p56 C4 ㉝
As its opening hours suggest (note that the kitchen may close early on slow nights), Favorit provides everything from lunch for office workers in a hurry to nightcaps for clapped-out clubbers in a room that comes with the flavour of an American diner. It's popular for quick lunches (a glass of wine to wash down a selection of small dishes), but it's also a fine place to while away a lazy afternoon or long evening.

Fruitmarket Gallery

45 Market Street (226 1843/www. fruitmarket.co.uk). Bus 36/Nicolson Street–North Bridge buses.

Street life Victoria Street

Victoria Street has a lot going for it. A cobbled brae that curves down from George IV Bridge towards the Grassmarket, it pretty much typifies the Old Town. It has its share of pubs, clubs, shops and eateries, while a discreet set of steps takes you up to Victoria Terrace set above the buildings on the street's north side. Not only does this afford a great view of the descending sweep of the brae, but also links through to the top of the Lawnmarket – a shortcut that brings to mind both Edinburgh's history of post-medieval nooks and crannies and also its hilly geography.

With bar-club Espionage (p85), cavernous Irish theme bar Finnegan's Wake at No.9b (0131 226 3816), and the Liquid Room club and music venue (p85) all virtually adjacent, the street can get pretty lively. The more considered drinker heads for the rare whisky and cask ale at the Bow Bar instead (p67).

Shoppers also wander down this way for antique books in the Old Town Bookshop at No.8 (p81), and antique lace and linen at Pine & Old Lace at No.46 (0131 225 3287). The area is well served for food and drink supplies thanks to the legendary I J Mellis, Cheesemonger (p78), the Whisky Shop at No.28 (0131 225 4666, www.whiskyshop.com), and Demijohn at No.32 (p78) specialising in vinegars, oils, liqueurs and whiskies.

For eats, the Grain Store (p72) does well with Scottish produce while alternatives include the long-running Indian restaurant Khushi's (p73).

Finally, no discussion of Victoria Street can pass without mention of Aha Ha Ha, technically at 99 West Bow (p77), for all your joke, novelty costume and rubber chicken needs.

Bow Bar p67

Open 11am-5.30pm Mon-Sat; noon-4.30pm Sun. **Café. Map** p56 C2 ㉞
The Fruitmarket modern art gallery challenges the viewer to ponder what they've just seen long after they've left the gallery itself. Just as well, then, that this light, airy café is on the premises, providing some space to think along with some excellent salads, light meals and delicious cakes.

Grain Store
30 Victoria Street (225 7635/www.grainstore-restaurant.co.uk). Bus 2, 23, 27, 41, 42. **Open** noon-2pm, 6-10pm Mon-Thur; noon-2pm, 6-11pm Fri; noon-3pm, 6-11pm Sat; noon-3pm, 6-10pm Sun. **£££. French-Scottish. Map** p56 B3 ㉟
Looking out from first-floor level down a curving, cobbled brae, the Grain Store is a comforting presence. Stone-walled, wooden-floored and candlelit, it's been a city favourite for years. The menu is generally Franco-Scots with the odd Euro foray, but there are few better places to neck half a dozen Loch Fyne oysters, followed by venison,

lamb or fresh fish. It's also an ideal location for lingering lunches (£10 for two courses, £13.50 for three) over a bottle of wine.

Herbe Bistro
NEW *44-46 George IV Bridge (226 3269/www.herbebistro.co.uk).* **Open** 11am-2.30pm, 5-9.30pm Tue-Sat. **££. Bistro. Map** p56 B4 ㉟
This site has seen several eateries come and go in recent years but fingers crossed that Herbe lasts. There is a takeaway snack bar on the ground floor while the main dining space is a split-level affair one storey down. Herbe is run by the people behind the highly regarded Marque Central (now closed). Here they take a less formal approach with unfussy decor and a straightforward bistro menu done well.

Igg's
15 Jeffrey Street (557 8184/www.iggs.co.uk). Bus 35/Nicolson Street–North Bridge buses. **Open** noon-2.30pm, 6-10.30pm Mon-Sat. **££. Spanish. Map** p57 D2 ㊲

La Garrigue

31 Jeffrey Street (557 3032/www. lagarrigue.co.uk). Bus 35/Nicolson Street–North Bridge buses. **Open** noon-2.30pm, 6.30-9.30pm Mon-Sat. **££. French. Map** p57 D2 ⓭

The quality rustic decor of Edinburgh's specialist Languedoc restaurant – tables and chairs are by the late, great furniture-maker Tim Stead – are in keeping with chef Jean Michel Gauffre's food philosophy. Highlights include 'three meat cassoulet' with pork, lamb and duck (plus toulouse sausage, of course), but there are meat-free options for vegetarians.

Lot

4 Grassmarket (225 9924/www.the-lot.co.uk). Bus 2, 23, 27, 41, 42. **Open** 11am-9.30pm Mon-Sat; noon-6pm Sun. **£. International. Map** p56 A4 ⓰

Hidden away in a converted church, the Lot is a not-for-profit bistro and arts venue run by An Airde, a charity that promotes Christian musicians. There are gigs upstairs, including local and international jazz nights put on by the Jazz Centre (see website), while downstairs is a neat dining room. Pop in for a coffee or enjoy a full evening meal from the short but eclectic menu: small haggis, neeps and tatties to start, say, followed by Thai green curry.

Maison Bleue

36-38 Victoria Street (226 1900). Bus 2, 23, 27, 41, 42. **Open** noon-3pm, 5-10pm Mon-Thur; noon-3pm, 5-11pm Fri-Sun. **££. French. Map** p56 B3 ⓫

The menu at atmospheric Maison Bleue is split into bouchées (one equates to a starter, two or three to a main), bouchées doubles (more substantial) and brochettes (chargrilled skewers). Set menus are good value, especially during early evening. A second branch opened with Marrakech influenced decor in 2006.

Medina

45-47 Lothian Street (225 6313). Nicolson Street–North Bridge buses. **Open** 10pm-3am daily. **Bar. Map** p56 C4 ⓬

Aside from a recent move towards a more seafood-slanted menu, not much has changed at Iggy Campos's upmarket Iberian restaurant since it first opened back in 1989. The table linens are still white, the glassware still shines, and the food still relies on good ingredients presented with Spanish flair. The two-course set lunch (£14.50) is excellent value. For the more informal Barioja, see p67.

Khushi's

9 Victoria Street (220 0057/www. khushis.com). Bus 35. **Open** noon-11pm Mon-Sat; noon-10pm Sun. **££. Indian. Map** p56 B3 ⓭

Edinburgh's oldest Indian restaurant, dating to 1947, settled in this impressive Old Town space in 2006. You go up marble stairs into a large duplex dining area but – this being Khushi's – you can still BYOB. The menu carries no surprises (the signature dish is lamb bhuna) but service is brisk and the atmosphere buzzes along. Best for a fun night out.

Capital expenditure

Scottish Parliament

The fact that Edinburgh makes such a big deal of its history meant it was never going to be an easy task for Catalan architect Enric Miralles when he was picked from a field of hundreds to design the Scottish Parliament on Canongate (348 5200, www.scottish.parliament.uk). The building was eventually opened by the Queen on 9 October 2004, three years behind schedule and nearly £400 million over budget.

Ask around town and locals will tell you that the whole enterprise was a monumental waste of taxpayers' money. Visitors, on the other hand, tend to like the building, as peculiar as it is beautiful, and architecture critics have also been kind: it won the Stirling Prize, Britain's most prestigious architecture award, in 2005.

Unfortunately, Miralles died of a brain tumour in July 2000, four years before the project was finished, and never got a chance to join the debate. Even more of a shame, as the controversy has probably put paid to any risk taking in building design for the foreseeable future.

If you have the time, take the 45-minute parliament tour (£3.50/£1.75, not available Tue-Thur when Parliament is sitting), which explores areas that are not normally accessible to the casual visitor. Even if you don't have the time or inclination to venture inside, the building's exterior, along with the garden areas and water features, provides plenty of points of interest.

Among them is the Canongate Wall, which is covered with quotations from centuries of Scottish writers engraved into blocks of different types of Scottish stone. At the end of the wall is a line drawing of the Old Town based on a sketch made by Miralles himself.

The sister venue to Negociants, Medina is a late and often lively basement with a North African theme. Although it's a kind of club-bar crossover, with DJs, drinks promos and a young profile, you can just lie on the cushions, relax and listen to music (Latin night on Mondays, for example). There's usually a cover charge, but it's no bank-breaker.

Negociants

45 Lothian Street (225 6313). Nicolson Street–North Bridge buses. **Open** 11am-1am Mon-Thur, Sun; 11am-3am Fri, Sat. *Food served* noon-midnight daily. **Bar. Map** p56 C4 ④③

Negociants feels as if it's been here forever. The fixtures and fittings are French-ish, but the band posters – it's a students' favourite – are more Britpop than brasserie. It's pleasantly spacious and light, with plenty of mirrors and big windows. There has been a marked improvement in the evening menu of late: you can now chow down on risotto, coq au vin or a salad niçoise. Equally laid-back sister operation Medina is downstairs.

North Bridge Brasserie

Scotsman Hotel, 20 North Bridge (556 5565/www.thescotsmanhotel. com). Nicolson Street–North Bridge buses. **Open** noon-2.30pm, 6-10pm Mon-Thur, Sun; noon-2.30pm, 6-10.30pm Fri, Sat. **££. Brasserie. Map** p56 C2 ④④

Housed in the former offices of the *Scotsman* newspaper, this upmarket hotel gave the local scene a real boost when it opened in 2001. Since then, its brasserie has settled down into an established hangout for lunch, dinner or drinks. It looks suitably sleek and imposing, with the requisite modern fittings and huge displays of flowers at the door. Food ranges from shepherd's pies to charcuterie platters.

Outsider

15-16 George IV Bridge (226 3131). Bus 23, 27, 42, 45. **Open** noon-11pm **££. Modern European. Map** p56 B4 ④⑤

A bigger and altogether more urbane sister to the Apartment, the Outsider has been a hit since it opened in 2002. The food is similar to the Apartment, but the Outsider scores extra points for its views over the Castle and the Old Town from the rear of the building. With a sometimes overweening attitude towards fashion, however, it's possibly not the best choice for grumpy old men (or women).

Royal Oak

1 Infirmary Street (557 2976/www. royal-oak-folk.com). Nicolson Street– North Bridge buses. **Open** 1pm-2am Mon-Sat; 12.30pm-2am Sun. **Pub.** No credit cards. **Map** p56 C3 ④⑥

Fall through the doors of this tiny, two-floor pub and you're virtually guaranteed to be regaled with a flurry of fiddles, squeezeboxes and guitars. There are nightly folk sessions here, with the Wee Folk Club taking over the Lounge Bar on Sundays for an organised programme of guest artists. No frills: just beer and tunes.

Saffrani

11 S College Street (667 1597). Bus 35/Nicolson Street–North Bridge buses. **Open** noon-2pm, 5.30-11pm Mon-Fri; 5.30-11pm Sat, Sun. **£. Indian. Map** p56 C4 ④⑦

Tucked away up a street to the side of the university's classical Old College, this site has played host to a number of restaurants over the last decade. Saffrani has been in situ since 2004, and looks like it should be around for a while. It resembles a fairly unassuming Indian restaurant from the outside, but owner Khalil Mansoori displays a welcome sense of adventure in the kitchen: try halibut with spinach and fenugreek leaves, a signature dish. Far superior to the average curry house.

Spoon

15 Blackfriars Street (556 6922). Bus 35/Nicolson Street–North Bridge buses. **Open** 9am-5pm Mon-Sat. **Café. Map** p57 D3 ④⑧

This fresh, modern café has a reputation for decent food and delicious smoothies. The clientele is more varied than you might expect given its proximity to the Royal Mile; indeed, the café can be a great escape from the tourist madness a few yards away. The menu features light breakfasts, panini, soups and ever-changing specials. Spoon is also licensed, so you can have a glass of wine to go with that focaccia.

Tower

Royal Museum of Scotland, Chambers Street (225 3003/www.tower-restaurant.com). Bus 23, 27, 42, 45. **Open** noon-4.30pm, 5-11pm daily. **££. International/seafood**. **Map** p56 C4 ⑭

A 1998 offering from star restaurateur James Thomson, this is definitely one for the beautiful people. Perched atop the Museum of Scotland, Tower offers self-conscious chic, good views and a terrace (weather permitting). The menu is flexible – combine a salad and a side if you like – with an emphasis on fresh seafood and well-hung meat.

The menu also boasts some serious wines, with 180 bins or thereabouts. Most are fairly affordable, but there's always the 1982 Margaux for those moments of madness.

Whistlebinkies

7 Niddry Street (557 5114/www.whistlebinkies.com). Nicolson Street–North Bridge buses. **Open** 5pm-3am Mon-Thur; 1pm-3am Fri-Sun. **Pub**. **Map** p56 C3 ⑳

Edinburgh's primary live music pub, Whistlebinkies takes in rock and pop acts along with resident singer-songwriters. Monday is open-mic night and Tuesdays are for up-and-coming bands; the rest of the week, you could find anything from earnest troubadours to indie wannabes.

Witchery by the Castle

352 Castlehill (225 5613/www.thewitchery.com). Bus 2, 23, 27, 41, 42. **Open** noon-4pm, 5.30-11.30pm daily. **£££. Scottish/International**. **Map** p56 A3 ㉛

Ecco Vino p70

One 16th-century venue, two dining rooms and tons of ambience. James Thomson opened the Witchery back in 1979, its wood panelling, red leather and candlelit interior immediately lending it a reputation for destination dining. The possibly even more romantic Secret Garden followed in 1989. Neither is cheap, and some critics grumble that the cooking (whole grilled Dover sole and roast loin of Scottish deer are typical mains) isn't always top class, but it's still of a high standard, served with a legendary wine list. Try a post-theatre supper to experience the Witchery without breaking the bank.

Shopping

Aha Ha Ha
99 West Bow (220 5252). Bus 2, 23, 27, 41, 42. **Open** 10am-6pm Mon-Sat. **Map** p56 B3 ⓾
Probably the city's best-known joke shop. You can't miss it: just look for the oversized Groucho moustache and glasses above the front door. It also sells magic tricks and costumes.

Analogue
102 West Bow (220 0601/www. analoguebooks.co.uk). Bus 2, 23, 27, 41, 42. **Open** 10am-5.30pm Mon-Sat. **Map** p56 B3 ⓾
Analogue deals in books on design and contemporary culture. As well as glossy tomes on fashion, illustration, graffiti and graphic design, there's a gallery space and interesting ranges of T-shirts, magazines and prints.

Anta
91-93 West Bow (225 4616/www. anta.co.uk). Bus 2, 23, 27, 41, 42. **Open** 10am-6pm Mon-Sat. **Map** p56 B3 ⓾
A family-run Scottish design company, Anta sells a selection of hand-painted stoneware and textiles.

Armstrongs
83 Grassmarket (220 5557). Bus 2, 23, 27, 41, 42. **Open** 10am-5.30pm Mon-Thur; 10am-6pm Fri, Sat; noon-6pm Sun. **Map** p56 B4 ⓾

Everyone from the Kaiser Chiefs to Kylie has stopped to browse at this massively popular Edinburgh institution. Clothing here spans the last 100 years, with everything from ballgowns to kaftans. Kilts are cheap here too.

Bagpipes Galore
82 Canongate (556 4073/www. bagpipe.co.uk). Bus 35, 36. **Open** 9.30am-5.30pm Mon-Sat; 10am-5pm Sun (July-Sept only). **Map** p57 E2 ⓾
A huge range of new and second-hand pipes, plus a beginner's tutoring kit for under £30. Probably best to ask the neighbours first.

Beyond Words
42-44 Cockburn Street (226 6636/ www.beyondwords.co.uk). Bus 35/ Nicolson Street–North Bridge buses. **Open** 10am-6pm Mon-Sat; 1-6pm Sun. **Map** p56 C3 ⓾
Scotland's only photographic bookshop stocks coffee table-friendly tomes featuring everything from landscapes to celebrity portraits.

Big Ideas
82 West Bow (226 2532/www.big ideasforladies.co.uk). Bus 2, 23, 27, 41, 42. **Open** 10am-5.30pm Mon-Fri; 9.30am-5.30pm Sat. **Map** p56 B3 ⓾
This friendly shop stocks a good range of well-designed smart and casual clothes in plus sizes.

Cadenhead's Whisky Shop
172 Canongate (556 5864/www. wmcadenhead.com). Bus 35, 36. **Open** 10.30am-5.30pm Mon-Sat. **Map** p57 E2 ⓾
Scotland's oldest independent bottler, established in 1842, has a fine selection of whiskies, encompassing both rare brands and more recognisable names. The company is also known for its Old Raj gin.

Cookie
29a-31 Cockburn Street (622 7260). Bus 35/Nicolson Street–North Bridge buses. **Open** 9.30am-6pm Mon-Wed, Fri, Sat; 9.30am-7pm Thur; noon-5pm Sun. **Map** p56 C3 ⓾

Its arrays of colourful dresses, tops and skirts lend Cookie the feel of an authentic vintage shop. However, the stock here is all new, and features plenty of unusual labels.

Corniche

2-4 Jeffrey Street (556 3707/ www.corniche.org.uk). Bus 35/ Nicolson Street–North Bridge buses. **Open** 10.30am-5.30pm Mon-Sat. **Map** p57 D2 ⑤①

Corniche has been introducing new labels to the city for years. Designers such as Westwood and Gaultier are represented, with menswear and womenswear pieces, alongside local girl Holly Campbell Mitchell.

Deadhead Comics

27 Candlemaker Row (226 2774/www. deadheadcomics.com). Bus 2, 23, 27, 41, 42. **Open** 10am-6pm Mon-Sat; noon-6pm Sun. **Map** p56 B4 ⑤②

Behind the gloomy exterior lies a fine selection of American superhero titles, as well as lesser-known indie works and second-hand comics.

Demijohn

32 Victoria Street (225 3265/www. demijohn.co.uk). Bus 2, 23, 27, 41, 42. **Open** 10am-6pm Mon-Sat; 12.30-5pm Sun. **Map** p56 B3 ⑤③

Dubbed 'the liquid deli', this unusual Victoria Street shop lets you try before you buy. Liqueurs, wines and spirits from around the world are joined by an excellent selection of olive oils and vinegars; you can even choose your own bottle to be filled. Hampers packed with goodies are a new addition to its wares.

Fab Hatrix

13 Cowgatehead (225 9222/www. fabhatrix.com). Nicolson Street–North Bridge buses. **Open** 10.30am-6pm Mon-Sat. **Map** p56 B4 ⑤④

Top hats, cloches, trilbies, bowlers, berets, straw hats and just about every other kind of smart headgear is stocked in this bright, inspiring store, along with a selection of wraps, scarves and accessories.

15 The Grassmarket

15 Grassmarket (226 3087). Bus 2, 23, 27, 41, 42. **Open** noon-6pm Mon-Sat. No credit cards. **Map** p56 A4 ⑤⑤

This treasure trove of a shop has an impressive array of Victoriana, from curtains to coats, with a particularly noteworthy selection of trilbies and vintage suits for gents.

Forbidden Planet

40-41 South Bridge (558 8226/ www.forbiddenplanet.co.uk). Nicolson Street–North Bridge buses. **Open** 10am-5.30pm Mon-Wed, Fri, Sat; 10am-6pm Thur; 11am-5pm Sun. **Map** p56 C3 ⑥⑥

All manner of action figures, science-fiction and fantasy novels, comics, DVDs and toys compete for shelf space at this fantasy chain.

Fudge House

197 Canongate (556 4172/www. fudgehouse.co.uk). Bus 35, 36. **Open** 10am-5.30pm Mon-Sat; 11am-5.30pm Sun. **Map** p57 D2 ⑥⑦

Huge blocks of fudge in every imaginable flavour, all made on site – heaven for sweet-toothed shoppers. There's also a coffee shop on site.

Geoffrey (Tailor) Kiltmakers & Weavers

57-61 High Street (557 0256/ www.geoffreykilts.co.uk). Bus 35/Nicolson Street–North Bridge buses. **Open** 9am-5.30pm Mon-Wed, Fri, Sat; 9am-7pm Thur; 11am-5pm Sun. **Map** p57 D3 ⑥⑧

One of the city's finest Highland outfitters is also home to 21st Century Kilts. Launched in 1996, this innovative range is made from materials such as denim and leather and is favoured by celebrity kilt wearers such as Robbie Williams and Vin Diesel.

IJ Mellis, Cheesemonger

30a Victoria Street (226 6215/ www.ijmellischeesemonger.com). Bus 2, 23, 27, 41, 42. **Open** 10am-5.30pm Tue-Thur; 10am-6pm Fri, Sat. **Map** p56 B3 ⑥⑨

Street life Cockburn Street

Cockburn Street causes wry amusement among locals of a certain age. They remember when it was full of head shops and clothes stores, a real hangout for young people back in the 1970s. And now? It has a new generation of music shops and clothes stores and has become a location of choice for one of the city's youth culture subsets: not quite goth and not entirely emo, they are mostly teenagers and they do generally favour black. You know the ones.

The greatest concentration can be found at the top of Fleshmarket Close (which lent its name to the Ian Rankin novel) during the school summer holidays but don't let that deter you. Down this street you can find actual vinyl at Underground Solu'shn (p82), as well as one of the city's best specialist bookstores in Beyond Words with its photographic monographs (p77).

There is a multitude of places to buy fashions that will look ridiculous on anyone over 25, notably Route One's skate chic at No.29 (0131 226 2131, www.routeone.co.uk) or the loud and pretty Cookie at No.29a-31, good for dresses and bags (0131 622 7260). Meanwhile other stores sell all kinds of knick-knacks, from Japanese gewgaws to fetishwear and bongs – you can browse for hours. If it all gets a bit too much, duck into a pub for a pint instead: the Scotsman Lounge at No.73 (0131 226 7726) is convivial, has music every night and opens at 6am; the Halfway House down Fleshmarket Close (0131 225 7101, www.halfwayhouse-edinburgh.com) is tiny but award-winning.

Foodwise, Viva Mexico at No.41 (0131 226 5145, www.viva-mexico.co.uk) has been doing enchiladas and burritos since Margaret Thatcher's second term.

IJ Mellis, Cheesemonger p78

Wandering past this shop will either make you wince or grin, so pungent is the smell of the cheeses within. Delicious farmhouse cheeses from all over Europe sit alongside a selection of Scottish favourites.

Just Scottish

4-6 North Bank Street (226 4806). Bus 2, 23, 27, 41, 42. **Open** 9.30am-5.30pm Mon-Sat. **Map** p56 B3 **70**

Top highlights among the tasteful, Scottish-themed gifts on sale here include Shirley Pinder's beautiful, eclectic scarves.

Napiers Dispensary

18 Bristo Place (225 5542/www. napiers.net). Bus 2, 41, 42. **Open** 10am-6pm Mon; 9am-6pm Tue-Fri; 9am-5.30pm Sat; 12.30-4.30pm Sun. **Map** p56 C4 **71**

Napiers, which dates back to 1860, offers treatments from herbalists, acupuncturists and other practitioners. The shop is well stocked with homeopathic and herbal medicines, as well as natural cosmetics.

Ness Scotland

336-340 Lawnmarket (225 8815/ www.nessbypost.com). Bus 2, 23, 27, 41, 42. **Open** 10am-6pm daily. **Map** p56 B3 **72**

Compared to some of the dreary Royal Mile stores, Ness feels reassuringly modern. Knitwear and accessories are available in vibrant colours at reasonable prices; highlights include Harris tweed corsages. There's another branch on High Street.

Oddities

16 Victoria Street (220 2255/www. odditiesclothing.com). Bus 2, 23, 27, 41, 42. **Open** 10am-6pm Mon-Sat; 1-5pm Sun. **Map** p56 B3 **73**

Oddities has been supplying a mixture of cult, underground and street brands (including Ladysoul and Silas) to style-savvy shoppers for the last ten years. Look out for the in-house range.

Old Town Bookshop

8 Victoria Street (225 9237/www. oldtownbookshop.com). Bus 2, 23, 27, *41, 42.* **Open** 10.30am-6pm Mon-Sat. **Map** p56 B3 **74**

Antiquarian maps and prints sit alongside a wide collection of historical, children's and general used titles at this Victoria Street shop.

Psycho-Moda

22 St Mary's Street (557 6777). Bus 35/Nicolson Street–North Bridge buses. **Open** 11am-6pm Mon-Sat. **Map** p57 D3 **75**

Situated just off the Royal Mile, this small boutique deals in own-label clothing for women, including dresses in luxurious fabrics.

Ripping Music & Tickets

91 South Bridge (226 7010/www. rippingrecords.com). Bus 35/Nicolson Street–North Bridge buses. **Open** 9.30am-6.30pm Mon-Sat; noon-5.30pm Sun. **Map** p56 C3 **76**

Ripping stocks a good selection of rock, pop, dance and indie CDs, but the main attraction is the gig tickets. From local nights to stadium shows, everything that's available is pinned up in the window display.

Royal Mile Whiskies

379 High Street (225 3383/www. royalmilewhiskies.com). Bus 35/ Nicolson Street–North Bridge buses. **Open** 10am-6pm Mon-Sat; 12.30-6pm Sun. **Map** p56 B3 **77**

Staff at this award-winning malt whisky shop are likely to encourage you to sample a few of the 300-plus varieties on offer before you buy.

Russian Shop

18 St Mary's Street (556 0181). Bus 35/Nicolson Street–North Bridge buses. **Open** 10am-6pm Mon-Sat. **Map** p57 D3 **78**

Russian dolls and all sorts of decorative items line the shelves of this cosy Old Town shop.

Rusty Zip

14 Teviot Place (226 4634). Bus 2, 41, 42. **Open** 10am-5.30pm Mon-Thur; 10am-6pm Fri, Sat; noon-6pm Sun. **Map** p56 C4 **79**

Geoffrey (Tailor) Kiltmakers & Weavers p78

Whether you're looking for an antique wedding dress or psychedelic swirls to wear to a '70s retro night, there's plenty here to tempt.

Scottish Designer Knitwear

42 Candlemaker Row (220 4112/ www.joyce.forsyth.btinternet.co.uk). Bus 2, 23, 27, 41, 42. **Open** 11am-4.30pm Tue-Sat. **Map** p56 B4 ⑳
Vibrant, colourful creations from Scottish knitwear designer Joyce Forsyth, such as dramatic flared jackets and matching hats.

Swish

22-24 Victoria Street (220 0615/www. swishonthe.com). Bus 2, 23, 27, 41, 42. **Open** 10am-6pm Mon-Sat; noon-5pm Sun. **Map** p56 B3 ㉛
Cool urban styles for men and women by Bench, Free Soul and the like, plus funky T-shirts for kids.

Tangram Furnishers

33-37 Jeffrey Street (556 6551/www. tangramfurnishers.co.uk). Bus 35/ Nicolson Street–North Bridge buses. **Open** 10am-5.30pm Mon-Thur; 10am-5pm Fri. **Map** p57 D2 ㉜
Tangram deals in super-stylish furniture, lighting and rugs from leading European manufacturers.

Underground Solu'shn

9 Cockburn Street (226 2242/www. undergroundsolushn.com). Bus 35/Nicolson Street–North Bridge buses. **Open** 10am-6pm Mon-Wed, Fri, Sat; 10am-7pm Thur; noon-6pm Sun. **Map** p56 C3 ㉝
Unbeatable for vinyl dance imports, with a huge choice of house, garage, techno and jungle sounds. The vibe is friendly rather than intimidating and the shop also sells tickets for forthcoming club nights.

Royal Mile Armoury

334 Lawnmarket (225 8580). Bus 2, 23, 27, 41, 42. **Open** 9am-6pm Mon-Sat; 10am-5pm Sun. **Map** p56 B3 ㉞
The lethal-looking window displays contain all the reproduction weapons

you'll ever need, while a not-very-Scottish replica gladiator's helmet will set you back £150.

Nightlife

Bongo Club

37 Holyrood Road (558 7604/www. thebongoclub.co.uk). Nicolson Street–North Bridge buses. **Open** times vary. **Admission** £3-£10. **Map** p57 E2 ⑧⑤

A convergence point for the city's aspirant music, art and club scenes, the Bohemian Bongo moved to the former Edinburgh University students' union building in 2003. More or less anything goes at this café-venue. The calendar usually features a mix of eclectic club nights (reggae at Messenger Sound System, hip-hop at Headspin, punky noise at Fast), the occasional gig (look out for Scottish Hobo Society nights, which draw the cream of local performers) and all manner of other odds and sods. The venue is used for comedy during the Fringe.

Bannermans

212 Cowgate (556 3254/www. bannermansgigs.co.uk). Nicolson Street–North Bridge buses. **Open** noon-1am Mon-Sat; 12.30pm-1am Sun. **Admission** £4. **Map** p56 C3 ⑧⑥

The cavernous network of wee rooms that make up this well-worn boozer have hosted all manner of musicians over the years. Formerly a folkie favourite, it's now a bolt-hole for the indie fraternity, small enough to feel busy when you're starting off and positively riotous when a band can draw a crowd. There's something going on most nights of the week.

Cabaret Voltaire

36 Blair Street (220 6176/www. thecabaretvoltaire.com). Nicolson Street–North Bridge buses. **Open** *Gigs* 7-10pm most nights. *Club* 11pm-3am daily;. **Admission** free-£15. **Map** p56 C3 ⑧⑦

This brick-lined basement space makes the most of the enthusiastic local support for innovative new music,

Going underground

Most locals and visitors happily wander around on the surface of the Old Town, blissfully unaware of what lies underneath. The answer is, quite a lot.

In the late 18th century, two major developments saw the construction of North Bridge, linking the High Street with the east end of Princes Street, and then South Bridge spanning the Cowgate. South Bridge is far larger than most people would credit, obviously a bridge where it crosses the Cowgate but not so obviously one for the rest of its length. But in fact the vast majority of its arches are hidden behind tall tenements and were floored over to provide extra space for the businesses operating on 'ground level'.

The legacy is a long-abandoned underground labyrinth that was in use well into the 19th century, first for commercial purposes then later as housing for the poor.

So much is obvious when you visit the Caves (8-12 Niddry Street South, 0131 557 8989, www.thecaves.eu), a private venue with club nights that occasionally serves as a film location. Its main room looks as if it has been hewn from the bedrock. But for a closer look various companies do guided walks through the South Bridge vaults, notably Mercat Tours (0131 225 5445, www.mercat tours.com) and Auld Reekie Tours (0131 557 4700, www. auldreekietours.com).

The other main subterranean attraction is Mary King's Close under the High Street, effectively a neighbourhood of small and abandoned alleys dating to the 17th century or earlier. The City Chambers was built right over the top of them in the mid 18th century. Atmospheric, spooky tours are operated by Real Mary King's Close (08702 430160, www.realmarykingsclose.com).

providing the shot in the arm that the city's music circuit has needed for a while. The promoters get in top-name DJs like Erol Alkan and Hervé, as well as bands such as the Whip and the Long Blondes. There are great club nights here after the gigs have finished, and once a month the place is home to Glasgow's legendary Optimo club.

Espionage

4 India Buildings, Victoria Street (477 7007/www.espionage007.co.uk). Bus 2, 23, 27, 41, 42. **Open** *7pm-3am daily.* **Admission** free. No credit cards. **Map** p56 B3 ⑥

This nightclub-and-bars complex on Victoria Street extends over five levels. The upper storeys house the Lizard Lounge bar, the middle level contains the Moroccan-themed Kasbar, while the lower floors are rather clubbier. Drinks promos and long hours draw a student-heavy, up-for-it crowd.

Forest

3 Bristo Place (220 4538/www.the forest.org.uk). Bus 2, 41, 42. **Open** 10am-midnight daily. **Admission** free. No credit cards. **Map** p56 C4 ⑧

The Forest provides an antidote to the creeping commercialism of other venues. Housed in a converted church, it contains an art gallery, a non-profit café and a club-cum-music venue at which all-comers are encouraged to get up on the stage. It hardly needs adding that the quality control can be a little unreliable, but all events are free.

Jazz Bar

1a Chambers Street (220 4298/ www.thejazzbar.co.uk). Nicolson Street–North Bridge buses. **Open** Gigs from 9pm daily. **Admission** free-£5. **Map** p56 C4 ⑨

One of the victims of the massive Old Town fire of 2002 was the Bridge Jazz Bar on Cowgate. Proprietor Bill Kyle turned to the local jazz scene and asked for its help backing a new venture to replace the much-loved old place; aficionados dug deep, and the Jazz Bar duly arrived on Chambers Street.

There's jazz here seven nights a week, Kyle bringing in players from near and far to provide the entertainment.

Liquid Room

9c Victoria Street (225 2564/www. liquidroom.com). Bus 2, 23, 27, 41, 42. **Open** Call for details **Admission** £5-£15. No credit cards. **Map** p56 B3 ㉛

On a busy night, the Liquid Room is as claustrophobic as a riot in a prison cell. Happily, the lack of cat-swinging capacity doesn't prevent it from being a great gig venue: everyone from the Kills to Robyn has received a rapturous reception here. The club nights are generally just as popular; Luvely on the first Saturday of each month goes down a treat with house fans.

Massa

36-39 Market Street (226 4224). Bus 36/Nicolson Street–North Bridge buses. **Open** 10.30pm-3am Mon, Wed, Sun; 8pm-3am Thur; 10pm-3am Fri, Sat. **Admission** free-£5. No credit cards. **Map** p56 C4 ㉜

It may have lost out on the hugely enjoyable Tackno night to rival Ego (see above), but Massa is still one of the more popular watering holes for weekenders who don't pick their clubs by genres. Admission is normally cheap, and drinks won't break the bank.

Out of the Bedroom

Canon's Gait, 232 Canongate (556 4481). Nicolson Street–North Bridge buses. **Gigs** Out of the Bedroom 8pm Thur. **Admission** free. **Map** p57 D3 ㉝

This nifty little basement space is now the home of Out of the Bedroom (www.outofthebedroom.co.uk), a regular weekly event bringing together aspiring local singer/songwriters.

Arts & leisure

Bedlam Theatre

11b Bristo Place (information 225 9873/box office 225 9893/www.bedlam theatre.co.uk). Bus 2, 41, 42. **Open** call for details. **Tickets** £2.50-£7.50. **Map** p56 C4 ㉞

The Bedlam Theatre is home to the Edinburgh University Theatre Company, which produces a rolling programme of student drama that can total as many as 40 shows a year. EUTC alumni include Ian Charleson, star of *Chariots of Fire*, actress and TV presenter Daisy Donovan, and Greg Wise, otherwise known as Mr Emma Thompson.

Dance Base

14-16 Grassmarket (225 5525/www. dancebase.co.uk). Bus 2, 23, 27, 41, 42. **Open** call for details **Tickets** prices vary. **Map** p56 A4 ⑨⑤

This beautifully airy, purpose-built state-of-the-art venue in the shadow of Edinburgh Castle has become the focal point for the capital's thriving dance community. With four studios housing an extensive programme of classes and workshops, all levels and areas of interest are accommodated. Ever wanted to learn Highland or gumboot dancing? Feldenkrais and the Alexander technique? This is the place. Regular performances have yet to happen here, though it's full of life nonetheless.

Reid Concert Hall

Bristo Square (650 2427/www.music. ed.ac.uk). Bus 2, 41, 42. **Concerts** Check website for details. **Tickets** free-£7. **Map** p56 C5 ⑨⑥

On selected days during term time, wander in and enjoy a free lunchtime concert from students at the University of Edinburgh's music faculty, or established performers such as the Edinburgh Quartet.

Scotsman Screening Room

Scotsman Hotel, 20 North Bridge (www.scotsmanscreenings.com). Nicolson Street–North Bridge buses. **Tickets** *Movie* £8.50. *Movie & meal* £39. **Map** p56 C2 ⑨⑦

The 46 leather armchairs lend this intimate and luxurious cinema the feel of a private viewing room; unsurprising, since that's what it is during the week. The Sunday night public programme concentrates on classic films that rarely get an outing on the big screen. Tickets are a tad pricey but probably worth it, especially when combined with dinner in the hotel's critically acclaimed Vermilion restaurant.

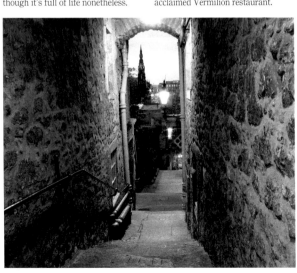

Princes Street

New Town

Although estate agents and property developers may tell you otherwise, Edinburgh's New Town has firm boundaries; the area comprises the regimented grid of streets and gardens that runs from **Princes Street** down to **Cumberland Street**. The result of two huge successive construction projects, it represents 18th-century Britain's biggest and best piece of town planning, and still holds some of the finest Georgian architecture in the country.

The neighbourhood is dotted with impressive boutiques and intimate cafés, as well as the usual gamut of high-street shopping emporia. However, it's still chiefly a residential area, especially in its northern extremities. Now, as then, the New Town is home to some of Edinburgh's richest residents,

from arriviste traders and trust-fund students to distinguished members of the Scottish aristocracy. Indeed, those who believe Scotland is run by a small, conspiratorial elite look towards these streets for their evidence.

Sights & museums

Georgian House

7 Charlotte Square (226 3318/ www.nts.org.uk). Princes Street buses. **Open** *Mar* 11am-4pm daily. *Apr-June, Sept, Oct* 10am-5pm daily. *July, Aug* 10am-6pm daily. *Nov* 11am-3pm daily (last admission 30 mins before closing). Closed Dec-Feb. **Admission** £5; £4 reductions. **Map** p88 C3 ●

The house is run by the National Trust for Scotland and provides a window into how the upper classes lived during the 18th century. The rooms are packed with period furnishings and

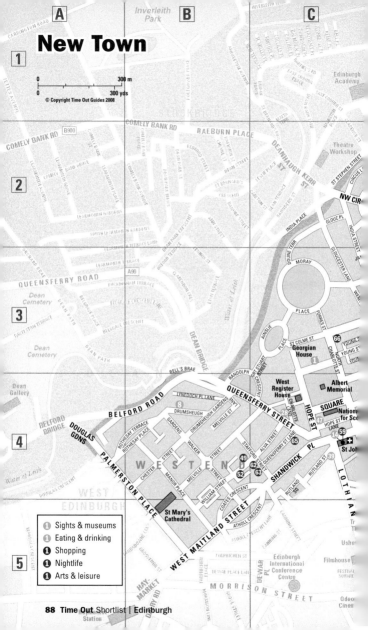

New Town

0   300 m
0   300 yds

© Copyright Time Out Guides 2008

- **1** Sights & museums
- **1** Eating & drinking
- **1** Shopping
- **1** Nightlife
- **1** Arts & leisure

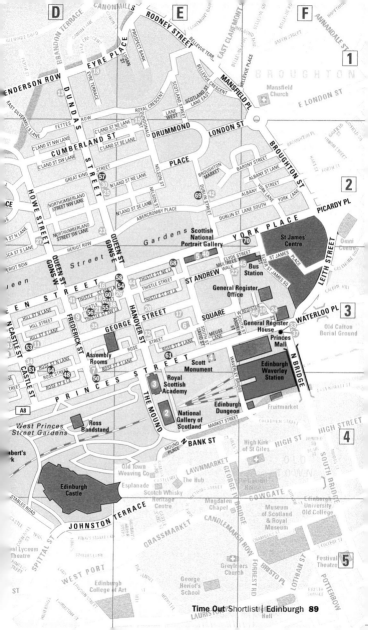

Georgian House p87

detail, right down to sugar cones, locked tea caddies, chamber pots and newspapers. The basement contains an informative video presentation; well-informed guides in each room are happy to answer questions. Just across the square is the headquarters of the National Trust for Scotland which features four beautifully restored townhouses with galleries and a pleasant courtyard café in summer.

National Gallery of Scotland

The Mound (624 6200/www.national galleries.org). Princes Street buses. **Open** 10am-5pm Mon-Wed, Fri-Sun; 10am-7pm Thur. **Admission** free; £6-£8 for special exhibitions. **Map** p89 E4 ❷

Edinburgh has a wealth of institutions serving the visual arts, but perhaps none is quite as grand as the National Gallery of Scotland. The gallery boasts excellent collections of paintings and sculptures, and the sheer wealth of great works is undeniable, from Byzantine-like Madonnas through the Northern Renaissance and High Renaissance (highlights include Raphael's *Bridgewater Madonna* and a handful of pieces by Titian) and right on to the early 20th century. Check the excellent website for details of the regular temporary exhibitions and related special events.

Royal Scottish Academy

The Mound (225 6671/www.royal scottish academy.org). Princes Street buses. **Open** 10am-5pm Mon-Sat; noon-5pm Sun. **Admission** free. *Exhibitions* £2-£4. **Map** p89 E4 ❸

William Playfair's vast building is effectively a large-scale temporary exhibition space, supplementing big-ticket blockbusters of the likes of Monet and Titian with shows devoted to less well-known artists both ancient and modern. A number of annual events focus on Scottish art; chief among them is the RSA Annual Exhibition, an open show held each spring, though it's also worth looking out for the Royal Scottish Society of Painters in Watercolour's semi-open exhibition, which runs for a month during the summer. Special events sometimes accompany the shows; call ahead for details.

Scott Monument

East Princes Street Gardens (529 4068/www.cac.org.uk). Princes Street buses. **Open** *Apr-Sept* 9am-6pm Mon-Sat; 10am-6pm Sun. *Oct-Mar* 9am-3pm Mon-Sat; 10am-3pm Sun. **Admission** £3. **Map** p89 E3 ❹

The monument houses a vast white marble statue of the city's beloved author Sir Walter Scott (by Edinburgh sculptor John Steell) as well as 64 statuettes, mostly of Scott's characters but with a few notable figures from Scottish history thrown in for good measure. The claustrophobic hike to the top is rewarded with superb views.

Scottish National Portrait Gallery

1 Queen Street (624 6200/www. nationalgalleries.org). Princes Street buses. **Open** 10am-5pm Mon-Wed, Fri-Sun; 10am-7pm Sun. **Admission** free. *Exhibitions* £1-£5. **Map** p89 E3 ❺

Sir Richard Rowand Anderson's impressive building originally housed the National Museum of Antiquities, but it now contains various busts and portraits of Scottish heroes, heroines and notable historical figures from the 16th century through to the present day. The foyer is decorated with stunning murals depicting key moments in Scottish history; further in, paintings of kings and queens – Mary, Queen of Scots and Bonnie Prince Charlie among them – offer a rich visual guide to the rise and fall of the Scottish monarchy. Temporary exhibitions provide added entertainment.

Eating & drinking

Abbotsford

3 Rose Street (225 5276). Princes Street buses. **Open** 11am-11pm Mon-Sat; 12.30-11pm Sun. *Food served* noon-3pm, 5.30-9.30pm Mon-Sat; 12.30-3pm, 5.30-9.30pm Sun. **Pub**. **Map** p89 E3 ❻

The Abbotsford may count the likes of Sainsbury's and Fopp among its neighbours these days, but it's been a no-nonsense drinking den since 1901: dark wood, bench tables, a fine central island bar, a decorative ceiling, four real ales and virtually no concessions to modernity. The food is better than you might imagine.

Amicus Apple
17 Frederick Street (226 6055/www. amicusapple.com). Princes Street buses. **Open** 11.30am-1am Mon-Sat; noon-1am Sun. **Bar**. Map p89 D4 ⑦
When it opened in summer 2006, this central cocktail bar introduced a new aesthetic to Edinburgh (designer stools, white leather banquettes, a pop-erotic mural) and brought a dedicated attitude to a menu of good drinks and fine bar snacks (and even a small restaurant space). Cool but not pretentious, and seconds from Princes Street.

Bonham
35 Drumsheugh Gardens (623 9319/ www.thebonham.com). Bus 13, 19, 37, 41, 47. **Open** 7-10am, noon-2.30pm, 6.30-10pm Mon-Fri; 7.30-10am, noon-2.30pm, 6.30-10pm Sun. **££**. **French**. Map p88 B4 ⑧
Although it is just a few minutes' walk from the bustling west end of Princes Street, the Bonham hotel feels delightfully secluded. The menu served in its light and spacious dining room reflects head chef Michel Bouyer's French origins, but offers a decidedly modern take on his native cuisine. Set lunches (£13.50 for two courses, £16 for three) are good value.

Café Marlayne
76 Thistle Street (226 2230). Princes Street buses. **Open** noon-2pm, 6-10pm Tue-Sat. **££**. **Café**. Map p89 D3 ⑨
Wicker chairs and wooden tables create a relaxed environment at this café, where you can count on finding solid French cuisine based around such raw materials as pigeon breast, crab, lamb and beef fillet. Puddings are delicious too; the pear and frangipane tart is a triumph.

Café Royal Circle Bar
19 West Register Street (556 1884). Princes Street buses. **Open** 11am-11pm Mon-Wed; 11am-midnight Thur; 11am-1am Fri, Sat; 12.30-11pm Sun. *Food served* 11am-10pm Mon-Sat; 12.30-10pm Sun. **Pub**. Map p89 F3 ⑩
An island bar dominates this attractive and elegant Victorian pub, where the walls are decorated with Royal Doulton tiles of famous inventors. It gets very busy after work, and is positively packed if Scotland are playing a home rugby international. The bar food is of a very high standard, but for more formal eats, try the beautiful Café Royal Oyster Bar next door (17A West Register Street, 556 4124).

Centotre
103 George Street (225 1550/www. centotre.com). Princes Street buses. **Open** *Italian Bar* 8am-11pm Mon-Thur; 8am-midnight Fri, Sat; 11am-5pm Sun. *Café* 7.30am-10pm Mon-Thur; 7.30am-11pm Fri, Sat; 11am-5pm Sun. **££**. **Italian**. Map p89 D3 ⑪
Victor and Carina Contini are part of the family behind the celebrated Valvona & Crolla (p104). However, in 2004, the duo decided to set up on their own in this former bank, still grandiose but done out with modern fixtures and fittings. The culinary aim is simple: to produce high-quality Italian food. At the front, the Italian Bar caters to coffee fiends, wine-sippers and snackers.

Circus Wine Bar & Grill
NEW *58a North Castle Street (226 6743/www.circuswinebarandgrill.co.uk). Princes Street buses.* **Open** *Restaurant* noon-2.30pm, 7-10pm Mon-Fri; 7-10pm Sat. *Bar* 5-11pm Mon-Thur; 5pm-1am Fri, Sat. **££**. **Wine bar/grill**. Map p89 D3 ⑫
Cosmo, a very posh Italian, reinvented itself as a Michelin-oriented venue in 2006, a move that didn't take. Soon after, it morphed into this upmarket grill where it's possible to have a two-course lunch for £15 or blow £42 on a 16oz chateaubriand at dinner. Smart-casual dress, elegant surroundings,

Street life George Street

Princes Street is now an architectural hotchpotch and Queen Street has turned into an arterial traffic route. By comparison, George Street is the most engaging thoroughfare in the southern reaches of the New Town, where the Georgian development morphs into the modern city centre.

Originally named for King George III, it was intended to be the New Town's main drag when the area was planned in the latter half of the 18th century. Bracketed by St Andrew Square in the east and Charlotte Square in the west, it has become a favoured location for upmarket stores, new and refurbished hotels, café-bars and restaurants in the last few years.

The east end has the Parish Church of St Andrew and St George which dates to 1784, then comes the venerable George Hotel. Its hugely refurbished café-bar-restaurant EH2 Tempus (p96) has allowed it to keep pace with relatively recent hotel-bar-nightclub arrivals in the neighbourhood like Le Monde and Tigerlily.

Meanwhile the Greco-Roman pile opposite was once a bank, built in 1847, but is now home to one of the city's most architecturally extravagant bar-restaurant complexes, the Dome (p95).

Keep heading west past Hanover Street and you hit women's fashion retail heaven. In one short burst of pavement on the north side you'll find LK Bennett (No.45-45a), Hobbs (No.47), Phase Eight (No.47b), Jigsaw (No.49), Laura Ashley (No.51), Karen Millen (No.53) and Coast (No.61). Gents, meanwhile, have the outfitting options of Austin Reed, Moss Bros or Crombie's. Further west you'll find restaurants like Centotre (p92) and good-time café-bar venues like the Living Room (p98) and 2007 debutante the Ivory Lounge (220 6180, www.the 1440.co.uk).

In a nutshell? Shopping by day, party time by night.

Centotre p92

good Scottish beef – or just pop in for a glass of decent syrah.

Clark's Bar

142 Dundas Street (556 1067). Bus 13, 23, 27. **Open** *11am-11pm Mon-Wed; 11am-11.30pm Thur-Sat; 12.30-11pm Sun. No credit cards.* **Pub**. **Map** p89 D1 ⑬

Sparse and traditional, this old howf opened in 1899 and hasn't changed in years; the decor still features red leather seats, shiny brass table tops and a dark red ceiling. You'll find a reasonable malt whisky selection, a few cask ales, and basic bar food such as toasties and baguettes.

Cornerstone Café

St John's Church, corner Princes Street & Lothian Road (229 0212/www. stjohns-edinburgh.org.uk). Princes Street buses. **Open** *9.30am-4pm Mon-Sat. No credit cards.* **Café**. **Map** p88 C4 ⑭

A popular lunch haunt for weary shoppers and office staff, the Cornerstone can be found in the basement of St John's Episcopalian Church (1818), bang on the corner of Princes Street and Lothian Road. It serves up robust canteen-style meals such as baked potatoes, tortilla and pasta. In summer, you can sit outside on the terrace and contemplate the adjacent cemetery.

Cumberland

1-3 Cumberland Street (558 3134/ www.cumberlandbar.co.uk). Bus 13, 23, 27. **Open** *11am-1am Mon-Sat; 12.30pm-1am Sun. Food served noon-9pm Mon-Thur, Sat, Sun; noon-3pm Fri.* **Bar**. **Map** p89 E2 ⑮

The Cumberland is perhaps the most user-friendly of the city's acclaimed cask ale bars. It feels light and spacious during the day, and the leafy beer garden is an absolute joy in the summer. There's a fair choice of wine and bar food, in addition to the nine or so ales on tap. All in all, it's the opposite of a misogynist drinking den.

Dining Room

Scotch Malt Whisky Society, 28 Queen Street (220 2044/www.smws.com). Bus 4, 8, 10, 11, 12, 15, 15A, 16, 17, 26, *44, 45.* **Open** *Non-members: pre-theatre menu 5-6.30pm Mon-Sat. A la carte noon-3.30pm Thur.* **££**. **Members' club**. **Map** p89 D3 ⑯

Complementing the Leith original, the Scotch Malt Whisky Society opened a second venue in a restored Georgian townhouse with some modern interior design touches. The ground floor holds a rather splendid dining room. Non-members are currently restricted to the pre-theatre menu (reasonably priced at £12.50 for two courses, £15 for three) apart from on Thurdays, but members can invite as many people as they like for a full meal. A day's membership can be bought for £10.

Dome

14 George Street (624 8624/www. thedomeedinburgh.com). Princes Street buses. **Open** *10am-late daily. Food served noon-10pm Mon-Wed, Sun; noon-11pm Thur-Sat, 7-9.30pm Thur.* **££**. **Modern Scottish**. **Map** p89 E3 ⑰

In the 1840s, the Commercial Bank of Scotland built this grand old pile as its head office; it remained a bank almost until the Dome took it over in 1996. There's a striking classical frontage, and the central hall is a soaring, decadent space with a marble mosaic floor. The whole thing is crowned by the eponymous dome, housing a bar and restaurant (the Grill Room); the building also has a separate 1930s-style cocktail bar.

Duck's at Le Marché Noir

14 Eyre Place (558 1608/www.ducks. co.uk). Bus 8, 17, 23, 36. **Open** *noon-2.30pm, 6-10pm Tue-Thur; 6.30-10pm Fri, Sat.* **££**. **French**. **Map** p89 D1 ⑲

At this intimate and polished space (owned, if you were wondering, by Malcolm Duck), food comes with a French accent: goat's cheese tartlet to start, perhaps, followed by a pork fillet casserole. The award-winning wine list incorporates everything from easy-drinking lunchtime plonk from £16.50 to serious (and seriously expensive) vintage French reds.

EDINBURGH BY AREA

Cumberland p95

Dusit

*49a Thistle Street (220 6846/www.
dusit.co.uk). Princes Street buses.* **Open**
noon-3pm, 6-11pm Mon-Sat; noon-11pm
Sun. **££**. **Thai**. **Map** p89 D3 ⑲
Edinburgh hasn't so much experienced
a wave of new Thai restaurants in the
last few years as a continuous spring
tide of green curry and tom yum soup.
Although it is comparatively pricey,
Dusit is among the most accomplished
and interesting of the bunch. For the
most part traditional, it does make a
few departures (a dash of whisky here
and there, for example).

EH2 Tempus

*George Hotel, 25 George Street
(240 7197/www.eh2tempus.co.uk).
Bus 45, 11, 16, 10, 17, 15, 23.*
Open 11am-1am Mon-Sat; noon-1am
Sun. *Food served* 11am-10pm Mon-
Sat; noon-10pm Sun. **££**. **Scottish**.
Map p89 E3 ⑳
To keep up with the Joneses, or at least
the brash competition nearby, the long-
established George Hotel reinvented
its bar-restaurant area to create EH2

Tempus in 2006. A big space with
large modernist paintings, it implies a
clientele of 21st-century gentry with an
informal attitude. You want decent
sausage and chips? You can have 'em.
Or oysters followed by ribeye steak.
The most grown-up venue of its kind
on George Street.

Fishers in the City

*58 Thistle Street (225 5109/www.
fishersbistros.co.uk). Princes Street
buses.* **Open** noon-10.30pm daily. **££**.
Seafood. **Map** p89 D3 ㉑
The owners of Fishers in Leith ven-
tured into the city centre in 2001 with
this smart, modern seafood eatery.
Hardy perennials include the excellent
creamy fish soup, oysters and a
seafood platter; alternative mains
might include west coast scallops with
smoked haddock Welsh rarebit.

Forth Floor

*Harvey Nichols, 30-34 St Andrew's
Square (524 8350/www.harvey
nichols.com). Princes Street buses.*
Open *Brasserie* 10am-5pm Mon; noon-
3pm, 6-10pm Tue-Sat; 11am-5pm Sun.
Restaurant noon-3.30pm Mon, Sun;
noon-3pm, 6-10pm Tue-Sat. **£-££**.
Modern European. **Map** p89 E3 ㉒
Even the anti-fashion brigade has had
to admit that Harvey Nicks' fourth-
floor restaurant and brasserie are
pretty good. The views over the Forth
are tremendous, the decor is funky, and
the kitchen operates at an elevated
standard. During the day it caters
for footsore shoppers, but at night
there's a real buzz. The restaurant has
a slightly more elaborate menu than
the brasserie, but it's all effectively one
space with a discreet partition.

Glass & Thompson

*2 Dundas Street (557 0909). Bus 13,
23, 27.* **Open** 8am-6pm Mon-Sat;
10.30am-4.30pm Sun. **Café**.
Map p89 D2 ㉓
For more than a decade, G&T has been
on every list of Edinburgh's best cafés.
Given the New Town location and premium prices, it's not the most populist
of places, but the food is excellent: the

Kay's p98

cakes are sublime, while the assorted tarts and platters would put some local restaurants to shame. The decor is modern, with a couple of outside tables for sunny days.

Guildford

1-5 West Register Street (556 4312). Princes Street buses. **Open** 11am-11pm Mon-Thur; 11am-midnight Fri, Sat; 12.30-11pm Sun. *Food served* noon-2.30pm, 6-9.30pm Mon-Thur; noon-3pm, 6-10pm Fri, Sat; 12.30-3pm, 6-9.30pm Sun. **Pub**. Map p89 F3 ㉔
Established in 1898 (the building dates back a further 60 years), the Guildford is one of Edinburgh's most accessible Victorian pubs, just a hop, skip and jump away from Waverley station. The rotating selection of cask ales is excellent, the whisky choice is decent and the bar food is better than average: try to eat in the small gallery overlooking the main bar.

Haldanes

13b Dundas Street (556 8407/www. haldanesrestaurant.com). Bus 13, 23,
27. **Open** noon-1.45pm, 5.45-9.30pm Tue-Fri; 5.45-10pm Sat. **£££**.
French/Scottish. Map p89 D2 ㉕
Chef and proprietor George Kelso built Haldanes' reputation as one of the city's most accomplished Franco-Scottish restaurants. In early 2006, it moved from Albany Street to these New Town premises, which incorporate a louche lounge bar that offers decent daytime ciabattas, and a warren of adjoining lower basement dining spaces with stone walls and the odd Jack Vettriano print. Kelso has stuck to his tried and tested style (tian of crab, panache of monkfish).

Henderson's Bistro

25 Thistle Street (225 2605/www. hendersonsofedinburgh.co.uk). Princes Street buses. **Open** noon-8.30pm Mon-Wed, Sun; noon-9.30pm Thur-Sat.
Bistro. Map p89 E3 ㉖
The Henderson's that so many people know and love (the Salad Table, established in 1963) is just around the corner, but is effectively a basement canteen. You queue, you choose and

you pay. Another glass of wine? Repeat the process. Thankfully, the Bistro is just a few yards away: it serves up the same kind of food (including soups, salads, chunky stews and pasta), but this is brought to you by waiting staff. It comes with less hassle involved, but it is admittedly a less atmospheric room.

Iglu

2b Jamaica Street (476 5333/www. theiglu.com). Bus 24, 29, 36, 42. **Open** *Bar* noon-1am daily. *Restaurant* noon-3pm, 6-10pm daily. **££. Gastropub. Map** p89 D2 ㉗

The ground floor bar is pleasingly modern (with free Wi-Fi access); upstairs is a small organic restaurant, added in 2005 by energetic proprietor Charlie Cornelius (who also runs the Wild in Scotland tour business). Dishes include wood pigeon, venison, salmon and vegetarian options, all from carefully sourced ingredients. Not 'haute', but worthwhile and fun.

Indigo Yard

7 Charlotte Lane (220 5603/www. indigoyardedinburgh.co.uk). Princes Street buses. **Open** 8.30am-1am Mon-Fri; 9am-1am Sat, Sun. *Food served* 8.30am-10pm Mon-Fri; 9am-10pm Sat, Sun. **Bar. Map** p88 C4 ㉘

Has it really been a decade or so since Indigo Yard made such a splash in the West End? It's showing a little wear and tear these days, but it still endures, popular both with post-work drinkers during the week and a more mixed clientele during the day and at weekends. Available to tables on the ground floor or the mezzanine, the menu offers pretty good breakfasts, fusion-style mains and some pure comfort food (sausages from Crombie's, for example).

Kay's

39 Jamaica Street (225 1858). Bus 24, 29, 36, 42. **Open** 11am-midnight Mon-Thur; 11am-1am Fri, Sat; 12.30-11pm Sun. *Food served* noon-2.30pm Mon-Sat; 12.30-2.30pm Sun. **Pub. Map** p88 C3 ㉙

Drink has been a mainstay here for nearly two centuries: before morphing into a pub in 1976, these premises

housed a wine merchant for more than 150 years. Now, along with a reputation as a patrician New Town howf, this palpably historic spot offers an excellent choice of single malt whiskies and a perfect environment in which to sample them.

Kweilin

19-21 Dundas Street (557 1875/www. kweilin.co.uk). Bus 13, 23, 27. **Open** noon-2pm, 5-11pm Tue-Sat; 5-11pm Sun. **££. Chinese. Map** p89 D2 ㉚

Kweilin's longevity (it's been open since 1984) bodes well for the quality of its Cantonese food, and the kitchen delivers. The simple, calming decor and somewhat aspirational atmosphere mean that it's perhaps not the best place to familiarise the kids with dim sum, but grown-ups will enjoy wrestling with crab claws to start, before tackling some roast duck or properly handled sea bass as a main.

Living Room

113-115 George Street (0870 442 2718/www.thelivingroom.co.uk). Princes Street buses. **Open** 11am-1am Mon-Sat; noon-1am Sun. *Food served* noon-10pm Mon, Tue, Sun; noon-11pm Wed; noon-11.30pm Thur; noon-midnight Fri, Sat. **Bar. Map** p89 D3 ㉛

The Living Room, part of a UK-wide chain, arrived in 2003 and quickly built a reputation as a somewhat more mature venue (pianist, sober dark wood fittings) in a part of the city where office nights out are common. While there is a restaurant, the clubbish bar area is the main feature.

Nargile

73 Hanover Street (225 5755/www. nargile.co.uk). Princes Street buses. **Open** noon-2pm, 5.30-10pm Mon-Thur; noon-2pm, 5.30-11pm Fri, Sat. **££. Turkish. Map** p89 E3 ㉜

Decor-wise, this city centre Turkish eaterie is bright, modern and cliché-free. Meze features prominently on the extensive menu, but kebabs, couscous, veggie options, seafood and specials such as chicken tossed in mustard and honey are also on offer, as are Turkish

Fishers in the City p96

Location, location

Recreate your favourite Scottish movie moments.

Princes Street – Trainspotting

Edinburgh's most bustling shopping street: the perfect location to make like Ewan McGregor in *Trainspotting*. To recreate the opening scene of Danny Boyle's drug-addled classic, your shoplifting extravaganza has to be followed by a marathon sprint down Leith Street to Calton Road, where you should really make every effort to narrowly avoid being run over at some point.

Edinburgh Academy, Henderson Row – The Prime of Miss Jean Brodie

The more masochistic of film fanatics may be pleased to learn that the Donaldson's building at the Edinburgh Academy in Stockbridge was the location used as the school in *The Prime of Miss Jean Brodie*. You could try strutting up to the building, lips pursed, hands balled into fists, announcing to passers-by in your best Maggie Smith accent: 'My gels are the crème de la crème.'

Heriot Row, New Town – Shallow Grave

Once you've developed a taste for the classier side of Edinburgh, the next step for any diehard film buff is to buy a Georgian flat in the New Town and interview potential flatmates, *Shallow Grave* style. Questions should be direct and straightforward: 'What on earth could make you think that we would want to share a flat like this with someone like you?' Let Danny Boyle's 1994 film serve as a reminder, though, that chopping up and burying your dead flatmates is probably not the best of ideas.

wines. Sit-down cuisine from this corner of the globe is still pretty rare in Scotland, so praise is due to manager and co-owner Seyhan Azak for carving out this unique and enduring fixture.

Number One

Balmoral Hotel, 1 Princes Street (557 6727/www.thebalmoralhotel.com). Princes Street buses. **Open** 6.30-10pm daily. **£££**. **Modern European**. **Map** p89 F3 ㉝

An enviable address, a keen reputation and a very talented chef (Jeff Bland) all conspire to make this a first-class dining experience, one of only two venues in Edinburgh with a Michelin star. The spacious dining room pulls off the trick of being contemporary and classic at once, as the menu brings you into the heady territory of foie gras roulade with pineapple chutney, followed by poached beef sirloin with horseradish gratin.

Oloroso

33 Castle Street (226 7614/www. oloroso.co.uk). Princes Street buses. **Open** *Bar* 11am-1am daily. *Restaurant* noon-2pm, 7-10.15pm daily. **£££**. **International**. **Map** p89 D3 ㉞

Since opening in 2001, this destination bar-restaurant has, under Tony Singh's watchful eye, consolidated its reputation for quality cooking. The restaurant leads on its beef, veal and seafood grills and modish à la carte menu, and there's a roof terrace from which to enjoy the ephemeral Scottish summer. That said, the bar is usually buzzing, and many people come simply to drink or snack.

Opal Lounge

51a George Street (226 2275/www. opallounge.co.uk). Princes Street buses. **Open** 5pm-3am Mon-Fri, Sun; noon-3am Sat. *Food served* 5-10pm Mon-Fri, Sun; noon-10pm Sat. **££**. **Asian**. **Map** p89 D3 ㉟

Opal Lounge has been going great guns since its arrival in 2002. The food is predominantly eastern: sushi, bento boxes, noodle bowls and little 'bites' of tempura or Thai fishcakes. A good

choice for lunch, the contemporary, minimal and relaxed basement space becomes much buzzier in the evenings, thanks to a roster of DJs (including a Vegas-themed night on Fridays) and a fine cocktail list.

Oxford

8 Young Street (539 7119/www. oxfordbar.com). Princes Street buses. **Open** 11am-1am Mon-Sat; 12.30pm-midnight Sun. No credit cards. **Pub**. **Map** p89 D3 ㊱

Cramped, dowdy and clannish, the Oxford's bar area offers no space at all, and while the adjacent room has been given a lick of paint lately, it's still pretty basic. Sometimes it feels as if you have to be a member to drink here. So why come? Because it ploughs its own furrow, and doesn't give a toss about the white noise of contemporary style. It enjoys minor celebrity status as a favoured haunt of Ian Rankin's Inspector Rebus (and, for that matter, Rankin himself).

Palm Court

Balmoral Hotel, 1 Princes Street (556 2414/www.thebalmoralhotel.com). Princes Street buses. **Open** 9am-1am daily. **££££**. **Tea room/bar**. **Map** p89 F3 ㊲

Now renamed the 'Bollinger Bar at Palm Court', this is an imposing spot for afternoon tea. Choose between regular and champagne afternoon teas (2.30-5.30pm daily) and book ahead, then kick back and feel like a moneyed aristocrat of the old school for an hour or two.

Plaisir du Chocolat

48 Thistle Street (225 9900/www. plaisirduchocolat.com). Princes Street buses. **Open** 10am-6pm Tue-Sat. **Chocolatier**. **Map** p89 D3 ㊳

Having moved from Canongate, this upmarket chocoholic's heaven has eschewed its former café status and now concentrates exclusively on cocoa products: truffles, gateaux and myriad other intricate creations. The wares command the high prices expected of a French-run chocolate shop of lore – this ain't no Dairy Milk.

Opal Lounge p101

Pompadour

Caledonian Hilton Hotel, Princes Street (222 8888/www.hilton.com). Princes Street buses. **Open** 12.30-10pm Tue-Fri; 7-10pm Sat. **££**. **French**. Map p88 C4 ㊳

While faddish eateries come and go, the Pompadour endures. The dining room is effortlessly traditional in a dainty rococo manner, with the odd concession to modernity. With a classic French repertoire and a great sense of history, it's very popular with tourists and couples on romantic breaks. With a bit of luck, newish head chef Kenny Coltman will lead Pompadour away from its 'Edinburgh institution' reputation and towards greater things once more.

Queen Street Café

Scottish National Portrait Gallery, 1 Queen Street (557 2844/www. natgalscot.ac.uk). Bus 4, 8, 10, 11, 12, 15, 15A, 16, 17, 26, 44, 45. **Open** 10am-4.30pm Mon-Sat; 11am-4.30pm Sun. **Café**. Map p89 E3 ㊵

The very fabric of this fantastic Victorian-Gothic building has a reassuring air of tradition. The café is good for gossip and a scone, or light meals such as soups, pasta, salads or focaccias after a look round the gallery. Although the food won't come with any fashionista flourishes attached, the standard is high.

Rick's

55a Frederick Street (622 7800/ www.rick’sedinburgh.co.uk). Princes Street buses. **Open** 7am-1am daily. *Food served* 7.30am-11pm Mon-Wed, Sun; 7am-11pm Thur-Sat. **Café-bar**. Map p89 D3 ㊶

On busier evenings, the café-bar at Rick's hotel tends to attract girls with a certain look (that blonde hair, that black top) and guys with a certain demeanour (that aspirational wristwatch), but it's still a lively spot to hang out. You can grab a very decent breakfast (kippers with poached egg is spot on); later in the day, the menu offers the likes of oysters, venison and duck breast.

Stac Polly

29-33 Dublin Street (556 2231/www. stacpolly.co.uk). Bus 10, 11, 12, 23, 27. **Open** noon-2pm, 6-9.30pm Mon-Fri; 6-9.30pm Sat. **££**. **Scottish**. Map p89 E2 ㊷

Like many restaurants trying to collar Scottishness as a unique selling point, the clubbish if rustic Stac Polly does offer haggis (in filo pastry with plum and red wine sauce). However, it also serves dishes such as duck with pineapple relish, and its Caledonian credentials are more in its general approach than in the way it draws on the homelier elements of the traditional Scots kitchen. Set lunches are excellent value at £14.95 (two courses) and £18.95 (three).

Tonic

34a N Castle Street (225 6431/www. devilskitchen.co.uk). Princes Street buses. **Open** noon-1am daily. *Food served* noon-4pm daily. **Cocktail bar**. Map p89 D3 ㊸

Tonic's identikit style bar look and 13-page cocktail list (combined with a meagre choice of wines) may spark doubts about its approach. However, the kitchen may well surprise you: since going into partnership with a catering firm, it has begun offering a nice line in one-dish lunchtime meals (focaccias, salads, chargrilled burgers and a few more elaborate efforts). Menus are put away as the convivial evening clientele appears.

Urban Angel

121 Hanover Street (225 6215/www. urban-angel.co.uk). Princes Street buses. **Open** 10am-10pm Mon-Thur; 10am-11pm Fri, Sat; 10am-5pm Sun. **£**. **Café-restaurant**. Map p89 E3 ㊹

Urban Angel has a smart country-city crossover look, with wooden floors and white walls. It maintains high ethical standards, using organic, free-range and Fair Trade ingredients. In the daytime, it's a café and takeaway serving up great brunches, sandwiches and salads, but it comes into its own in the evening as a relaxed and popular restaurant. Try the fantastic tapas to start, followed by a bowl of crayfish risotto. There are also some top-notch veggie options available.

Valvona & Crolla Vin Caffè

Multrees Walk, St Andrew's Square (557 0088/www.valvonacrolla.com). Princes Street buses. **Open** 9.30am-9pm Mon-Wed; 9.30am-10pm Thur, Fri; 9am-10.15pm Sat; noon-5pm Sun. **£-££. Italian. Map** p89 F3 ㊺

Valvona & Crolla launched the ambitious Vin Caffè, a modern space with a café on the ground floor and restaurant upstairs, back in 1999. The latter offers dark wood, leather banquettes and acclaimed (if not inexpensive) food. Dishes include some excellent pizzas, griddled venison and pasta dishes as simple as taglierini with cream, butter and parmesan.

Voodoo Rooms

NEW *19a West Register Street (556 7060/www.thevoodoorooms.com). Princes Street buses.* **Open** noon-1am daily. *Food served* noon-10pm daily. **££. International. Map** p89 F3 ㊻

There are classic pubs in Edinburgh that date back to the Victorian era and woe betide anyone who messes with them. However, in an ornate space above the Café Royal, the Voodoo Rooms made its 2007 debut offering not just a long gallery bar but also a dining area (Creole-slanted) and a clubby music venue. One esteemed local food critic was so appalled she left before she ordered. Good for a beer or a bop however.

Whigham's Wine Cellars

13 Hope Street, Charlotte Square (225 8674/www.whighams.com). Princes Street buses. **Open** noon-midnight Mon-Thur; noon-1am Fri, Sat. *Food served* noon-10pm daily. **££. Wine bar. Map** p88 C4 ㊼

The old alcoves, candles and low ceilings give this well-established basement wine bar a cosy, intimate feel, but it's not completely subterranean: a 2004 expansion into next door's basement created a brighter, more open

space. The menu tends towards good bistro fare (including a signature seafood platter); the wine list is a decent international mix.

Shopping

In the shadow of the Castle, the north side of Princes Street is lined with standard chain stores such as Topshop and M&S, while a nearby upmarket alternative drag has emerged on George Street featuring the likes of Space NK, Hobbs and Jo Malone. But for even more exclusive labels head to Multrees Walk, where you'll find the likes of Louis Vuitton, Emporio Armani and Mulberry. If you venture beyond the high street, you'll find an inspiring range of boutiques, stocking everything from urban labels to local designers, and wonderful delis.

Alistair Wood Tait

116a Rose Street (225 4105). Princes Street buses. **Open** 10am-6pm Tue-Fri; 9.30am-5.30pm Sat. **Map** p89 D4 ㊽

Tait sells its own collections, featuring Scottish gemstones mounted in platinum, silver and gold. Look out, too, for antique pieces, including traditional Scottish pebble brooches.

Arkangel

4 William Street (226 4466/www. arkangelfashion.co.uk). Bus 3, 3A, 4, 12, 25, 26, 31, 33, 44. **Open** 10am-5.30pm Mon-Wed, Fri, Sat; 10am-6.30pm Thur. **Map** p88 B4 ㊾

This boutique feels like some giant dressing-up box, with unusual clothes as well as a fabulous range of jewellery. Designs come from big names such as Butler & Wilson, Ruyi and Les Nereides.

Boudiche

15 Frederick Street (226 5255/ www.boudiche.com). Princes Street buses. **Open** 10am-6pm Mon-Wed, Fri, Sat; 10am-7pm Thur; noon-5pm Sun. **Map** p89 D4 ㊿

Princes Street

From its crystal chandeliers to the luxury lingerie on sale, the vibe at Boudiche is deeply decadent. Brands include La Perla Black Label, Damaris, Spoylt and Elle Macpherson Intimates.

Cruise Woman

31 Castle Street, (220 4441/www.cruise clothing.co.uk). Princes Street buses. **Open** 9.30am-6pm Mon-Wed, Fri, Sat; 10am-7pm Thur; 11.30am-5.30pm Sun. **Map** p89 D3 ⑤⑴
Voted Most Stylish Retailer 2005 at the Scottish Style Awards, Cruise has been catering to fashion-conscious Scots for 20 years. Brands stocked include the likes of Prada, Gucci, Dolce & Gabbana and Galliano.

Fling

18 William Street (226 4115/www. fling-scotland.com). Bus 3, 3A, 4, 12, 25, 26, 31, 33, 44. **Open** 9.30am-6pm Mon-Fri; 9.30am-5.30pm Sat. **Map** p88 B4 ⑤⑵
There's more to Fling than leather, but it's a good place to start. All products are produced in Scotland; highlights include the leather-bound notebooks, travel bags and a dinky – if rather unnecessary – wallet for holding a pack of chewing gum.

Hamilton & Inches

87 George Street (225 4898/www. hamiltonandinches.com). Princes Street buses. **Open** 9.30am-5.30pm Mon-Fri; 9.30am-5pm Sat. **Map** p89 D3 ⑤⑶
Scotland's best-known jewellers, Hamilton & Inches have a royal warrant as silversmiths to the Queen. The wares are every bit as grand as the Georgian shop: watches, silverware and a stylish (if pricey) selection of contemporary and classic jewellery.

Henderson's

92 Hanover Street (225 6694/ www.hendersonsofedinburgh. co.uk). Princes Street buses. **Open** 8am-7pm Mon-Fri; 10am-6pm Sat. **Map** p89 E3 ⑤⑷
Henderson's has been promoting natural food in Scotland for more than 40 years through its shop and restaurant. You'll find a good supply of breads,

cheeses and healthy snacks; in particular, keep an eye out for the wonderful vegetarian haggis rolls.

Jane Davidson

52 Thistle Street (225 3280/www.jane davidson.co.uk). Princes Street buses. **Open** 9.30am-6pm Mon-Wed, Fri, Sat; 9.30am-7pm Thur. **Map** p89 D3 **65**
This chic boutique has been attracting in-the-know locals since 1969, with designs by Christian Lacroix, Diane von Furstenberg, Missoni and more.

Joseph Bonnar

72 Thistle Street (226 2811/www. josephbonnar.com). Princes Street buses. **Open** 10.30am-5pm Tue-Sat. **Map** p89 D3 **66**
Fancy antique and period jewellery for those occasions when you really want to splash out.

Margiotta's

122-124 Dundas Street (476 7070). Bus 13, 23, 27. **Open** 7.30am-10pm Mon-Sat; 8am-10pm Sun. **Map** p89 D2 **67**
This popular deli has branches around the city, selling standard groceries along with good selections of wines, cheeses, olives and gourmet snacks.

Neal's Yard Remedies

102 Hanover Street (226 3223/www. nealsyardremedies.com). Princes Street buses. **Open** 10am-6pm Mon-Wed, Fri, Sat; 10am-7pm Thur; 1-5pm Sun. **Map** p89 E3 **68**
Lovely soaps, moisturisers and bath oils are among the body and beauty essentials on sale, made using essential oils and other natural ingredients. (The ultra-rich Frankincense Nourishing Cream is highly recommended.) The treatment rooms offer a host of options.

One World Shop

St John's Church, Princes Street (229 4541/www.oneworldshop.co.uk). Princes Street buses. **Open** 10am-5.30pm Mon-Wed, Fri, Sat; 10am-7pm Thur. **Map** p88 C4 **69**
Offerings at Edinburgh's Fairtrade shop include crafts, textiles, toys, clothing and foods.

Pam Jenkins

41 Thistle Street (225 3242/www. pamjenkins.co.uk). Princes Street buses. **Open** 10am-5.30pm Mon-Sat. **Map** p89 D3 **60**
A dangerously tempting array of designer shoes and accessories from well-known names such as Jimmy Choo, Christian Louboutin, Nicole Farhi and Kate Spade. Shoe-lovers, enter at your peril.

Romanes & Pattersons

122 Princes Street (225 4966). Princes Street buses. **Open** 9am-6pm Mon-Sat; 10am-6pm Sun. **Map** p89 E3 **61**
Now part of the Edinburgh Woollen Mill group of shops, Romanes & Pattersons has been trading in tartan since 1808. Prices are fair.

Sam Thomas

18 Stafford Street (226 1126). Bus 3, 3A, 4, 12, 25, 26, 31, 33, 44. **Open** 9.30am-6pm Mon-Wed, Fri, Sat; 9.30am-6.30pm Thur; 12.30-5pm Sun. **Map** p88 C4 **62**
The price tags in this friendly boutique are, pleasingly, a little lower than you might expect. Clothes, including hard-to-find labels such as Great Plains and Avoca, are laid out neatly on colour co-ordinated rails.

Studio One

10-16 Stafford Street (226 5812). Bus 3, 3A, 4, 12, 25, 26, 31, 33, 44. **Open** 9.30am-6pm Mon-Wed, Fri, Sat; 9.30am-7pm Thur; 11am-5pm Sun. **Map** p88 C4 **63**
A wealth of interesting household items and quality gifts line the shelves at Studio One, from scented candles and soaps to paper lanterns and a selection of colourful rugs.

Tiso

123-125 Rose Street, New Town (225 9486/www.tiso.com). Princes Street buses. **Open** 9.30am-5.30pm Mon, Tue, Fri, Sat; 10am-5.30pm Wed; 9.30am-7.30pm Thur; 11am-5pm Sun. **Map** p89 D3 **64**
Effectively Scotland's outdoors superstore, Tiso stocks a massive variety of clothing, equipment, books and

maps. The Leith store even has a mini climbing wall and a Gore-Tex waterproof test shower.

Nightlife

Caledonian Backpackers

3 Queensferry Street (476 7224/www. caledonianbackpackers.com). Princes Street buses. **Open** 6pm-1am Mon-Thur, Sun; 4pm-5am Fri, Sat. *Food served* noon-7pm daily. **Admission** £4-£5 Fri, Sat. No credit cards. **Map** p88 C4 65

It may be the rough and ready bar of a New Town backpackers' hostel, but thanks to canny local promoters such as Baby Tiger (www.baby-tiger.net), the eclectic bills of indie, rock, folk, pop and experimental electronica it occasionally stages are worth a look.

Eighty Queen Street

80 Queen Street (226 5097/www. eighty-queen-street.com). Princes Street buses. **Gigs** 9pm Wed; 2pm, 9pm Sat; 2pm Sun. *Food served* noon-7pm daily. **Admission** free. **Map** p88 C3 66

This spacious cellar bar offers regular sets of unobtrusive modern jazz, with guest artistes often featuring on Saturdays. It's worth dropping by on Wednesdays for the well-established open mic sessions.

Frenchies

89 Rose Street North Lane (225 7651). Princes Street buses. **Open** 1pm-1am Mon-Sat; 2pm-1am Sun. No credit cards. **Map** p89 D4 67

Coming across more like a local pub in a Highland village than a bar in the Scottish capital, Frenchies is the oldest gay hangout in Edinburgh. Despite its central location the bar is quite difficult to spot, as the entrance is just a small doorway in between boarded-up windows. It's a charm, however. Happy hour runs from 6-8pm daily.

Jam House

5 Queen Street, New Town (226 4380/ bookings 226 5875/www.thejamhouse. com). Princes Street buses. **Gigs** 10pm Wed-Sun. **Admission** free-£10. **Map** p89 E3 68

Housed in the beautiful former BBC Broadcasting House, this music-and-dining venue is a real looker, a grand and expansive space with tables on the main floor and seating upstairs. The problems are with the anodyne programming, cover bands mixing with turns from the likes of Hue & Cry.

New Town Bar

26b Dublin Street (538 7775/www. bar-twist.co.uk). Bus 4, 8, 10, 11, 12, 15, 15A, 16, 26, 44, 45. **Open** *Bar* noon-1am Mon-Thur; noon-2am Fri, Sat; 12.30pm-1am Sun. *Club* 10pm-2am Fri-Sat. *Food served* noon-7pm Mon-Sat; 12.30-7pm Sun. **Map** p89 E2 69

After a brief spell as Twist, New Town Bar has reverted back to its former self, albeit incorporating the major refurbishment that has made it a far more welcoming prospect than it once was. It's a mellow regulars spot during the day, and the kitchen serves snacks to laptop-carrying customers (there's free Wi-Fi access). The basement club has a female DJ in residence on Fridays and Saturdays.

Stand

5 York Place (558 7272/www.the stand.co.uk). Playhouse or Princes Street buses. **Shows** 9pm (doors 7.30pm) Mon-Sat; 1pm (doors 12.30pm), 9pm (doors 7.30pm) Sun. **Tickets** free-£10. No credit cards. **Map** p89 F2 70

The Stand's big weekend comedy shows see its 160-capacity basement space at its uproarious best; arrive early for a good seat. However, weekday shows can offer some surprises. Established performers such as Miles Jupp and Craig Hill cut their teeth at Monday's popular Red Raw newcomers' night (£1); Wednesdays are generally devoted to more diverse forms of comedy, including sketch shows and satire. Increasingly, though, Thursday shows are the ones to catch, with Frankie Boyle often taking on compère duties. Sunday afternoons have a more laid-back vibe, with battered sofas, a simple menu and free improv.

Inverleith House p110

Stockbridge

Village backwater, Georgian vision, bohemian enclave, workers' utopia: Stockbridge has been many things to many people over the centuries. But while housing trends and shopping fashions continue to come and go, Stockbridge still feels less like an urban neighbourhood and more like a village that just happens to have a city on its doorstep.

Independent businesses thrive here: cafés, pubs and small restaurants galore, and a handful of small local stores and well-stocked charity shops along Raeburn Place make for a pleasant afternoon's browsing. The architecture is as varied as the shopping opportunities and several centuries' worth of building styles can be seen during the course of a gentle stroll

around the area. Of particular note are the schools; neo-classsical Edinburgh Academy and gargoyle-heavy **Fettes**, which was apparently JK Rowling's inspiration for Hogwarts.

A great way to experience Stockbridge's sedate charm is to take a walk along the **Water of Leith**, a 28-mile stretch of river that cuts through the neighbourhood. The river is easily accessible: you can join it at the **Gallery of Modern Art** and wander to Stockbridge, or pick it up in Stockbridge at Pizza Express and meander along its course to Canonmills without leaving the path. There are a couple of herons that live along this stretch and can frequently be seen fishing in the river. And during the annual

Stockbridge Festival, which normally runs for nine days towards the end of June, the river plays host to an annual duck race, so don't be surprised if you see the odd stray bobbing along from Stockbridge to Canonmills one summer's day.

Sights & museums

Dean Gallery

Belford Road (624 6200/www.national galleries.org). Bus 13 (or free shuttle bus from the Mound). **Open** 10am-5pm daily. **Admission** free; £1-£6 for special exhibitions. **Map** p111 A5 ①

The Dean Gallery is conveniently situated directly across the road from the Scottish National Gallery of Modern Art (p112); you can easily combine a visit to both in a day. The exhibitions it hosts are often enlightening, and the gallery currently holds one of Britain's largest collections of surrealist and Dadaist artworks, including pieces by Dali, Giacometti, Miró and Picasso.

Inverleith House

Royal Botanic Garden, Inverleith Row (552 7171/www.rbge.org.uk). Bus 8, 17, 23, 27. **Open** *Nov-Feb* 10am-3.30pm Tue-Sun. *Mar-Oct* 10am-5.30pm Tue-Sun. *During festival* 10am-5.30pm daily. **Admission** free. **Map** p111 C1 ②

The house was refurbished in 2004 with funding from the National lottery and exhibitions taking place in the gallery space often make reference to the natural world. Inverleith House also hosts temporary exhibitions by some big-hitters of modern art, including Edinburgh-born Callum Innes, Ulrich Rückriem, Agnes Martin, minimalist sculptor Carl Andre and Turner Prize nominee Jim Lambie, as well as shows by a range of up-and-coming local talent.

Royal Botanic Garden

20A Inverleith Row (5527171/www. rbge.org.uk). Bus 8, 17, 23, 27. **Open** *Nov-Feb* 10am-4pm daily. *Mar, Oct* 10am-6pm daily. *Apr-Sept* 10am-7pm daily. **Admission** *Garden* free.

Dean Gallery

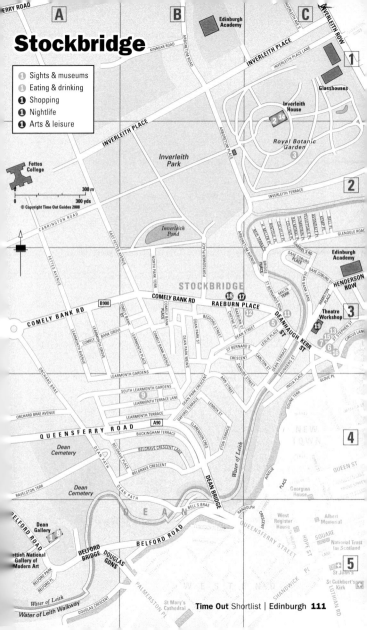

Stockbridge

1 Sights & museums
1 Eating & drinking
1 Shopping
1 Nightlife
1 Arts & leisure

© Copyright Time Out Guides 2008

Scottish National Gallery of Modern Art

EDINBURGH BY AREA

Glasshouses £3.50; £1-£3 reductions.
Map p111 C2 ❸
The Royal Botanic Garden has delight-
ed both plant-lovers and those just out
for a casual stroll, for almost two
centuries. The Botanics is one of
Edinburgh's most peaceful tourist
attractions, but it's also a noted centre
for botanical and horticultural research,
and houses the oldest botanical library
in Britain. Kids love it too.

Scottish National Gallery of Modern Art

*Belford Road (624 6200/www.national
galleries.org). Bus 13 (or free shuttle
bus from the Mound).* **Open** 10am-5pm
daily **Admission** free; £1-£6 for
special exhibitions. **Map** p111 A5 ❹
Occupying a building designed in the
1820s as an institution for fatherless
children, the permanent collection
features numerous well-established
artists, with a strong showing from the
so-called 1980s Glasgow Boys: Peter
Howson, Steven Campbell, Adrian

Wiszniewski, Ken Currie and others.
The ground level is usually devoted to
special exhibitions, with the upper
floor accommodating works by big
international names such as Matisse,
Picasso and Pollock. The entire supporting wall on the stairs linking the
two floors has been given over to the
artist Douglas Gordon, who has neatly
printed the names of every person he
has ever met and whose name he can
remember. Outisde, the landscaped
gardens make a great picnic location.

Eating & drinking

Avoca

*4-6 Dean Street (315 3311). Bus 24,
29, 42.* **Open** 11am-midnight Mon-
Thur, Sun; 11am-1am Fri, Sat. *Food
served* noon-2.30pm, 5.30-8.15pm Mon-
Thur; noon-7.15pm Fri-Sun. **£. Pub.**
Map p111 C3 ❺
Despite bearing the name of a village
in County Wicklow, this is no Oirish
theme bar. Instead, it's a compact,

Royal Botanic Garden p110

modern pub in one of the city's most bourgeois quarters, with wooden fittings, friendly staff and decent bar food (including late breakfasts).

Bailie

2 St Stephen Street (225 4673). Bus 24, 29, 42. **Open** 11am-midnight Mon-Thur; 11am-1am Fri, Sat; 12.30pm-midnight Sun. *Food served* 11am-9pm Mon-Thur, Sat; 11am-5pm Fri; 12.30-9pm Sun. **£. Pub. Map** p111 C3 ⑥
This old-style basement pub – all striking blacks and reds, focused on a central island bar – somehow manages to combine New Town money with Stockbridge bohemia. Food is typical pub grub (fish and chips, steak pie) with a few more ambitious dishes. The only change of late is that the old regulars look testier than ever, presumably because they have to go outside to smoke.

Bell's Diner

7 St Stephen Street (225 8116). Bus 24, 29, 36, 42. **Open** 6-10.30pm Mon-Fri, Sun; noon-10.30pm Sat. **£. Diner. Map** p111 C3 ⑦
It's said that modern sharks evolved something like 144 to 208 million years ago, and have been such a great success in terms of natural selection that they haven't changed much since. And so to Bell's Diner, a burger joint par excellence since 1972; in terms of Edinburgh restaurant turnover, this actually makes it fitter than your average Great White. It's small and simple, cooking up fabulous burgers (including vegetarian options), good steaks and hearty desserts to delight your inner child.

Café Newton

Dean Gallery, 73 Belford Road (623 7132/www.natgalscot.ac.uk). Bus 13. **Open** 10am-4.30pm daily. **£. Café. Map** p111 A5 ⑧
With more than a nod to the grandeur of the Viennese coffee houses (and a rather spectacular Victoria Arduino coffee machine), Café Newton is worth

Gallery Café

a visit just to look. But the lemon polenta cake is rather wonderful, and the rest of the offerings are also good (soup, platters, specials and more). The only downside is that it's smaller than it looks and gets crowded.

Channings

12-15 S Learmonth Gardens (315 2225/www.channings.co.uk). Bus 19, 37, 41, 47. **Open** noon-2.30pm, 6-10pm Mon-Fri; 12.30-3pm, 6-10pm Sat, Sun. **£££. Scottish/French**. Map p111 B4 ⑨

One of a small chain of boutique hotels in the city, Channings (p111) has two eateries: a wine bar with a good choice of light meals and snacks, and – more importantly – a fine dining room under the supervision of Hubert Lamort, serving some of the best modern Franco-Caledonian cuisine in the city (pan-fried scallops to start; roast squab with couscous, dried fruits, harissa and sweet jus as a main, perhaps). Located up the hill from the main Stockbridge 'village', it feels very discreet.

Gallery Café

Scottish National Gallery of Modern Art, 75 Belford Road (332 8600/ www.natgalscot.ac.uk). Bus 13. **Open** 10am-4.30pm daily. **£. Café**. Map p111 A5 ⑩

A perennially popular eatery, and not just with the city's art hounds. People come from all over town for the selection of soups, salads and a couple of hot dishes, as well as a decent cheese selection. The light basement space is busy but the café's real appeal becomes apparent in the summer, when diners can sit on the terrace next to the garden outside the classical 19th-century building.

Hector's

47-49 Deanhaugh Street (343 1735). Bus 24, 29, 42. **Open** noon-midnight Mon-Wed, Sun; noon-1am Thur-Sat. *Food served* noon-3pm, 5-10pm Mon-Fri; noon-4pm Sat, Sun. **£. Bar**. Map p111 C3 ⑪

Formerly a pioneering designer restaurant, this establishment is now a less ostentatious style bar, good for cosy chats by candlelight or nestling by the fire. The menu features the usual suspects (nachos, burgers, salads). A handy stop if you've been wandering around the nearby Royal Botanic Garden.

EDINBURGH BY AREA

Hogwarts to Hollywood

What a long, strange trip it's been. In 2007, Jo Rowling kept her place on the list of dollar billionaires published by the prestigious *Forbes* magazine in the United States, her net worth pegged at $1 billion. Not bad for someone who took the first step towards that unimaginable pile of cash by writing a novel longhand, while living on benefits, in a couple of Edinburgh cafés just a dozen years earlier.

The Gloucestershire-born Rowling moved to the city at the end of 1994 with her infant daughter. Behind her she had a degree from the University of Exeter, spells of study or work in Paris, London and Porto, and a failed marriage.

The idea for Harry Potter had been kicking around for some time, having first popped into Rowling's head on a train from London to Manchester. Even then it was conceived as a seven-part series, charting young Harry's necromancing from the ages of 11 to 17 while a pupil at Hogwarts, which was supposedly inspired by Fettes College (p109).

It was only in 1995, however, that Rowling started scribbling in places like the Elephant House Café (p70) on George IV Bridge and Nicolson's on Nicolson Street (now a Chinese buffet restaurant), while her daughter napped. And it took until the summer of 1997 for *Harry Potter and the Philosopher's Stone* – aided by a grant from the Scottish Arts Council – to see the light of day.

From there the phenomenon developed: another six books between 1998 and 2007, plus the highest grossing film series ever. There's still one more movie to go, even after the release of *Harry Potter and the Half-Blood Prince* scheduled for late 2008.

One of the biggest literary and entertainment stories of all time ended where it began, however: Rowling finished the seventh and final book in Edinburgh, albeit in rather grander circumstances. She was staying at the Balmoral Hotel (p172) and left behind a little graffiti on a bust in her room: 'JK Rowling finished writing *Harry Potter and the Deathly Hallows* in this room (652) on 11th January 2007.'

For Rowling, life moves on. She has another two children with her second husband Neil Murray, and the family maintains homes in Edinburgh, London and, fitting for a fairy tale of this nature, a castle in Perthshire. These days she spends a lot of her time doing charity work, but says she will continue to write. Not in cafés around the Old Town, though.

Stockbridge Restaurant

Maxi's

33 Raeburn Place (343 3007/www. eveningatmaxis.com). Bus 24, 29, 42. **Open** 8.30am-5pm Mon-Fri; 8.30am-6pm Sat; 10am-5pm Sun. **£**. **Café**. **Map** p111 C3 ⑫

A friendly and popular café with a few deli bits and bobs for sale, Maxi's is approaching its tenth anniversary. A light and airy space with blond wood tables, it's modern but still accessible. Stop for breakfast or a quick coffee, or dawdle over a bottle of red with a panini and a salad. In the evenings (Thur-Sat), another pair of hands takes over to offer a bistro dinner menu, with a focus on local ingredients; mains might include pot roast shoulder of pork, or beef and cider pie. A decent neighbourhood eaterie.

Stockbridge Restaurant

54 St Stephen Street (226 6766/www. thestockbridgerestaurant.com). Bus 24, 29, 36, 42. **Open** 7-9.30pm Tue-Sat. **££**. **Modern European**. **Map** p111 C3 ⑬

If the Edinburgh restaurant market is maturing, then the growing profile of this small, smart, basement eaterie, run by chef Jason Gallagher since 2004, is part of the trend. The dishes betray no lack of ambition: grilled halibut fillet with a crab crust, for instance. But it's no city centre hangout: it's a neighbourhood establishment, albeit in a fairly swish locality, providing great food without hubris. Local foie gras for local people? Drop by anyway.

Terrace Café

Royal Botanic Gardens, Inverleith Row (552 0616/www.rbge.org.uk). Bus 8, 17, 23, 27. **Open** *May-Sept* 9.30am-6pm daily. *Oct-Apr* closes earlier; phone for details. **£**. **Café**. **Map** p111 C1 ⑭

This café next to Inverleith House (p110) is a handy pit-stop. There are seats inside and out, light lunches of the quiche-and-salad or baked-potato variety, plus sandwiches and cakes. If the weather is good try and grab a table outside: the views of the central Edinburgh skyline are unparalleled.

Watershed

44 St Stephen Street (220 6189). Bus 24, 29, 42. **Open** *4pm-midnight Mon-Wed; noon-1am ThurSat;12.30pm-1am Sun. Food served 4-8pm Mon-Fri; noon-8pm Sat; 12.30-8pm Sun.* **Pub.** Map p111 C3 ⑮

The Watershed's recent facelift has cheered up its fading style-bar image with a blast of design eclecticism that the new management says 'just seemed like a good idea at the time': a celebration of Koh Samui beach-bar chic in an Edinburgh basement. It has a reasonable bar food menu at lunchtime and in the afternoon; as with many other venues of this ilk, it gets buzzier and pubbier in the evening.

Zanzero

NEW *15 North West Circus Place, (220 0333/www.zanzero.com). Bus 24, 29, 42.* **Open** *9am-11pm daily.* **£.** **Italian.** Map p111 C3 ⑯

From the people who brought you Centotre (p92), Zanzero arrived in 2007 and despite its garish green décor, it provokes diners into saying things like, "Woah that mozzarella's bloody good." Essentially a modern Italian caffè where the focus falls on the quality of the ingredients rather than the Baroque complexities of their preparation, you can drop in for a free range egg roll from 10am or come in later and have a three-course evening dinner. Shiny happy peopleville.

Shopping

Galerie Mirages

46A Raeburn Place (315 2603). Bus 24, 29, 42. **Open** *10am-5.30pm Mon-Sat; noon-4.30pm Sun.* Map p111 B3 ⑰

Sheila Dhariwal travels the globe in search of interesting jewellery to stock in her gallery, but also makes her own designs using antique beads. A good selection of silver pieces is also on offer.

Herbie of Edinburgh

66 Raeburn Place, (332 9888/www.herbieofedinburgh.co.uk). Bus 24, 29, 42. **Open** *9.30am-7pm Mon-Fri; 9am-6pm Sat.* Map p111 B3 ⑱

Galerie Mirages

This friendly neighbourhood deli has plenty of fresh-baked breads and an extensive range of cheeses that you can try before you buy.

Arts & Leisure

Theatre Workshop

34 Hamilton Place, (226 5425/www.theatre-workshop.com). Bus 23, 27, 36. Map 111 C3 ⑲

A thriving house of radical touring theatre, and an epicentre for boho Stockbridge life since 2000, the building's focus is now on its own professional company, the first professional mixed physical ability ensemble in Europe. Its shows tackle single-issue politics head-on, from anti-globalisation marches to disabled activism. Aesthetic sensibilities, alas, are sometimes buried in the desire to get the message across. More recently, though, it has been winning back the critics with acclaimed productions of shows such as *Arabian Nights* and *the Wind in the Willows*.

Nelson Monument

Calton Hill & Broughton

It was from the top of Calton Hill that Robert Louis Stevenson drew much of the inspiration that fuelled his writing on Edinburgh and although *The Strange Case of Dr Jekyll and Mr Hyde* was set in London, its atmosphere of moral hypocrisy was charged with what Stevenson saw from here.

The hill is on the edge of old Edinburgh and is home to the City Observatory. In the run-up to Hogmanay, it's the destination for the annual torchlight procession, culminating in a fireworks display and boat-burning. **The National monument** is also a great place from which to view the spectacular fireworks that close the Edinburgh International Festival each year.

Sights & museums

Nelson Monument

Calton Hill (556 2716/www.cac.org.uk). Playhouse buses. **Open** *Apr-Sept* 10am-6pm Mon-Sat. *Oct-Mar* 10am-3pm Mon-Sat. **Admission** £3. No credit cards. **Map** p119 C3 ❶
If the views from Calton Hill aren't grand enough for your liking, you can get an even better vantage point from the top of the Nelson Monument, designed in the shape of Nelson's telescope. Be warned, though: despite its sturdy structure the viewing deck can feel very exposed on windy days.

Eating & drinking

Barony

81-83 Broughton Street (558 2874). Bus 8, 13, 17/Playhouse buses. **Open**

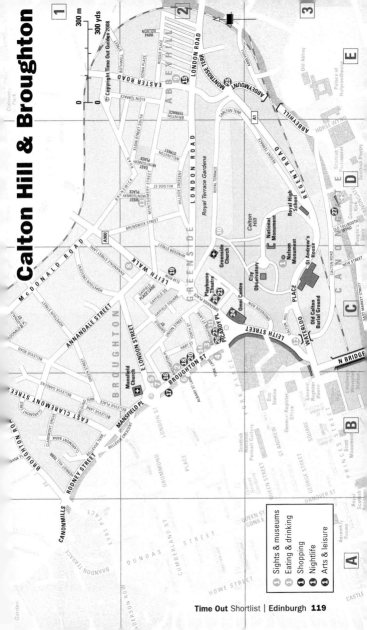

Calton Hill & Broughton

NORTON PARK

300 m
300 yds

© Copyright Time Out Guides 2008

EASTER ROAD

ABBEYHILL

LONDON ROAD

MONTROSE TERR

ABBEYMOUNT

ELGIN TERRACE

BOTHWELL ST

EDINA PLACE

ROSSIE PLACE

CARLTON TERR

A1

BRINTON TERRACE

ELGIN STREET SOUTH

EAST MONTGOMERY PLACE

WELLINGTON STREET

HILLSIDE CRESCENT

HILLSIDE ST

LONDON ROAD

Royal Terrace Gardens

ROYAL TERRACE

WEST MONTGOMERY PLACE

BRUNTON PLACE

MONTGOMERY STREET

REGENT ROAD

BRUNSWICK STREET

A900

ABBEYHILL

HORSE WYND

Palace of Holyroodhouse

Old Abbey

Scottish Parliament

WINDSOR STREET

GREENSIDE

Royal High School

Calton Hill

National Monument

Nelson Monument

St Andrew's House

McDONALD ROAD

LEITH WALK

HOPETOUN CRESCENT

ANNANDALE STREET LANE

GAYFIELD PLACE LANE

ELM ROW

GAYFIELD SQ

Greenside Church

City Observatory

Playhouse Theatre

Omni Centre

Old Calton Burial Ground

CALTON ROAD

OLD TOLLBOOTH WYND

People's Story

Museum of Edinburgh

CANONGATE

NEW STREET

EAST MARKET STREET

ANNANDALE STREET

BELLEVUE ROAD

MACDONALD RD

BROUGHTON

E LONDON STREET

GAYFIELD STREET

UNION STREET

HART STREET

BROUGHTON ST

PICARDY PL

YORK PLACE

LEITH STREET

WATERLOO PLACE

REGENT ROAD

N BRIDGE

Mansfield Church

Mansfield PL

MANSFIELD PL

EAST CLAREMONT STREET

BELLEVUE GARDENS

BELLEVUE TERR

BELLEVUE LANE

BELLEVUE CRESCENT

CLAREMONT GROVE

CLAREMONT BANK

HERIOT HILL TERR

RODNEY STREET

BROUGHTON ROAD

CANONMILLS

EYRE PLACE

BRANDON TERRACE

DRUMMOND PLACE

LONDON ST

ST ANDREW

Scottish National Portrait Gallery

Queen Street Gardens

QUEEN STREET

QUEEN ST GDNS E

GEORGE STREET

HANOVER ST

General Register Office

General Register House

Bus Station

Scott Monument

PRINCES STREET

Royal Scottish

Assembly Rooms

CUMBERLAND ST

DUNDAS STREET

HOWE STREET

HENDERSON ROW

CASTLE

Garden

Legend

- Sights & museums
- Eating & drinking
- Shopping
- Nightlife
- Arts & leisure

11am-1am Mon-Sat; 12.30-11pm Sun. *Food served* 11am-10pm Mon-Sat; 12.30-10pm Sun. **Pub**. **Map** p119 C2 ②

The Barony is a traditional-looking pub, but by no means without character or charisma. The clientele is pretty mixed, and wouldn't seem entirely out of place in one of the more contemporary café-bars nearby. There's pub grub, various cask ales (with regular guest offerings), plus occasional live music performances.

Baroque

39-41 Broughton Street (557 0627/ www.baroqueedinburgh.com). Bus 8, 13, 17. **Open** 10am-midnight Mon-Wed, Sun; 10am-1am Thur-Sat. *Food served* 10am-9pm Mon-Sat; 10am-8pm Sun.* **Café-bar**. **Map** p119 C2 ③

You can trace the last ten years of Edinburgh's café-bar trends through this one venue alone. Baroque was a complete design riot when it first opened, but trimmed back the excess a few years later and then added free Wi-Fi access in 2005. Open to the street in summer, the bar has all the usual booze choices alongside a basic menu.

Basement

10a-12a Broughton Street (557 0097/ www.thebasement.org.uk). Bus 8, 13, 17/Playhouse buses. **Open** noon-1am daily. *Food served* noon-10.30pm daily. **Bar**. **Map** p119 C2 ④

Broughton Street's original style bar is pretty unchanged since it opened in 1994, except for the odd improvement decor-wise. With a dim-lit, split-level room and separate dining space, it can get buzzy in the evenings, when the music is loud. The menu changes during the week, but avocado salad or steak pie are good benchmarks.

Bella Mbriana

NEW *7–11 East London Street (558 9581). Bus 8, 13, 17.* **Open** 5-10.30pm Mon; noon-2.30pm, 5-10.30pm Tue-Thur; noon-2.30pm, 5-11.45pm Fri; noon-11.45pm Sat; noon-10pm Sun. **££**. **Italian**. **Map** p119 B2 ⑤

Claremont p124

Edinburgh's three generic cuisines are Chinese, Indian and Italian. Given the volume of phone book they occupy, stand-outs are relatively rare; 2007 debutante Bella Mbriana, by the bottom of Broughton Street, may be on to a winner though. There is nothing complex about this place, in menu or decor, but chef Rosario Sartore used to run the despicably underrated Partenope in Dalry Road. Here he has created another informal and worthwhile Neapolitan eaterie.

Blue Moon Café

36 Broughton Street (556 2788/www. bluemooncafe.co.uk). Bus 8, 13, 17/ Playhouse buses. **Open** 11am-midnight Mon-Fri; 10am-midnight Sat, Sun. **Café**. Map p119 B2 ⑥
Gay-run but straight-friendly, the Blue Moon is a popular meet-and-eat place during the week, but the atmosphere steps up a notch to accommodate the pre-club crowd. The food tends to be simple and filling (burgers, nachos, macaroni cheese), while there are some good bottled lagers and economy wines. If you want to know anything about the city's gay scene, just ask the friendly staff.

Cask & Barrel

115 Broughton Street (556 3132). Playhouse buses. **Open** 11am-12.30am Mon-Wed, Sun; 11am-1am Thur-Sat. *Food served* noon-2pm daily. **Pub**. Map p119 B2 ⑦
Beer heaven: this old-fashioned pub offers local brews, obscure artisan cask ales from around the UK, and bottled beers from Germany and the Low Countries. Wherever you choose to sit or stand, you'll be able to watch the football on one of the screens.

Embo

29 Haddington Place, Leith Walk (652 3880/www.embodeli.com). Bus 7, 10, 12, 14, 16, 22, 25, 49. **Open** 8am-4pm Mon-Fri; 9am-4.30pm Sat. No credit cards. **Deli/café**. Map p119 C2 ⑧
Up a short flight of steps from the pavement on one of Leith Walk's terraces, Embo is a small but well-run

establishment. If you're in the area and fancy a high-quality focaccia, salad or wrap, then head here. The food on offer is very good, whether you decide to eat in or have a takeaway. The decor is simple but attractive.

Manna House

22-24 Easter Road (652 2349/ www.manna-house-edinburgh.co.uk). Bus 1, 35. **Open** 8am-7pm Tue-Thur; 8am-6pm Fri, Sat. £. No credit cards. **Pâtisserie**. Map p119 E2 ⑨
Manna House bears testament to the changes that property-price inflation has wrought in Edinburgh. Easter Road has always been a solid, working-class street, but the sheer cost of flats these days has brought in a wave of new residents. Businesses have moved in to cater for the new arrivals; among them is this brilliant pâtisserie, where shoppers can stop for coffee, cake, elaborate tarts or savouries.

No.3 Royal Terrace

3 Royal Terrace (477 4747/www. no3royalterrace.com). Bus 1, 4, 5, 15, 15A, 19, 26, 34, 44, 45. **Open** noon-2pm, 5.30-10pm daily. **££. Modern European**. Map p119 D2 ⑩
Occupying two floors of a Georgian townhouse, No.3 possesses a certain grandeur. Most diners are seated on the ground floor, complete with ornate bar and chandeliers; upstairs is generally reserved for busier evenings or private functions. The signature dish is charcoal-grilled steak, but there's a fair choice à la carte, too, plus a handy pre-theatre menu and a garden at the back.

Outhouse

12a Broughton Street Lane (557 6668). Bus 8, 13, 17/Playhouse buses. **Open** noon-1am daily. *Food served* noon-7pm daily. **Bar**. Map p119 C2 ⑪
Down an unlovely lane off Broughton Street, the Outhouse could easily be just another style bar. However, it works hard at attracting a lively clientele with regular DJs, and scores with the urban beer garden out back. There's not much of a view, but it is away from all the traffic pollution.

Pivo

2-6 Calton Road (557 2925). Nicolson Street–North Bridge buses. **Open** 7pm-3am Mon-Thur, Sun; 5pm-3am Fri, Sat. **Bar. Map** p119 C3 ⑫

It's not so much a Czech bar as a Czech-themed bar, but Pivo has the look (and the lager) all the same. Two minutes from the east end of Princes Street, it's a popular late-night DJ bar; if you want to savour that Staropramen in relative peace, best go early in the evening.

Renroc

91 Montgomery Street (556 0432/ www.renroc.co.uk). Bus 1, 7, 10, 12, 14, 16, 22, 25, 35, 49. **Open** 7.30am-6pm Mon-Wed; 7am-10pm Thur, Fri; 9.30am-10pm Sat; 10.30am-6pm Sun. **Café. Map** p119 D2 ⑬

If Manna House (p121) demonstrates the gentrification of the upper end of Easter Road, nearby Renroc goes one better, offering not only an extensive café menu but also a complementary health studio in its basement. Sample soups, sandwiches, panini and specials – ideally at one of the tables outside, which are something of a suntrap.

Tapas Tree

1 Forth Street (556 7118). Playhouse buses. **Open** 11am-11pm daily. **£. Tapas. Map** p119 C2 ⑭

This old Spanish dependable throws out classic tapas (serrano ham, tortilla española and so on), but doesn't rest on its laurels: there's a good-value lunch menu, a Spanish guitar night on Wednesdays and flamenco on Thursdays. The emphasis is on fun, free-flowing conversation and sharing; no wonder locals are grateful that the Tapas Tree keeps on going.

Shopping

Cornelius

18-20 Easter Road (652 2405). Bus 1, 35. **Open** noon-9pm Mon-Sat. **Map** p119 E2 ⑮

Another example of gentrification in a far from traditionally middle-class area (the southern end of Easter Road), Cornelius is a decent wine merchant in a neighbourhood that's previously been served only by cheap supermarkets and chains. There's an excellent choice of bottled beers.

Crombie's of Edinburgh

97-101 Broughton Street (557 0111/ www.sausages.co.uk). Bus 8, 13, 17. **Open** 8am-5.30pm Mon-Fri; 8am-5pm Sat. **Map** p119 B2 ⑯

This high-quality butcher is best known for its extensive array of sausages: boar, port and stilton, and pork, mango and apple are stocked alongside more traditional bangers.

Joey D

54 Broughton Street (557 6672/ www.joey-d.co.uk). Bus 8, 13, 17. **Open** 10.30am-6pm daily. **Map** p119 B2 ⑰

The cutting-edge garments here are best described as reconstructed. Tweed, boiler suits, jeans and other items are ripped up and put back together to create something more interesting.

Organic Pleasures

NEW *71 Broughton Street (558 2777/ www.organicpleasures.co.uk). Bus 8, 13, 17.* **Open** 11am-7pm Tue-Sat; 1-6pm Sun. **Map** p119 C2 ⑱

Organic Pleasures offers a range of non-toxic and hypo-allergenic items as well as bodycare products, lingerie and much more besides; the thinking lady's love boutique.

Valvona & Crolla

19 Elm Row, Leith Walk (556 6066/ www.valvonacrolla.com). Bus 7, 10, 12, 14, 16, 22, 25, 49. **Open** 8am-6pm Mon-Sat; 10.30am-5pm Sun. **Map** p119 C2 ⑲

Edinburgh's best-known destination for gourmet treats, this family-run Italian deli has been operating since the 1930s. Shelves are stacked from floor to ceiling with a delicious range of products, and there's a small café in converted stables at the back serving moreish breakfasts and delightful lunches.

Villeneuve Wines

49a Broughton Street (558 8441/ www.villeneuvewines.com).

Street life Broughton Street

Joey D

For a short thoroughfare, Broughton Street sure packs a punch. With the Blue Moon Café (p121) on the corner of Barony Street and the Edinburgh LGBT Centre it has long been a focus for the city's gay scene. What's more you can't really go far without bumping into a bar, restaurant or interesting shop.

The Street (p126) on the corner of Picardy Place kicks off the fun, a gay-friendly pre-club bar with a basic menu. A few doors down, Baroque (p120) has a similar pre-party feel, as does the Outhouse (p121) round the corner in Broughton Street Lane. The Basement (p120) back on the main drag was a true original, an influential style bar dating to 1994, and is still popular for its food. Or for other eating options try the Olive Tree Bistro at No.91 (557 8589,www.theolivebranch scotland.co.uk) or Bella Mbriana (p120) just round the corner in East London Street.

If you need to stock up on food, Crombie's does wonderful gourmet sausages (p122) while Real Foods at 57 (5571911, www.realfoods.co.uk) is the local port of call for all things wholesome. The Piccante fish and chip shop (478 7884) at No.19 balances the food karma with a banner boasting 'deep fried Mars sold here'; local fish and chip fans tend to patronise the Rapido (556 2041) at No.79.

For pubs try the Barony (p118), while engaging fashion shops include Joey D (p122) and Concrete Wardrobe at No.50a (558 7130). Also check out Seesaw at No.109 for Fairtrade baby clothes (556 9672, www.seesawtoys.co.uk). At the other end of the reproduction spectrum, Organic Pleasures (p122) is a store by women for women selling lingerie, sex toys and more.

New businesses abound: one of the latest additions cooking up a storm is Pani Solinska at No.73, a Polish-inspired restaurant and takeaway (07835 719411, www.panisolinska.com). For ventures old and new, Broughton Street is certainly worth a couple of hours of your time.

Bus 8, 13, 17. **Open** noon-10pm
Mon; 1-10pm Tue, Wed; 10am-10pm
Thur; 9am-10pm Fri, Sat; 1-8pm Sun.
Map p119 C2 ㉑
A well-stocked and reasonably priced
fine wine and whisky shop.

Nightlife

The area between Broughton
Street and Leith Walk is known as
the Pink triangle and it's where
you'll find the city's gay scene.
While it's true that many here
could go a little easier on the hair
gel and distressed denim, there's
a friendly, fun vibe throughout,
and none more so than in August
during the festival when armies of
thesp queens screech into town.

CC Blooms

*23-24 Greenside Place (556 9331).
Playhouse buses.* **Open** 6pm-3am
Mon, Fri, Sat; 8pm-3am Tue-Thur,
Sun. **Admission** free. No credit cards.
Map p119 C2 ㉑

Ah, CC's, where great romances start
and end, often in the same evening.
The capital's only full-time gay venue
may be offensive to both eye and ear
(disastrous pop galore!), but its cheeky
charm attracts girls and boys alike.
The weekend queues to get downstairs provide the perfect opportunity
to make your move. After all, as soon
as you get down there, the pair of you
will both be itching to leave.

Claremont

*133-135 East Claremont Street (556
5662/www.claremontbar.co.uk). Bus
8, 13, 17, 23, 27.* **Open** 11am-
midnight Mon-Thur; 11am-1am Fri,
Sat; 12.30-11pm Sun. *Food served*
11.30am-2.30pm, 6-10pm Mon-Sat;
12.30-6pm Sun. **Map** p119 B1 ㉒

A homo mecca for those with a fetish:
various Saturdays throughout the
month are turned over to bears, kilt-
wearers, transvestites and glamorous
goth types. During the rest of the
week, the Claremont attracts a
friendly, cruisey, male-dominated

Embo p121

Arthur's Seat

Take a hike up Edinburgh's extinct volcano.

It's a point that's been made before but it's worth making again: no other city in Europe has an extinct volcano within its limits. Arthur's Seat stands 823 feet (251 metres) above sea level within the 650-acre Holyrood Park and is Edinburgh's playground.

Climbing the hill is a regular and rewarding challenge for many Edinburghers, or if you're not local it's a great way to get your bearings. Some cross-country runners ascend the hill every day; conversely, drink-fortified teens have been known to climb the peak after a night on the tiles.

And every May Day hundreds of faithful souls take a pre-dawn jaunt to partake in the pagan tradition of washing their faces in the dew at sunrise, said to bring clear skin and great beauty. The origins of the ritual are unknown; as, for that matter, is the identity of the person who left 17 miniature coffins, each containing a tiny wooden doll, in a hillside cave during the 19th century. The eight surviving coffins can be seen in the National Museum of Scotland but the mystery of their origin has never been solved. Several paths lead to the top and all can be taken at an easy pace. A word of warning, though: it might be in the centre of the city, but the park has seen its share of tragic accidents. If you plan to climb Arthur's Seat, wear strong shoes that will not slip on the grass or slopes, and take an extra layer of clothing – even on mild days there's no shelter from the often fearsome wind.

It's worth ending your trek back from the top with a visit to the Sheep Heid Inn (43-45 The Causeway, 656 6951) – as close as you'll get to a historic country pub in Edinburgh. Legend has it that the inn got its name from a motif on a snuff box presented by King James VI before he legged it to London to become James I of Britain. Never mind all that though – for many, the enticing bar menu and selection of guest beers are ample reward for the near-traumatic exertion of the hike. Unsurprisingly it's popular at the weekends – booking is advised if you want to join the muddy hordes for Sunday roast.

crowd sporting denim or leather. On the food front, the inexpensive bar menu is great and chef Jean-Philippe makes exceedingly good cakes.

EGO

14 Picardy Place, New Town (478 7434/www.clubego.co.uk). Playhouse buses. **Open** 11pm-3am nights vary. **Admission** £5-£15. No credit cards. **Map** p119 C2 ㉓

The ground floor of this elegantly appointed ex-casino and dancehall plays host to a number of fine nights. Among them Tuesday's Vibe is the city's biggest weekly gay night, and on the first Saturday of each month Fever plays progressive house to a mixed, friendly crowd. Keep an eye out for one-offs and parties like electro-house monthly Touch.

Jongleurs

Unit 6/7, Omni Centre, Greenside Place (08707 870707/www.jongleurs. com). Bus 8, 12, 16, 17, 25. **Shows** 8.30pm Fri, Sat. **Tickets** £10-£12. **Map** p119 C2 ㉔

On the plus side, you're likely to find some of the biggest names in the business taking the mic at Jongleurs. But this is also, unashamedly, comedy for the masses; not for nothing has the club's empire spread from humble London beginnings to 17 branches around the UK. Ticket price includes entrance to the post-gig club.

Regent

2 Montrose Terrace (661 8198). Bus 1, 4, 5, 15, 15A, 19, 26, 34, 35, 44, 44A, 45. **Open** 11am-1am Mon-Sat; 12.30pm-1am Sun. **Map** p119 E2 ㉕

Proud of its credentials as a real ale pub, this gay boozer eschews the jukebox in favour of encouraging conversation. The atmosphere is very much in keeping with the pub's traditional decor, and staff are pleasantly friendly. Regent is an excellent alternative to the city's more frenetic bars and clubs, if a little bit out of the way. There's also free Wi-Fi access for those toting a laptop.

Street

2 Picardy Place (556 4272). Playhouse buses. **Open** 4pm-1am Mon; noon-1am Tue-Sat; 12.30pm-1am Sun. **Map** p119 C2 ㉖

This is a jewel in the crown of the local gay and lesbian communities; some diehard regulars even rate it as one of the best bars in the city. Sit upstairs on chrome and cream leather bar stools and gaze at the fish tank, or descend to the intimate bar below. Run by Trendy Wendy, the scene's most famous face, and Louise, ex-manager of Planet Out, it's not to be missed.

Studio 24

24-26 Calton Road (558 3758/ www.studio24edinburgh.co.uk). Nicolson Street–North Bridge buses. **Admission** £5-£10. No credit cards. **Map** p119 D3 ㉗

Studio 24 boasts a long and storied musical history (Mudhoney, Fugazi and Teenage Fanclub all made their Edinburgh debuts here). These days the flourishing underground goth and metal scene predominates, especially at Saturday's Mission night and its under-18s sister club Junior Mission. Despite continued resilience, Studio 24 has been threatened with closure as developers continue to 'gentrify' the Old Town. Check online before setting out.

Arts & leisure

Edinburgh Playhouse

18-22 Greenside Place (524 3333/ www.edinburghplayhouse.org.uk). Playhouse buses. **Tickets** £10-£36.50. **Map** p119 C2 ㉘

The 3,000-seat Playhouse is the regular home for touring West End musicals. In winter 2008 it will host *Mary Poppins*, among others. The Edinburgh International Festival regularly uses the auditorium, the largest of its kind in the UK, for bigger dance and opera productions, while grown-up rock stars and big-name comedians treat the Playhouse as a stopping-off point; Neil Young and the Sugababes have both visited recently.

Leith

The history of Leith, a couple of miles north-east of the Old Town, is almost as chequered as that of its neighbour. At various points a medieval fishing settlement, a crucial port, a shipbuilding centre and a crime-riddled suburb, it's now on the up, and in quite spectacular fashion. It's the home of Hibernian FC, but despite its proximity to central Edinburgh it's very much a separate place, with an atmosphere and a history all of its own.

In the 1980s, encouraged by cheap rents, a few intrepid restaurateurs and creative white-collar entrepreneurs decided to take the plunge and set up in Leith, leavening the social mix in the area while also encouraging others to follow. The area gradually began to improve, but things really started to take off when, in 1992, the docks were privatised, and new owners Forth Ports looked at alternative uses for the empty land. The huge Scottish Executive building was completed at Victoria Quay in 1995, followed in short order by the 1998 arrival of the Royal Yacht Britannia and the opening of the Ocean Terminal shopping mall in 2001.

However, the most dramatic changes in Leith have been residential. Numerous new apartment blocks have sprung up over the last decade, some affordable and some decidedly plush. And the docks are a key component in the grandiose plans for Edinburgh Forthside (www. edinburghforthside.co.uk), a long-term development that incorporates housing, schools, retail and leisure into what will eventually become virtually a new city by the sea.

Sights & museums

Royal Yacht Britannia

Ocean Terminal (555 5566/www.royalyachtbritannia.co.uk). Bus 1, 11, 22, 34, 35. **Open** *Apr-Jun, Sept, Oct* 10am-6pm daily (last admission 4.30pm). *July, Aug* 9.30am-6pm daily (last admission 4.30pm). *Nov-Mar* 10am-5pm daily (last admission 3.30pm). **Admission** £9.75; free-£7.75 reductions. **Map** p129 C1 ❶

Launched in 1953, the year of Queen Elizabeth II's coronation, the Royal Yacht Britannia was used by the Royal Family for state visits, holidays and diplomatic functions for more than four decades. It was decommissioned at the end of 1997 and now resides permanently in Leith, where it has consistently drawn big crowds; in autumn 2005 the old girl clocked up her two millionth visitor since opening to the public in late 1998.

Although the ship's exterior has an art deco beauty, stepping on board – enter from the second floor of Ocean Terminal, via the Britannia Experience – is like regressing into a 1950s nightmare of suburban taste. The chintzy drawing room is perhaps the worst offender in this regard. However, visitors do get to see the state dining room, which has entertained everyone from Rajiv Gandhi to Reagan, and the engine room, favoured more by grease monkeys. The price of admission includes an audio guide that's packed with anecdotes and points of reference.

Eating & drinking

Bar Diesel

19 Shore Place (476 6776/www.bardiesel.co.uk). Bus 1, 10, 16, 22, 35, 36. **Open** 11am-11pm Tue-Sat; noon-11pm Sun. **££**. **Grill**. **Map** p129 D2 ❷

This 18th-century warehouse, one street back from the Water of Leith, has hosted some pretty upmarket restaurants in its time, and the interior is still fairly swish. Bar Diesel took over the premises in 2007, offering an international menu: baked goat's cheese for a starter, then a buffalo burger or a steak, say, as a main. Vegetarians need not be deterred, though: some lovely pasta and crêpes are also available. It's not going to win a Michelin star anytime soon, but with reasonable prices and friendly service you could do a lot worse for a laid-back lunch.

Bar Sirius

7-10 Dock Place (553 5583). Bus 1, 10, 16, 22, 35, 36. **Open** noon-11.30pm Mon-Thur; noon-1am Fri-Sun. *Food served* noon-8pm daily. **£**. **Café-bar**. **Map** p129 D2 ❸

When Sirius arrived in Leith a decade ago, its like had never been seen before. But the original ostentation of its design was calmed down a little, and in spring 2006 a refurb freshened the whole place up once more. It's still very popular, both as a venue for a good night out and for café-bar eats.

Britannia Spice

150 Commercial Street (555 2255/www.britanniaspice.co.uk). Bus 1, 10, 16, 22, 35, 36. **Open** noon-2pm, 5-11.45pm Mon-Sat; 5-11.45pm Sun. **£**. **Asian**. **Map** p129 C2 ❹

This nautical-themed venue tries to cover the whole subcontinent rather than just India, with some Thai dishes thrown in for good measure. The menu includes all the usual suspects, but plenty more besides; you can have Himalayan trout or chicken jalfrezi, lamb biriani or Bangladeshi baked fish. A popular, populist and award-winning feature of the new Leith.

Café Truva

77 The Shore (554 5502). Bus 1, 10, 16, 22, 35, 36. **Open** 9am-6.30pm daily. **£**. **Turkish**. **Map** p129 D2 ❺

This wee Turkish delight of a café, located down by the Water of Leith, serves the kind of light meals and sweets that may remind you of past holiday excursions to that end of the Mediterranean: not only moussaka and meze, but also breakfasts, filo pastry savouries and baklava. Try to nab one of the outside seats on a sunny day.

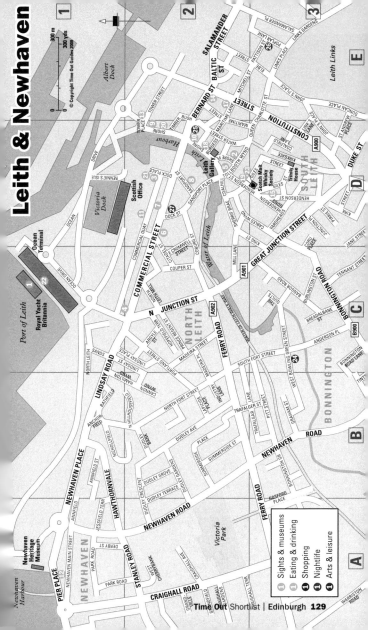

Leith & Newhaven

300 m
300 yds
© Copyright Time Out Guides 2009

Albert Dock

SALAMANDER STREET

BERNARD ST
BALTIC ST

CONSTITUTION STREET

Leith Links

Port of Leith

Ocean Terminal

Royal Yacht Britannia

Victoria Dock

Rennie's Isle

Scottish Office

Leith Gallery

Scotch Malt Whisky Society

Trinity House

SOUTH LEITH

DUKE ST

GREAT JUNCTION STREET

JUNCTION ST

COMMERCIAL STREET

NORTH LEITH

LINDSAY ROAD

FERRY ROAD

BONNINGTON ROAD

BONNINGTON

HAWTHORNVALE

NEWHAVEN PLACE

NEWHAVEN ROAD

NEWHAVEN

Newhaven Heritage Museum

Newhaven Harbour

PIER PLACE

STANLEY ROAD

CRAIGHALL ROAD

Victoria Park

| Sights & museums |
| Eating & drinking |
| Shopping |
| Nightlife |
| Arts & leisure |

Cairn Café at Tiso Edinburgh Outdoor Experience

41 Commercial Street (555 2211/ www.thecairncafe.co.uk). Bus 1, 10, 16, 22, 35, 36. **Open** 9am-5pm Mon-Wed, Fri, Sat; 9am-6pm Thur; 11am-3pm Sun. **£**. **Café**. **Map** p129 D2 ⑥

Tiso is Scotland's premier outdoors activity store; come for the gear that could get you up Ben Nevis or even more challenging mountains. This handy addition at the back serves up breakfast rolls, some serious panini, quiches, soups and salads, plus tasty pies and baked potatoes with a range of fillings. There's nothing very complicated or surprising; this is just a dependable café serving decent food in bright, breezy surroundings.

Daniel's

88 Commercial Street (553 5933/ www.daniels-bistro.co.uk). Bus 1, 10, 16, 22, 35, 36. **Open** 10am-10pm daily. **£**. **French**. **Map** p129 D2 ⑦

A long stretch of Leith's Commercial Street is occupied by refurbished warehousing. Plenty of bars and restaurants have been established here since the mid 1990s, and the casualty list is frightening. The survivor par excellence is Daniel Vencker, whose Alsatian-influenced modern French bistro still packs 'em in after all these years with delicious dishes such as pork knuckle on the bone.

Domenico's

30 Sandport Street (467 7266). Bus 1, 10, 16, 22, 35, 36. **Open** noon-10pm daily. **£**. **Italian**. **Map** p129 D2 ⑧

The food at this tiny, informal Italian combines heartiness with joie de vivre, and it makes up in personality what it lacks in finesse. Once you've struggled through the generous servings of antipasti (an assortment of charcuterie, cheeses and roast vegetables), the impending plate of spaghetti alla vongole might just finish you off. Book ahead and bring an appetite.

Loch Fyne Oyster Bar p132

Fishers

1 The Shore (554 5666/www.fishers bistros.co.uk). Bus 1, 10, 16, 22, 35, 36. **Open** noon-10.30pm daily. **££**. **Seafood**. **Map** p129 D2 ⑨
The nautical theme in Fishers' decor and fittings is pretty much justified by the fact that the docks are on the doorstep. Eat in the bar or the small adjacent raised area, where a starter such as crab stuffed with mozzarella and artichoke is almost a meal in itself. This has been one of the city's leading seafood restaurants since 1991, and you'll leave replete and happy.

King's Wark

36 The Shore (554 9260). Bus 1, 10, 16, 22, 35, 36. **Open** noon-11pm Mon-Thur; noon-midnight Fri, Sat; 11am-11pm Sun. *Food served* noon-3pm, 6-10pm Mon-Sat; 11am-3pm, 6-10pm Sun. **£**. **Pub**. **Map** p129 D2 ⑩
Built on the site of a 15th-century building, the current King's Wark was part of an early 17th-century royal complex used by King James VI of Scotland (who became King James I of England). The main room is simply a well-worn, welcoming pub, but there's a smaller space to one side for slightly more formal dining. The beer-battered fish and chips is always a winner, and Sunday brunch is terrific.

The Kitchin

NEW *78 Commercial Quay (555 1755/ www.thekitchin.com). Bus 1, 10, 16, 22, 35, 36.* **Open** 12.30-3.30pm, 6.45pm-midnight Tue-Sat. *Food served* 12.30-1.45pm, 6.45-9.15pm Tue-Sat. **£££**. **Scottish/French**. **Map** p129 D2 ⑪
A simple story: a bloke (Tom Kitchin) with an illustrious chef CV decided to have a go with his own place; his wife (Michaela Kitchin) also had bags of experience front of house. They opened in summer 2006 and by early 2007 had a Michelin star, catapulting them into the city's list of 'best eats'. A deceptively simple menu is allied with seriously good cooking and service.

Loch Fyne Oyster Bar

*25 Pier Place (559 3900/www.
lochfyne.com). Bus 11, 7, 16, 10.*
Open 9am–10pm Mon-Fri; 9am-
10.30pm Sat; 9am-10pm Sun. **££.**
Seafood. **Map** p129 A1 ⑫

For a business that started out on
the shores of a sea loch in Argyll, then
opened up dozens of restaurants in
England from 1998 onwards, Loch
Fyne took a long time to 'come home'
to Scotland. But in 2007 it launched a
light and spacious Edinburgh outlet
at an old fishworks on Newhaven
Harbour. The menu will be familiar to
anyone who has eaten in a Loch Fyne
before, but with good, simple seafood
on offer who's complaining?

Malmaison Bar

*1 Tower Place (468 5000/www.
malmaison.com). Bus 1, 10, 16,
22, 35, 36. Food served 10am-8pm daily.*
££. Bar. **Map** p129 E2 ⑬

The name is now well known thanks
to a string of boutique hotels across the
UK, but this was the very first of their
number (p182). The ground floor has a
fine contemporary bar space, with outdoor seating on the terrace that overlooks the water. The food is good, but
the Malmaison Brasserie next door has
a more extensive menu, serving up
dishes such as chargrilled burgers,
monkfish, great salads and a fabulous
Sunday brunch.

Noble's

*44a Constitution Street (555 1920).
Bus 1, 10, 16, 22, 35, 36.* **Open**
11am-midnight Mon-Wed, Sun;
11am-1am Thur-Sat. *Food served
noon-3pm Mon-Fri.* **£. Pub**.
Map p129 E2 ⑭

This old Victorian bar has gone
through many changes in its long life-
time, the latest being a serious refurbishment in 2006 that brought an
added sense of gravitas to the already

Malmaison Bar

Anti-style bars

More atmosphere, less attitude in Leith.

Pearce's

The history of style bars in Edinburgh is short and bipolar. Prior to the 1980s, there were none. Then came Negociants (p75) and the City Café (p69) with the wacky idea of serving food and drink in a café-bar crossover.

Into the 1990s and this started to seem like a very good plan. In 1994, the Basement (p120) was probably the first place to sport a self-conscious look of bold colours and chunky metal flourishes, then everyone got in on the act. You can still see the influence at Baroque (p120) or Sirius (p128).

The next generation was epitomised by clean lines, dark wood and dimmed lights at the likes of Opal Lounge (p101) and Rick's (p103), but the following wave soon jollied things up again by going lush. And for large ventures with lots of resources, they simply did lush-to-the-max – just check out Tigerlily (p178), Le Monde (p176), EH2 Tempus (p96) and the Ivory Lounge (126-128 George Street, 0131 220 6180, www.the1440.co.uk).

But in among this ostentation an alternative train of bar-room thought was gathering pace, an anti-style phenomenon centred around Leith.

In 2003, Boda opened on Leith Walk (229 Leith Walk, 553 5900). Its Swedish owners took over a fairly dull old bar, kept the layout, applied paint and depended on an interesting community attitude to carry them through. This was so successful that over the next four years they opened Sofi's in Henderson Street, the Victoria on Leith Walk, and Pearce's on Elm Row (for all, see www.bodabar. com). These establishments have attractions unheard of in the pleasure palaces of George Street: Sofi's has a jogging group, Pearce's has a children's play area, and all do moose sausages.

As for other pubs with a fresh outlook, the Regent (p125) is gay, does bargain food, free Wi-Fi and cask ale, while the Roseleaf (23-24 Sandport Place, 0131 476 5268, www.roseleaf.co.uk) is under new ownership with pub grub, an amenable atmosphere and not a gilded column in sight.

ornate interior (which boasts stained glass and a maritime frieze). There's now plush leather seating, and a more upmarket style in both the food served and the general tenor.

Plumed Horse

NEW *50-54 Henderson Street (554 5556/www.plumedhorse.co.uk). Bus 1, 10, 16, 22, 35, 36.* **Open** noon-1.30pm, 7-9pm Tue-Sat. **£££. Modern European**. Map p129 D3 ⑮
Tony Borthwick ran a Michelin-starred restaurant in Dumfriesshire but opted to move to Edinburgh at the end of 2006. His new venture confounded expectation. Foodies and critics looked for immediate excellence; he provided something small, low-key and well crafted, but it took a while to find its feet. There is no big front-of-house crew or kitchen brigade here, but Tony and company still do a grand job. Odd location, likeable venue.

Pond

2-4 Bath Road (467 3825). Bus 1, 10, 16, 22, 35, 36. **Open** 3pm-1am Mon-Fri; 1pm-1am Sat, Sun. **£. Pub.** Map p129 E2 ⑯
The encroachment of new apartment blocks has now put paid to the Pond's former reputation as 'the pub at the end of the universe', but it's still in a fairly unlovely street between Leith Links and the docks (albeit less than half a mile away from the Shore and the heart of Leith). It has the look of a hand-knitted university common room, but with a decent pint and some bombay mix in your hand, and a seat on one of the sofas, it can seem like a home from home.

Port O' Leith

58 Constitution Street (554 3568). Bus 1, 10, 16, 22, 35, 36. **Open** 9am-1am Mon-Sat; 12.30pm-1am Sun. No credit cards. **£. Pub.** Map p129 E2 ⑰
Both this pub and its proprietor, Mary Moriarty, are legends on the Edinburgh pub scene. It's a small and neatly kept pub, patronised by everyone from merchant mariners to locals and students. You could sit for hours

looking at the details: ships' flags, lifebelts, snuff for sale and so on. With bucketloads of character, it captures the true essence of Leith.

Restaurant Martin Wishart

54 The Shore (553 3557/www. martinwishart.co.uk). Bus 1, 10, 16, 22, 35, 36. **Open** noon-2pm, 6.45-9.30pm Tue-Sat. **Set meal** £50 3 courses. **££££. Scottish/ French**. Map p129 D2 ⑱
Located in the historical heart of Leith, Wishart's establishment has retained a Michelin star since 2001, and the food is sublime: subtle frothy pumpkin purée with vegetable shavings, served in a small glass vase as an amuse-bouche; intense jerusalem artichoke soup as a starter, with a dainty bouill-abaisse to follow. Then, for dessert, achingly good almond and pear tart with Armagnac ice-cream. The sommelier is brilliant, the front of house staff are approachable and efficient, and the kitchen crew are the best in the city. Marks out of ten? Eleven.

Scotch Malt Whisky Society Members' Room

The Vaults, 87 Giles Street (554 3451/ www.smws.com). Bus 1, 10, 16, 22, 35, 36. **Open** 10am-5pm Mon; 10am-11pm Tue, Wed; 10am-midnight Thur-Sat; 11am-10pm Sun. *Food served* noon-5pm Mon; noon-9pm Tue-Sat; 12.30-3pm Sun. **££. Bar**. Map p129 D3 ⑲
The SMWS was set up in 1983 to buy individual casks of whisky from distilleries, bottle them and sell them to members. It remains largely unchanged: the atmosphere is still tranquil, the food is still good and the range of rare whiskies is the city's best. It's open to members only; membership starts at £75 a year.

Shore

3-4 The Shore (553 5080/www.the shore.biz). Bus 1, 10, 16, 22, 35, 36. **Open** 11am-midnight Mon-Sat; noon-11pm Sun. *Food served* noon-2.30pm, 6.30-10pm Mon-Fri; noon-3pm, 6.30-10pm Sat, Sun. **£. Gastropub**. Map p129 D2 ⑳

Scotch Malt Whisky Society
Members' Room

The Shore has a small, bustling bar and tables outside on the pavement – on finer days, you can even take your drink across the street to the quayside and sit watching the Water of Leith flow into the docks. It's essentially a gastropub; the bar menu is fabulous, and a small adjoining room operates as a restaurant, serving some excellent fresh fish and seafood dishes. There is often live music in the bar.

Skippers

1a Dock Place (554 1018/www.
skippers.co.uk). Bus 1, 10, 16, 22, 35,
36. **Open** 12.30-2pm, 7-10pm Mon-Fri,
Sun; 12.30-2pm, 6.30-10pm Sat. **££.**
Seafood. Map p129 D2 ㉑
Skippers has been around for over 25 years, and was a real pioneer in the pre-refurbished docklands. It has an excellent reputation for its bistro-style seafood cookery; dishes such as cullen skink or fish cakes are fixtures on the menu, but the catch of the day will influence the specials on offer.

Sky Bar

Ocean Terminal, Ocean Drive
(555 2646). Bus 1, 10, 16, 22, 35,
36. **Open** noon-midnight Mon-Thur,
Sun; noon-1am Fri, Sat. *Food served*
noon-10pm daily. **££**. **Bar**.
Map p129 C1 ㉒
On the first floor of Ocean Terminal mall, the Sky Bar has great views out over the Western Harbour and the Royal Yacht Britannia. Good for cocktails, it's best when you can go outside to the balcony and look out over the water. Shoppers seem wary of even the slightest breeze, so it's often fairly quiet out there. One of the more unusual places to drink in the city.

Vintners Rooms

Vaults, 87 Giles Street (554 6767/
www.thevintnersrooms.com). Bus 1,
10, 16, 22, 35, 36. **Open** noon-2pm,
7-10pm Tue-Sat. **£££. Modern**
European. Map p129 D3 ㉓
At the corner of a Leith backstreet you'll find this former wine warehouse with a history dating back to the late 16th century. Its first floor is home to

the Scotch Malt Whisky Society (p134), while the ground floor hosts the Vintners Rooms, a classy French-style fixture since 1985. Diners have the choice of tables in the homelier bar area or in a small adjacent room with elaborate plasterwork. The latter tends to be a little stark during the day, but is better at night.

Shopping

Edinburgh Architectural Salvage Yard

31 West Bowling Green Street (554
7077/www.easy-arch-salv.co.uk). Bus 7,
11, 14, 21. **Open** 9am-5pm Mon-Fri;
noon-5pm Sat. Map p129 C3 ㉔
The Edinburgh Architectural Salvage Yard has been supplying Edinburgh's citizens with period pieces for more than 20 years. Georgian, Victorian, art nouveau and art deco styles are all represented here, in the form of everything from door handles to bath tubs and even fireplaces.

Flux

55 Bernard Street (554 4075/www.
get2flux.co.uk). Bus 12, 16, 22, 35, 36.
Open 11am-6pm Mon-Sat; noon-5pm
Sun. Map p129 D2 ㉕
Quirky, British-made crafts are a speciality here, with an ever-changing range of gifts, jewellery and art.

Georgian Antiques

10 Pattison Street (554 7286/www.
georgianantiques.net). Bus 21. **Open**
8.30am-5.30pm Mon-Fri; 10am-2pm
Sat. Map p129 E3 ㉖
Spread over 50,000sq ft of floor space in a converted whisky bond, this is the largest collection of quality antiques and collectibles in town.

Kinloch Anderson

4 Dock Street (555 1390/www.
kinlochanderson.com). Bus 1, 11, 16,
22, 34, 35, 36. **Open** 9am-5.30pm
Mon-Sat. Map p129 D2 ㉗
Kinloch Anderson may be the city's most renowned kiltmaker, although it's far from the cheapest. The shop also includes a small tartan museum.

Marchmont

South Edinburgh

Starting at the new Quartermile residential development on Lauriston Place, South Edinburgh stretches off like a slice of cake, taking in everything from the green spaces of the Meadows and Blackford Hill to tenemented suburbs such as Marchmont and Bruntsfield. There are students galore here, thanks to the campus outposts of Edinburgh and Napier universities and the presence of Edinburgh College of Art; their influence ensures that the area boasts plenty of takeaways, pubs and second-hand bookshops. But what really defines much of South Edinburgh is the middle-class reserve apparent in any leafy backstreet in the Grange or Morningside, where the grandest houses sit discreetly behind the highest walls.

Sights & museums

Edinburgh College of Art

*Lauriston Place (221 6000/www.
eca.ac.uk). Bus 23, 27, 35, 45.*
Open hours vary. **Admission**
free. **Map** p138 B3 ➊
The Edinburgh College of Art operates a year-round programme of exhibitions. For many, the highlight is the annual degree show in June, when the public can eye up (and, hope the artists, purchase) works of future art stars. However, the college puts on regular shows by artists from all over the world; check online for details.

Surgeons Hall Museums

*Royal College of Surgeons of Edinburgh,
18 Nicolson Street (527 1649/www.
rcsed.ac.uk). Nicolson Street–North
Bridge buses.* **Open** *Aug* 10am-4pm
Mon-Fri; noon-4pm Sat, Sun. *Sept-July*
noon-4pm Mon-Fri. **Admission** £5,
£3 reductions. **Map** p139 D2 ➋

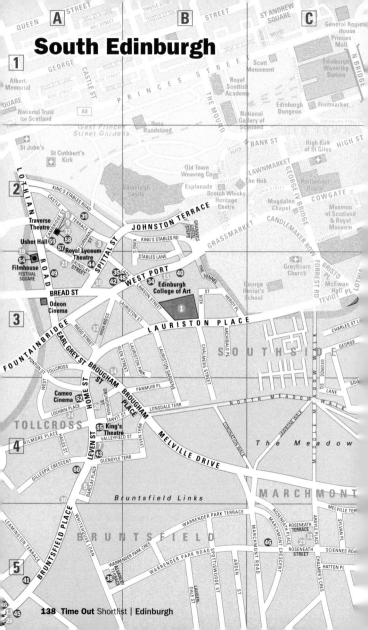

South Edinburgh

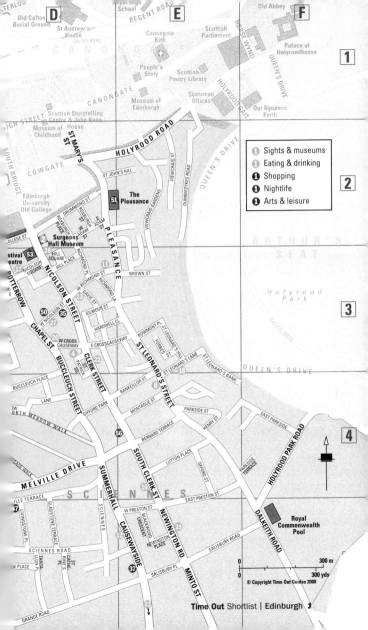

Surgeons Hall Museums p137

Here you can trace the history of medicine in the city from 1505, through to the development of modern surgical techniques. One of the real curios is a pocketbook covered with the tanned skin of William Burke who, with accomplice William Hare, killed at least 16 Edinburgh citizens in 1827-8 and sold their bodies for dissection. The main attraction is the celebrated pathology collection, the largest in the UK (see box p141). The museum helpfully suggests that some people might find the pickled remains 'unsettling', and under-15s must be accompanied by an adult.

Eating & drinking

Abstract

NEW 33-35 Castle Terrace (229 1222/ www.abstractrestaurant.com). Bus 1, 2, 10, 11, 15, 15A, 16, 17, 23, 24, 27, 34, 35, 45. **Open** noon-2pm, 6-10pm Tue-Sat. **££. International**. Map p138 A2 ❸

Abstract is easily Edinburgh's most exciting and dramatic opening of 2007. First chef Loic Lefebvre endured a Gordon Ramsay televisual ordeal at the original Abstract in Inverness, but ignored *F Word*'s advice and stuck with his own menu. Then Lefebvre and the proprietors opened in Edinburgh, for which locals are still grateful. Then he quit and went home to France; fortunately, quality didn't suffer. Modern decor and contemporary food with élan, the two-course lunch menu is a total bargain.

Ann Purna

45 St Patrick Square (662 1807). Nicolson Street–North Bridge buses. **Open** noon-2pm, 5.30-11pm Mon-Fri; 5.30-11pm Sat; 5-10pm Sun. **£. Indian**. Map p139 D3 ❹

The family-run Ann Purna has a wholly vegetarian, South Indian-style menu and a relaxed and homely feel. It's very close to the George Square and Buccleuch Place buildings of Edinburgh University, and is extremely popular with both staff and students: the bargain business lunch is extraordinarily good value.

Apartment

7-13 Barclay Place (228 6456). Bus 11, 15, 15A, 16, 17, 23, 45. **Open** 5-11pm Mon-Fri; noon-11pm Sat, Sun. **£. Fusion**. Map p138 A4 ❺

Apartment's success obviously depends on the food, but its status as an informal designer eaterie for middle-class Edinburgh hipsters also owes much to its location: Bruntsfield, Marchmont and Merchiston are right on the doorstep. Expect to find key dishes such as the chunky, healthy lines or CHLs (chargrilled chunks on a skewer); the rest of the menu has a modern, fusion feel. A spring 2006 makeover showed that the management isn't resting on its laurels. See p75 for the Outsider, its Old Town sister.

Atrium

10 Cambridge Street (228 8882/ www.atriumrestaurant.co.uk). Bus 1, 2, 10, 11, 15, 15A, 16, 17, 23, 24, 27, 34, 35, 45. **Open** noon-2pm, 6-10pm Mon-Fri; 6-10pm Sat. **£££. International**. Map p138 A2 ❻

Waking the dead

When standing in the renowned pathology collection at **Surgeons Hall Museums** (p137) you can use the line 'I see dead people' in its literal sense rather than as a filmic reference. What you'll see are parts of dead people in jars, quite often diseased or damaged, preserved for posterity and the education of medical students. Despite there being a trauma warning on the website very few people actually seem to be unsettled by the bits and bobs – or bits of Bob – which may be due in part to the graceful surroundings.

The building dates back to the 1830s and was designed by William Playfair who did many other neo-classical piles around the city, including the Royal Scottish Academy (p91). The pathology collection is housed in a particularly elegant space – the actual Surgeons Hall – where whispers, soft footsteps and wide eyes seem the order of the day rather than shrieks.

There is far more to see here than human giblets, however. A working college, it hosts conferences, meetings and exams, and since late 2006 has even boasted its own smart hotel next door, Ten Hill Place (0131 662 2080, www.tenhillplace.com), though you don't need to be a surgeon to stay.

There have been temporary exhibitions in recent years on a variety of topics from Scottish women's hospitals to Joseph Bell, the president of the college in the late Victorian era who was Conan Doyle's inspiration for Sherlock Holmes. Meanwhile the permanent displays tell the tale of surgery in Edinburgh over the last 500 years and more.

There is an entire section on sport and wellbeing, as well as a collection of dental artefacts bequeathed by Glaswegian dentist John Menzies Campbell and housed in its own purpose-built wing. Looking at how dentistry was done back in the day will either exacerbate your phobia, or make you extremely grateful for recent developments in anaesthesia and technology the next time you book a check-up.

Atrium p140

Sharing a building with the Traverse Theatre, Andrew Radford's flagship restaurant changed the rules of Edinburgh's fine dining scene when it opened back in 1993. These days its design still looks contemporary, with low-key lighting, dark wood and clean lines all adding to the sense of occasion and otherness. Destination dining that's stood the test of time, Atrium is still well worth a visit.

Bennet's

8 Leven Street (229 5143). Bus 11, 15, 15A, 16, 17, 23, 45. **Open** 11am-1am daily. *Food served* noon-2pm, 5-8.30pm Mon-Sat; noon-5pm Sun. **Pub**. Map p138 A4 ⑦

Bennet's is a marvel of Victorian design. A long wooden bar occupies one side of the room (with alcoves along the top of the gantry accommodating a huge selection of single malts), while the opposite wall has fitted red leather seats and even more wooden fittings. Come here to enjoy the cask ales, hearty pub grub and stained glass, but don't bother with the overspill room out back.

Blonde

75 St Leonard's Street (668 2917/ www.blonderestaurant.com). Nicolson Street–North Bridge buses. **Open** 6-10pm Mon; noon-2.30pm, 6-10pm Tue-Sun. ££. **Modern Scottish/ European**. Map p139 E4 ⑧

This modern neighbourhood restaurant, named after its blond-wood interior, has been a real asset to the area since opening in 2000. The menu takes an eclectic approach: dishes such as mussels in coconut milk, lime and basil to start, then beer-braised venison as a main course. The wine list is brief and affordable, and the waitresses are as sharp as tacks.

Blue Bar-Café

10 Cambridge Street (221 1222/www. bluescotland.co.uk). Bus 1, 2, 10, 11, 15, 15A, 16, 17, 23, 24, 27, 34, 35, 45. **Open** noon-2.30pm, 5.30-10.30pm Mon-Thur; noon-2.30pm, 5.30-11pm Fri, Sat. ££. **Café-bar**. Map p138 A2 ⑨

Upstairs from the Atrium restaurant (p140) and also run by Andrew Radford, Blue was a real smash when it opened in 1997. It's moved in and out of vogue over the years, but is still

The Japanese team in this small, uncluttered establishment produces a range of tasty dishes, many of which won't spook the Scottish palate too much. There's assorted tempura, user-friendly makizushi (rice rolled in seaweed), and bowls of noodles, for example, so raw fish isn't compulsory. But if you want a more adventurous culinary experience, you'll find tuna or salmon sashimi and squid nigirizushi on the menu too.

Borough

72-80 Causewayside (668 2255/ www.boroughhotel.com). Bus 41, 42. **Open** *Bar* 11am-1am Mon-Sat; 12.30pm-midnight Sun. *Restaurant* noon-5pm, 6-9.30pm Mon-Fri; noon-5pm, 6-10.30pm Sat, Sun.
Bar/Modern European.
Map p139 E5 ⑫
The most obvious feature of this boutique hotel (p180) is the spacious lounge with newspapers to browse and leather sofas on which to slump. You can drink here, but you'd also do well to eat. There's generally a good standard of Modern European cooking (also available in the adjacent restaurant space that's dotted with discreet booths), and the brunch menu is probably the best in the city. It's calming when quiet, but DJs play on busier nights. The kitchen closes around 10pm.

Canny Man's

237 Morningside Road (447 1484). Bus 11, 15, 15A, 16, 17, 41. **Open** noon-11pm Mon-Wed; noon-midnight Thur, Sat; noon-1am Fri; 12.30-11pm Sun. *Food served* noon-3pm, 6.30-9pm Mon-Sat; 12.30-3pm Sun. **Pub**. No credit cards. Map p138 A5 ⑬
It's been around since 1871. It looks as if it was decorated by a mad maiden aunt from the Victorian era. It has a good wine list, an excellent bar menu (the open sandwiches are legendary), and a truly exceptional selection of single malt whiskies. The catch? It's a fair schlep into Morningside and the sign by the door says 'Dress smart but casual', and it means it. Also known as the Volunteer Arms.

hugely popular. On a good day, Blue produces the best café-bar food in town, and can whip you up a pretty good salmon and smoked haddock fishcake with salsa rossa. There's a large dining space at the front and a bar area to the rear of the premises. It's open all day.

Blue Blazer

2 Spittal Street (229 5030). Bus 1, 2, 10, 11, 15, 15A, 16, 17, 23, 24, 27, 34, 35, 45. **Open** 11am-1am Mon-Sat; 12.30pm-1am Sun. **Pub**.
Map p138 A3 ⑩
Sandwiched between the lads-night-out chaos of Lothian Road and the lap-dancing bars at the top of the West Port, the Blue Blazer is no more or less than a cosy place to hide away and chat with your friends over a decent pint, especially in the wee room through the back.

Bonsai

46 W Richmond Street (668 3847/ www.bonsaibarbistro.co.uk). Nicolson Street–North Bridge buses. **Open** noon-late daily. **£. Japanese**.
Map p139 D3 ⑭

Cloisters

*26 Brougham Street (221 9997).
Bus 11, 15, 15A, 16, 17, 23, 45.*
Open noon-midnight Mon-Thur,
Sun; noon-1am Fri, Sat. *Food served*
noon-2.30pm Mon; noon-8pm Tue-Sat;
12.30-6pm Sun. **Pub**. Map p138 A3 ⑭
The decor at Cloisters, housed in a former manse, is simple, but it's the rare
cask ale that's the selling point. It puts
on a good showing on the whisky front
as well, with around 80 varieties to
choose from.

Dragonfly

*52 West Port (228 4543/www.
dragonflycocktailbar.com). Bus 2,
35.* **Open** 4pm-1am daily. **Cocktail
bar**. Map p138 B3 ⑮
This address has hosted many a
venue over the years, but perhaps
plush cocktail bar Dragonfly will
stick. Some might see hints of a
Graham Norton stage set in the decor,
but there are absolutely no quibbles
with the quality of the drinks. A real
hit with the beautiful people, it's definitely not to be confused with the strip
joints nearby.

Dragon Way

*74-78 S Clerk Street (668 1328).
Nicolson Street–North Bridge buses.*
Open noon-2.30pm, 5-11pm Mon-
Sat; 4-11pm Sun. **£. Chinese**.
Map p139 E4 ⑯
Most diners are too gobsmacked by the
gilded birds and dragons on the walls,
the small waterfall and various other
decorative extravagances to notice the
menu, but once you add in the food,
you have a truly memorable restaurant. Dishes are generally Cantonese,
but with Peking and Sichuan influences. The kitchen also fits in specials,
which often depend on the seafood
catch of the day.

Elephants & Bagels

*37 Marshall Street, Nicolson
Square (668 4404/www.elephant-
house.co.uk). Nicolson Street–North
Bridge buses.* **Open** 8.30am-6pm
Mon-Fri; 9.30am-5pm Sat, Sun. **£**.
Café. Map p139 D3 ⑰
The baby sister of the Elephant House
(p70) doesn't sell many elephants, but
is big on the bagel side of things. It's
particularly popular with students
from the university, who take away
the sweet and savoury goodies for
impromptu picnics in nearby George
Square during the summer.

Engine Shed

*19 St Leonard's Lane (662 0040/
www.engineshed.org.uk). Nicolson
Street–North Bridge buses.* **Open**
10am-3.30pm Mon-Sat. **£. Vegetarian**.
No credit cards. Map p139 E3 ⑱
Based in a former train maintenance
depot, this vegetarian/vegan whole-
food café is a good pit-stop if you've
been hiking around Arthur's Seat.
Mains such as cashew nut pie and
spinach bake are wholesome and
hearty, and the bread is excellent, but
what really sets this venture apart is
its training role for adults with learn-
ing difficulties, who work on the other
side of the counter. Worth supporting.

Filmhouse Café Bar

*88 Lothian Road (229 5932/www.
filmhousecinema.com). Bus 1, 2, 10,
11, 15, 15A, 16, 17, 23, 24, 27, 34,
35, 45.* **Open** 10am-11.30pm Mon-
Thur, Sun; 10am-12.30am Fri, Sat.
Food served noon-10pm daily.
Bar. Map p138 A3 ⑲
The city's independent arthouse cinema (p152) has been around since
the 1980s, but a 2002 refurbishment
means the bar doesn't look dated.
With coffee, snacks, light meals and a
couple of good beers on tap, it's the
perfect place to meet friends before or
after a movie. If you're brave enough
to take on the city's cinema buffs,
there's a film quiz on the second
Sunday of every month.

Human Be-In

*2/8 West Crosscauseway (662 8860/
www.humanbe-in.co.uk). Nicolson
Street–North Bridge buses.* **Open**
10am-1am daily. *Food served* noon-
9pm daily. **Bar**. Map p139 D3 ⑳
The interior of this polished style bar
is all about the dark woods and clean

Blue Bar-Café p142

lines. There are cosy booths to the rear, as well as low, comfortable seats in front of the big windows that look out over the street, and there are outside tables in the summer. Food includes some fairly ambitious dishes (baked sea bream with clams, duck salad). However, many people come here just for a drink – especially on weekend evenings, when DJs play.

Jasmine

32 Grindlay Street (229 5757). Bus 1, 2, 10, 11, 15, 15A, 16, 17, 23, 24, 27, 34, 35, 45. **Open** noon-2pm, 5-11.30pm Mon-Thur; 1-2pm, 5pm-12.30am Fri; 1-11.30pm Sat, Sun. **£.** **International**. **Map** p138 A3 ㉑
Jasmine has been around for many years, but the premises have been spruced up and refurbished along the way, and currently feature lemon walls, dark wood flooring and ban-quette seating. Local workers are lured in with a bargain lunch menu; regulars rave about the almond chicken with orange sauce. The seafood specials here can also be great.

Kalpna

2-3 St Patrick Square (667 9890/ www.kalpnarestaurant.com). Nicolson Street–North Bridge buses. **Open** noon-2pm, 5.30-10.30pm Mon-Sat. **£.** **Indian**. No credit cards during lunchtime. **Map** p139 D3 ㉒
Restaurant trends have come and gone over the last few decades, but nothing much has changed at Kalpna. The sign above the door still reads 'You do not have to eat meat to be strong and wise', and the Gujarati vegetarian fare remains successful; try a thali if you're having trouble deciding. The interior is far from contemporary, but the food is a welcome departure from Indian cliché: freshly made, delicately spiced and often enjoyably inventive.

Kwok

44 Ratcliffe Terrace (668 1818). Bus 3, 3A, 7, 8, 29, 31, 37, 49. **Open** noon-2pm, 5-11.30pm Tue-Thur; 5pm-12.30am Fri, Sat; 5-11.30pm Sun. **£.** **Chinese**. **Map** p139 E5 ㉓
This great little Chinese eaterie gets less recognition than it should because of its location half a mile south of the Meadows, in lands where visitors generally fail to tread. Dark red decor and a backdrop of jazz and lounge music set the scene, and the brasserie-like atmosphere is quite unlike that of any other Chinese establishment in the city. The food is of an impressive qual-ity and freshness.

Made in France

5 Lochrin Place (221 1184). Bus 11, 15, 15A, 16, 17, 23, 45. **Open** 10am-4pm Mon-Sat. **Café. Map** p138 A4

This café arrived on the Tollcross scene at the end of 2004, but quickly established itself as a local favourite thanks to the Francophile enthusiasms of owners Craig and Amanda Nash. French cheeses, saucisson, nice terrines, authentic baguettes and tartiflettes are among the well-sourced temptations on offer. It's great for a croissant and coffee, or for a more substantial lunch.

Metropole

33 Newington Road (668 4999). Nicolson Street–North Bridge buses. **Open** 8.30am-10pm daily. **Café. Map** p139 E5

Deep in the heart of studentland, this café is lent an air of faded grandeur by its setting in a converted bank. You could pop in for a coffee and cake during the daytime or lunch on a baked potato or plate of lasagne, but it's also a good place to come for straightforward eats in the evening.

Montpeliers

159-161 Bruntsfield Place (229 3115/ www.montpeliersedinburgh.co.uk). Bus 11, 15, 15A, 16, 17, 23, 45. **Open** 9am-1am daily. *Food served* 9am-10pm daily. **££. International. Map** p138 A5

Although it has been around since 1992, the odd refurb has ensured that Montpeliers hasn't become dated or dowdy. The decor is currently clean cut, with sofas by the window and dark woods galore. The bar is to one side with the dining space partitioned off to the other; here, you can sample salads, steaks, burgers or comfort food (Irish stew, perhaps). The breakfast menu is also justly celebrated at what remains Bruntsfield's café-bar of choice.

Pear Tree House

36 West Nicolson Street (667 7533). Nicolson Street– North Bridge buses. **Open** 11am-midnight Mon-Thur; 11am-1am Fri, Sat; 12.30pm-midnight Sun. **Pub. Map** p139 D3

Literally over the road from Edinburgh University's George Square campus, the Pear Tree's cobbled beer garden has played host to generations of thirsty students in its time. Inside, the decor is classic trad Scots pub, but with a big screen for the football. Outside term time, it's fairly placid.

Suruchi

14a Nicolson Street (556 6583). Nicolson Street–North Bridge buses. **Open** noon-2pm, 5-11pm daily. **£. Indian. Map** p139 D3

Under the direction of Herman Rodrigues, Suruchi has consolidated its position as one of Edinburgh's best Indian restaurants. Here you'll find jazz gigs, food festivals, cultural displays and, alongside old favourites such as prawn masala, some innovative dishes that nod to the Scottish larder (salmon tikka, for instance, or the unlikely but decent haggis pakora). Vegetarians do well too, and even simple sundries such as coconut rice can be sublime.

Sweet Melinda's

11 Roseneath Street (229 7953/ www.sweetmelindas.co.uk). Bus 24, 41. **Open** 7-10pm Mon;

Dragon Way p144

noon-2pm, 7-10pm Tue-Sat. **££**.
Seafood/game. Map p138 C5 ㉙
The bright, compact Sweet Melinda's
is an oasis in the culinary desert of
Marchmont. It's not billed as a seafood
restaurant, but there are some good
fishy choices supplied by the acclaimed
fishmonger a few doors down the road:
scallops with chilli sauce, halibut and
crab risotto, Thai-style fish cakes. The
kind of neighbourhood restaurant
where diners walk in with limited
expectations and walk out with a smile.

Thai Lemongrass
*40-41 Bruntsfield Place (229 2225).
Bus 11, 15, 15A, 16, 17, 23, 45.* **Open**
noon-2.30pm, 5-11.30pm Mon-Thur;
noon-11.30pm Fri, Sat; 1-11.30pm
Sun. **££. Thai**. Map p138 A4 ㉚
When it first opened in 2002, this was
acclaimed as one of the best Thai eateries in the city. So why change a winning
formula? Staff in traditional costume
serve fresh dishes (from an extensive
menu) that command attention with
their punchy flavours, such as stir-fried
roast duck with basil leaves. There are
also some good seafood specials, and a
short vegetarian menu. Try the coconut
ice-cream to finish.

Thaisanuk
*21 Argyle Place (6597781/www.
thaisanuk.com). Bus 24, 41.* **Open**
6-11pm daily. **£. Thai**. No credit cards.
Map p138 C5 ㉛
Thaisanuk started life with a slightly
hand-knitted feel, as an appealing but
tiny room where the tom yum soup had
the zing of authenticity and the noodles
came in generous portions. After opening a takeaway in the west, the owners
extended the original in spring 2006.
Happily, it's still as laid-back and likeable as ever.

Traverse Theatre Bar
*10 Cambridge Street (228 5383/www.
traverse.co.uk). Bus 1, 2, 10, 11, 15,
15A, 16, 17, 23, 24, 27, 34, 35, 45.*
Open 10.30am-midnight Mon-Wed,
Sun; 10.30am-1am Thur-Sat. *Food
served* 10.30am-11pm daily. **Bar**.
Map p138 A2 ㉜
The bar at the Trav gets very busy
pre- and post-performance, especially
during the Fringe. The modern,
roomy establishment is generally
open-plan, but offers a more closed-off
dining space in one corner. It attracts
a typical café-bar crowd. You can pick
up anything from a veggie sausage

Borough p143

sandwich or a haggis baguette for breakfast, through to nachos, Thai fish cakes or a stilton and walnut salad at night. Another bonus is the free wireless internet access, allowing you to check your emails over a smoothie or a good glass of wine.

Two Thin Laddies

103 High Riggs (229 0653). Bus 11, 15, 15A, 16, 17, 23, 45. **Open** 8am-6pm Mon-Fri; 9am-5pm Sat, Sun. **Café**. No credit cards. **Map** p138 A3 ⑬
This friendly café in the heart of Tollcross opens early for those seeking breakfast en route to work, unlike those café-bars that don't emerge blinking into the daylight until 11am or noon. It's bright and wholesome, with a wide-ranging menu featuring bakes, salads and more, plus the enduring legend that is the Two Thin Laddies' macaroni cheese.

Shopping

Armchair Books

72-74 West Port (229 5927/www. mochaholic.org/acb). Bus 2, 35. **Open** 10am-7pm daily. **Map** p138 B3 ㉞
An archetypal second-hand bookshop, with thousands of old volumes stacked precariously on bookshelves in every available little space. Specialising in Victorian, illustrated and antiquarian books, it's a browser's paradise.

Boardwise

4 Lady Lawson Street (229 5887/ www.boardwise.com). Bus 2, 35. **Open** 10am-6pm Mon-Sat. **Map** p138 A3 ㉟
If you're after skateboarding stuff you're better off trying Focus (see p149), but if snowboarding, surfing or windsurfing's your game then you'll find everything you need here, alongside the standard imported skater and surfing clothing labels.

Coco

174 Bruntsfield Place (228 4526/www. cocochocolate.co.uk). Bus 11, 15, 15A, 16, 17, 23, 45. **Open** 10am-6pm Mon-Sat. **Map** p138 A5 ㊱
All of the chocolates produced and sold here are organic and ethically traded, and the helpful staff can describe the whole process from bean to bar. Check online for details of the ever-popular tasting evenings.

Designshop UK

116-120 Causewayside (667 7078/ www.designshopuk.com). Bus 2, 3, 3A, 5, 7, 8, 14, 29, 30, 31, 33, 37, 47, 49. **Open** 10am-6pm Tue-Sat. **Map** p139 E5 ㊲

Focus

Stocking covetable furniture and accessories from world-famous names such as Vitra and Panton, this is the ideal place to come if you're in your early thirties and looking to furnish a loft apartment in a putatively fashionable part of town.

Edinburgh Bike Co-op

8 Alvanley Terrace (228 3565/www. edinburghbicycle.com). Bus 11, 15, 15A, 16, 17, 23, 45. **Open** *Apr-Sept* 10am-7pm Mon-Fri; 10am-6pm Sat, Sun. *Oct-Mar* 10am-6pm Mon-Wed, Fri-Sun; 10am-7pm Thur. **Map** p138 A5 ❸
Scotland's first co-operatively run bike shop, open for almost 30 years, has an extensive selection of bikes, panniers, protective gear and other accessories. The friendly staff are happy to give advice on good local cycling routes.

Farmers' Market

Castle Terrace (557 9201). **Open** 9am-2pm Sat. **Map** p138 A2 ❸
Held weekly at the foot of Edinburgh Castle, this market caters to hungry foodies desperate for local produce. More than 50 specialist stalls sell meat, fish, free-range eggs, cheeses, fruit and veg and all manner of homemade chutneys, breads and chocolates.

Focus

44 West Port, Grassmarket (229 9009/ www.focuspocus.co.uk). Bus 2, 35. **Open** 10am-6pm Mon-Sat; noon-5pm Sun. **Map** p138 B3 ❹
Edinburgh's best skate shop is skater-owned and skater-run and staff know their stuff. Along with boards, Tshirts from the likes of Suburban Bliss and The Hundreds, as well as limited edition NikeSB trainers, make it a fixture with non-skating hipsters.

Freeze

116 Bruntsfield Place (228 2355/www. freeze-scotland.com). Bus 11, 15, 15A, 16, 17, 23, 45. **Open** 10am-6pm Mon-Sat; noon-6pm Sun. **Map** p138 A5 ❹
An extensive range of skiing stuff from salopettes to goggles to good old tube socks. Staff also sell snowboard gear and there's a workshop.

Herman Brown

151 West Port (228 2589). Bus 2, 35. **Open** 12.30-6pm Mon-Sat. **Map** p138 A3 ❹
The vintage clothing and accessories sold at this family-run shop have been carefully selected before being put on sale. There are plenty of classy finds at very good prices, plus a glamorous selection of jewellery.

Cycle city

Don a helmet and head for the hills.

Edinburgh, like Rome, is built on seven hills – so when it comes to gentle leisure cycling, it's not exactly in the class of Amsterdam and Copenhagen.

But it would be wrong to rule out Edinburgh as a cycling city, at least according to the folks at Spokes (3132114/www.spokes. org.uk), a local group that has lobbied since 1977 for better conditions for the area's cyclists. Provision is made for cyclists on the city's major roads, and Edinburgh is also the perfect centre for trips as far afield as St Andrews and the Borders. But those seeking a gentler pace need not be discouraged. Many of the city's former train lines have been turned into cycle paths, forming one of the most extensive off-road networks in the country. Trains, like bikes, don't care too much for hills, which makes for easy and safe cycling over a surprisingly large area.

To the north of the city is the **Water of Leith Walkway** (p109), which leads to the **Scottish National Gallery of Modern Art** (p112) in one direction and the port of Leith in the other. From the same starting point, you can get as far as the seaside at **Cramond** (p47).

On the other side of town, join the Union Canal towpath at Fountainbridge, then rejoin the walkway leading right out to Balerno. On the south side of **Holyrood Park** (p125), the charmingly named Innocent Railway Path will set you en route for Musselburgh. It's a slight misnomer however: make sure you wear a helmet where the paths cross the city's less reputable housing schemes. This affords at least some protection when local urchins engage in their popular 'throw a rock at a cyclist' game. The worst spots are on the cycle path running from Victoria Park to Crewe Toll, parallel with Ferry Road. As long as you avoid the hills and the missiles, bike riding in Edinburgh is a cinch compared to most other capital cities.

Biketrax (7-11 Lochrin Place, South Edinburgh, 228 6633, www.biketrax.co.uk) and Cycle Scotland (29 Blackfriars Street, Old Town, 556 5560, www.cycle scotland.co.uk) offer bike rentals; depending on the bike, expect to pay around £10-£20 a day or £50-£90 a week.

Lupe Pinto's Deli

24 Leven Street (228 6241/www.lupe pintos.com). Bus 11, 15, 15A, 16, 17, 23, 45. **Open** 10am-6pm Mon-Wed, Sat; 10am-7pm Thur, Fri; 12.30-5.30pm Sun. **Map** p138 A4 ⑭

Lupe Pinto's Deli stocks tequila, chillies and just about every other ingredient you might need to create a Mexican feast, along with Caribbean, Spanish and Asian produce.

McAlister Matheson Music

1 Grindlay Street (228 3827/www. mmmusic.co.uk). Bus 1, 2, 10, 11, 15, 15A, 16, 17, 23, 24, 27, 34, 35, 45. **Open** 9.30am-6pm Mon-Thur; 9.30am-6.30pm Fri; 9am-5.30pm Sat. **Map** p138 A3 ⑭

Classical music and opera are the firm focus here, and the shop stays open later when there's a concert on at Usher Hall.

Nippers for Kids

131 Bruntsfield Place (228 5086/www. nippersforkids.com). Bus 11, 15, 15A, 16, 17, 23, 45. **Open** 9.30am-5.30pm Mon-Sat. **Map** p138 A5 ⑮

Almost 20 years ago, Karen Mackay spotted a gap in the children's clothing market. Today, her company produces its own affordable designs, as well as stocking brands such as Uttam and Confetti.

Peter Green

37a-37b Warrender Park Road (229 5925). Bus 5, 24, 41. **Open** 10am-6.30pm Tue-Thur, Sat; 10am-7.30pm Fri. **Map** p138 C5 ⑯

This independent wine merchant in Marchmont also stocks large selections of spirits and beers alongside cases of reds, whites and rosés.

Victor Hugo

29 Melville Terrace (776 1827/www. victorhugodeli.com). Bus 24, 41. **Open** 8am-6pm Mon-Fri; 9am-6pm Sat. **Map** p139 D5 ⑰

A great place to get picnic provisions, this deli stocks produce from around the world: Polish fudge, Scots cheeses and Russian rye bread, for example.

West Port Books

145 West Port (229 4431). Bus 2, 35. **Open** 10am-6pm Mon-Sat. **Map** p138 B3 ⑱

At the time of going to press there was talk of changing the name to Edinburgh Books. Whatever it's called you'll still be able to while away a happy afternoon in this sizeable second-hand book shop, which houses over 25,000 volumes, not to mention a large selection of sheet music.

Wonderland

97 Lothian Road (229 6428/www. wonderlandmodels.com). Bus 1, 2, 10, 11, 15, 15A, 16, 17, 23, 24, 27, 34, 35, 45. **Open** 9.30am-6pm Mon-Fri; 9am-6pm Sat; noon-5pm Sun (Oct-Dec only). **Map p**138 A3 ⑲

Boasting a massive selection of model cars, trains and planes, dinosaurs, monsters and skeletons in all shapes and sizes, plus doll's houses, Scalextric sets and kites, Wonderland should keep the children amused.

Word Power

43 West Nicolson Street (662 9112/ www.word-power.co.uk). Nicolson Street–North Bridge buses. **Open** 10am-6pm Mon-Sat; noon-5pm Sun. **Map** p139 D3 ⑳

This radical bookstore sells titles from new writers and small presses alongside copies of *Stupid White Men* and *The God of Small Things*. Word Power is warmly supported by writers, and the shop hosts an annual Radical Book Fair in October.

Nightlife

Edinburgh Folk Club

60 Pleasance (650 2458/www. edinburghfolkclub.org.uk). Nicolson Street–North Bridge buses. **Gigs** 8pm Wed. **Admission** £6; £5 reductions. No credit cards. **Map** p139 D2 ㉑

The Pleasance's Cabaret Bar hosts the Edinburgh Folk Club's weekly sessions for 11 months in every 12; the exception is during the heady days of August, when the venue becomes subsumed by the Fringe.

Filmhouse

Arts & leisure

Cameo

38 Home Street (information 228 2800/bookings 0871 704 2052/ www.cameocinema.co.uk). Bus 11, 15, 15A, 16, 17, 23, 45. **Map** p138 A4 ⊕
Nestled in Tollcross, this indie cinema is a real treat, picking four films a week from the edges of the mainstream. Chat up the friendly staff at the bar which was totally refurbished in 2005, then take your pint through when the film begins. Sunday's weekly double-bill of classic cinema is just £5.

Edinburgh Festival Theatre

13-29 Nicolson Street (529 6000/ www.eft.co.uk). Nicolson Street–North Bridge buses. **Map** p139 D3 ⊕
The EFT began life as the Empire Palace Theatre, playing host to the biggest old-time variety stars during its early years. By the mid-1980s, it was another story; then the run-down Empire bingo hall, it suffered the indignity of staging shows by the likes of trash-sleaze merchants the Cramps. However, in 1994 major restoration turned the EFT into the most opulent of commercial receiving houses, with one of the biggest dance stages in the UK. Its programme includes a mixture of dance, opera and large-scale theatrical productions, and it's always a major venue for opera and dance during the Edinburgh International Festival.

Filmhouse

88 Lothian Road (information 228 2689/bookings 228 2688/www.film housecinema.com). Bus 1, 2, 10, 11, 15, 15A, 16, 17, 23, 24, 27, 34, 35, 45. **Map** p138 A3 ⊕
A mix of arty new films and classics is screened at the Filmhouse, which supplements its day-to-day programming with a variety of festivals (the annual Dead by Dawn is a gory treat) and extra screenings on Sundays

and Wednesdays organised by the long-running Edinburgh Film Guild (www.edinburghfilmguild.com). On the second Sunday of the month, you can go head-to-head with Edinburgh's cinema-going cognoscenti at the notoriously competitive quiz night. The café/bar serves a range of drinks and home-cooked food.

King's Theatre

2 Leven Street, Tollcross (529 6000/ www.eft.co.uk). Bus 11, 15, 15A, 16, 17, 23, 45. **Map** p138 A4 ⑤⑤
Built in 1905, this elegant old-time institution is managed, along with the Edinburgh Festival Theatre, by the Festival City Theatres Trust. The programme mixes musicals with star-studded serious drama, usually on pre- or post-West End tours. Highlights of recent seasons have included Simon Callow in *Present Laughter* and Penelope Keith starring in *The Importance of Being Earnest*.

Queens Hall

Clerk Street (box office 668 2019/ administration 668 3456/www. thequeenshall.net). Nicolson Street–North Bridge buses. **Map** p139 E4 ⑤⑥
Self-consciously squeezed in among a row of shops, this former church retains a distinctly spiritual vibe, right down to the pews on the ground floor. The venue attracts performers from all genres, and plays host to as many jazz, folk and rock gigs as it has classical recitals. The programmes staged by the Scottish Ensemble and the Paragon Ensemble are always worth a look.

Royal Lyceum

Grindlay Street (information 248 4800/ box office 248 4848/www.lyceum. org.uk). Bus 1, 2, 10, 11, 15, 15A, 16, 17, 23, 24, 27, 34, 35, 45. **Map** p138 A2 ⑤⑦
At its peak in the 1970s, the Lyceum was at the vanguard of a renaissance in local theatre, and a breeding ground for leading directors such as Bill Bryden and Richard Eyre. The intervening decades were less radical but audiences stayed loyal; since 2003,

artistic director David Mark Thomson has built the company into one of the most popular in Scotland. Notable moments include John Clifford's bold translation of Goethe's *Faust* and a pre-*Doctor Who* David Tennant starring in *Look Back in Anger*.

Traverse Theatre

10 Cambridge Street (228 1404/www. traverse.co.uk). Bus 1, 2, 10, 11, 15, 15A, 16, 17, 23, 24, 27, 34, 35, 45. **Map** p139 A2 ⑤⑧
Two performance spaces showcase a lively array of new plays from writers developed by the company – among them David Greig, David Harrower and Douglas Maxwell – as well as a rolling programme of touring shows. In August, it's always one of the hottest spots on the Fringe.

Usher Hall

Lothian Road (box office 228 1155/administration 228 8616/ www.usherhall.co.uk). Bus 1, 2, 10, 11, 15, 15A, 16, 17, 23, 24, 27, 34, 35, 45. **Map** p138 A2 ⑤⑨
At the time of going to press, the hall was closed for yet more refurbishment, due to be completed in August 2008. A great deal of time and money has already been spent returning the Usher Hall to its former glory; from the cosmetic refurbishments to the restoration of the colossal pipe organ. Impressive acoustics mean that the venue, which first opened in 1914, is in constant demand by everyone from the RSNO to bands such as Mogwai or jazz artists such as John Scofield. Most of the major music events at August's Festival take place here.

Zen Lifestyle

9 Bruntsfield Place (477 3535/www. zen-lifestyle.com). Bus 11, 15, 15A, 16, 17, 23, 45. **Open** 8am-10pm Mon-Fri; 9am-5.30pm Sat; 10am-5.30pm Sun. **Map** p138 A4 ⑥⓪
With a whole host of accolades to its name – eight national awards at the last count – this soothing urban retreat offers a comprehensive range of health and beauty treatments.

EDINBURGH BY AREA

Lauriston Castle

West Edinburgh

Aside from a handful of iconic attractions further out – Edinburgh Zoo, Murrayfield Rugby Stadium and Hearts FC – West Edinburgh is not an area that generally detains or diverts visitors to the city. But it's here, way out West, that various layers of Edinburgh's economic history fit together like some topological puzzle, just as a few old buildings hidden away in residential warrens hint at a less urban past. The most surprising feature may well be the Union Canal, its terminus tucked discreetly away just off Lothian Road. Well, that and the penguins…

Before railways made their impact on the city, the last word in 19th-century transport was the Union Canal. Built by Irish navvies and French stonemasons in 1822, it ran all the way from Lothian Road to Camelon, near Falkirk, linking with the Forth & Clyde Canal that ran on to Glasgow. Coal, building materials and passengers came in to Edinburgh; merchants' goods, horse manure and more passengers went out. Nowadays the canal towpath is popular with walkers, joggers and cyclists, and will take you from Lochrin Basin right through the city, out into West Lothian and beyond.

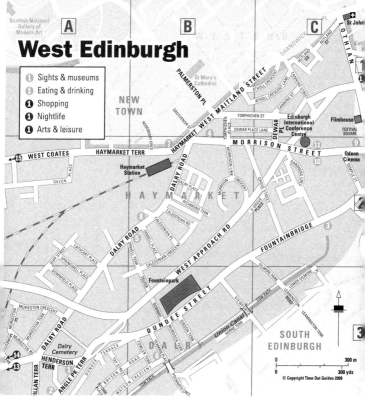

West Edinburgh

- ❶ Sights & museums
- ❶ Eating & drinking
- ❶ Shopping
- ❶ Nightlife
- ❶ Arts & leisure

Edinburgh Zoo is principally a family-orientated attraction, albeit one that puts an increasing emphasis on conservation. If the rest of the city seems a little too much like an audio-guided history lesson, you'll find the zoo's a great place for kids to let off steam. What's more, the penguin parade is one of the most bizarre and hilarious sights in the city no matter how old you are – check with staff for times.

The grounds of Lauriston Castle are also a good choice for a picnic and a day away from the city's bustle, though the 16th-century neo-Jacobean fortified property, its Edwardian interiors crammed full of perfectly preserved antiques, isn't quite so suitable for charging around in, not least because the house can only be viewed on a tour.

Eating & drinking

Athletic Arms

1-3 Angle Park Terrace (337 3822/ www.theathleticarms.co.uk). Bus 2, 3, 3A, 4, 25, 33, 44, 44A. **Open** noon-1am daily. *Food served* noon-5pm daily. **Pub**. **Map** p155 A3 ❶

Santini p159

Before today's style bars, Edinburgh had a few 'classic' pubs. Some of them were Victorian and ornate, while other places traded on a different reputation; the Athletic Arms was famous for serving the best pint of McEwan's 80/- in town. Some things remain unchanged; the beer here is still decent, and most locals still call the place the Diggers, after the gravediggers from the nearby cemetery who used to drink here.

Caley Sample Room

58 Angle Park Terrace (337 7204). Bus 2, 3, 3A, 4, 25, 33, 44, 44A. **Open** noon-midnight Mon-Thur; noon-1am Fri; 10am-1am Sat; 10am-11pm Sun. *Food served* noon-9pm Mon-Fri; 10am-10pm Sat; 10am-9pm Sun. **Pub.** Map p155 A3 ②

The Caley is red brick on the outside and roomy on the inside, with wooden benches and simple, functional decor. With good cask ales on offer, it invariably gets packed out before Hearts games at nearby Tynecastle.

Cargo

Edinburgh Quay, 129 Fountainbridge (659 7880/www.cargobar.co.uk). Bus 1, 34, 35. **Open** 11am-1am daily. *Food served* noon-10pm daily. **Bar.** Map p155 C2 ③

Cargo could be viewed as a cavernous 'retail leisure experience', catering to the outspill from the financial services sector offices nearby. But since opening in 2004, it's offered reasonable food and the chance to sit outside by the terminus of the Union Canal, all as part of an award-winning urban regeneration scheme. Busy, but nicely placed.

Chop Chop

248 Morrison Street (221 1155). Bus 2, 22, 30. **Open** 11.30am-2.30pm, 5.30-10.30pm Tue-Fri, Sun; 5-10.30pm Sat. **£. Chinese.** Map p155 B1 ④

This sparse room certainly isn't a romantic venue – or, indeed, an eaterie where you might linger at all – but it is a fixture on many a local foodie's list of places to get a quick bite to eat, with a secret weapon in the form of the excellent boiled or fried dumplings. It's a rewarding pit-stop on anyone's night out and perfect for larger groups, who can share a selection.

First Coast

99-101 Dalry Road (313 4404/ www.first-coast.co.uk). Bus 2, 3, 3A, 4, 25, 33, 44, 44A. **Open** noon-2pm, 5-10.30pm Mon-Sat. **££. Bistro.** Map p155 B2 ⑤

The MacRae brothers, who hail from the Isle of Skye, opened this Dalry Road bistro in 2003. Decor-wise, it's all done out in white and light blue, with touches of bare stone and dark wood. The food, like the general atmosphere, is approachable (haricot bean stew with chorizo, black pudding and pork belly, for example, plus truly excellent mash). Affordable wines add to the appeal.

Golden Rule

28-30 Yeaman Place (622 7112). Bus 22, 30. **Open** noon-midnight Mon-Sat; noon-11pm Sun. **Pub.** Map p155 B3 ⑥

Lochrin Basin p154

Edinburgh Zoo p155

The Golden Rule is a fine old-fashioned pub with a selection of cask ales, plus a more contemporary lounge bar downstairs with a glowing reputation for its excellent jukebox. The western tenemental suburbs of the city tend to be a bit of a desert when it comes to somewhere decent to have a pint, so this one stands out all the more.

La Bruschetta

13 Clifton Terrace (467 7464/www. labruschetta.co.uk). Bus 2, 3, 3A, 4, 12, 25, 26, 31, 33, 38, 44, 44A. **Open** noon-2pm, 6-10.30pm Tue-Sat. **£**. **Italian**. Map p155 B2 ⑦
There's nothing very elaborate about La Bruschetta; it's just a fabulous little Italian restaurant. The interior is neat and modern, but the focus is very much on owner Giovanni Cariello's food: familiar Italian dishes such as insalata caprese, spaghetti carbonara and risotto al frutti di mare. No surprises, then, but it is a joy to see this kind of thing done with such skill.

La Partenope

96 Dalry Road (347 8880). Bus 2, 3, 3A, 4, 25, 33, 44, 44A. **Open** 5-10.45pm Mon, Sun; noon-2pm, 5-10.45pm Tue-Fri; noon-10.45pm Sat. **££**. **Italian**. Map p155 B2 ⑧
Unlike some other Italian spots in town, Rosario Sartore's traditional Neopolitan restaurant has great specials, with seafood very much at the forefront of the menu. There are some interesting wines from southern Italy, waiters are upbeat and chatty, and decor-wise it looks just like an Italian restaurant should. The name relates to one of the sirens who killed herself after failing to cop off with Ulysses; Naples was built on the spot where her body washed up.

Rainbow Arch

8-16a Morrison Street (221 1288). Bus 2, 22, 30. **Open** noon-11.30pm daily. **£**. **Chinese**. Map p155 C2 ⑨
Rainbow Arch has the look and atmosphere of a traditional Chinese restaurant (as invented for westerners).

There are authentic Cantonese dishes, though, and the Chinese clientele bodes well for the quality of the food. The waitresses are friendly, the dim sum is great, and on most nights it stays open long past its advertised closing time, making it the place to go for a late prawn dumpling or two.

Roti

73 Morrison Street (221 9998/ www.roti.uk.com). Bus 2, 3, 3A, 4, 25, 33, 44, 44A. **Open** noon-2.30pm, 7-10.30pm Tue-Fri; 7-10.30pm Sat. **££. Indian. Map** p155 C2 ⓾
The brainchild of Tony Singh at Oloroso, Roti opened in 2005 but proved such a success that it moved to this larger space in 2007. The Indian-influenced menu goes way beyond curry clichés – beef vindaloo is marinated for 24 hours then braised for eight, or try duck breast with marrow and ginger. The alternative tiffin menu offers a tapas-like taste of various dishes, in the restaurant or bar.

Santini

8 Conference Square, Western Approach Road (221 7788). Bus 2, 3, 3A, 4, 25, 33, 44, 44A. **Open** noon-2pm, 6-10pm Mon-Fri; 6-10pm Sat. **££. Italian. Map** p155 C2 ⓫
Previously Santini and Santini Bis, a restaurant and bistro respectively. The two were combined in summer 2007 and occupy the ground floor of the One Spa building, behind the Sheraton Grand hotel. The food is an amalgamation of the two restaurants' menus – so expect anything from well-made pizza and pasta to baby chicken with polenta and parmesan. Contemporary, sharp and not for scruffs. There are branches in London and Milan.

Shopping

Paper Tiger

53 Lothian Road (228 2790/www. papertiger.ltd.uk). Bus 1, 2, 10, 11, 15, 15A, 16, 17, 23, 24, 27, 34, 35, 45. **Open** 9.30am-6pm Mon-Wed, Fri, Sat; 9.30am-7pm Thur; 11am-5pm Sun. **Map** p155 C1 ⓬

Uni verses

Visually speaking, and in terms of atmosphere, Napier University in the south-west of the city couldn't be further away from the battlefields of Flanders, but what went on here for a few months in 1917 did much to create the lines of poetry that were to shape later thinking about the conflict.

The premises were requisitioned by the British Army for use as a hospital, specifically for officers suffering from 'neurasthenia' or shellshock, and it was here that Siegfried Sassoon and Wilfred Owen met, and immediately hit it off.

Sassoon contributed one of his own most celebrated poems, 'The Dreamers', to *Hydra*, the hospital magazine that Owen edited. Owen, for his part, was inspired to write such pieces as 'Dulce et Decorum Est' and 'Anthem for Doomed Youth'. Their time at the hospital is explored in Pat Barker's critically acclaimed novel *Regeneration*.

The building where Sassoon and Owen spent their time together now houses Napier University's Business School; within it, the Craiglockhart Campus Library is home to the War Poets Collection (219 Colinton Road, 455 6021, www.napier.ac.uk). The permanent exhibition contains material on the Great War, concentrating on the poets, patients and staff at Craiglockhart during those years. It's open to all, and admission is free.

A friendly shop with another branch in New Town that is a good source of innovative stationery and wrapping paper and also stocks a large selection of interesting greetings cards. It also sells Freitag bags too.

Arts and leisure

Gorgie City Farm
Gorgie Road (337 4202). Bus 1, 2, 3, 21, 25, 33, 34, 38. **Open** *Mar-Oct* 9.30am-4.30pm daily. *Nov-Feb* 9.30am-4pm daily. **Admission** free; donations welcome. **Map** p155 A3 ⑬
This lovely, informal spot has the usual farmyard favourites: pigs, ducks and naughty little shetland ponies. plus a pet lodge (housing guinea pigs, rabbits, fish, tortoises and the like), a playground and a good café with highchairs.

Heart of Midlothian FC
Tynecastle Stadium, McLeod Street (0870 787 1874/www.heartsfc.co.uk). Bus 1, 2, 3, 3A, 4, 22, 25, 30, 33, 44, 44A. **Open** *Match days* 9.30am-3pm; *Shop* 9.30am-5.30pm Mon-Fri. *Tickets* £6-£35. **Map** p155 A3 ⑭

Hearts have been operating at close to capacity since their upturn in fortune in 2005, so getting tickets on match days might prove tricky. Book ahead, particularly for games against Celtic, Rangers and Hibs. European ties are played at Murrayfield.

Murrayfield Stadium
110 Roseburn Street (346 5000/tours 346 5100/www.scottishrugby.org). Bus 16, 26, 31. **Open** *Shop* 9am-5pm Mon-Sat; closed Sun; *Turnstiles* 2hrs before KO on match days. **Tickets** £10-£60. *Tours* £6; £3.50 reductions. **Map** p155 A2 ⑮
Scotland's most famous rugby venue still draws sell-out crowds – if you want to see any high-profile games try and buy tickets well ahead. Or if you're not fussed about big name clubs or internationals, a good option is going to see local clubs, like the Edinburgh Gunners, for which booking isn't necessary. Another option, assuming there's no big match that week, is a stadium tour. These are offered at 11am and 2.30pm from Monday to Friday and need to be booked two days in advance.

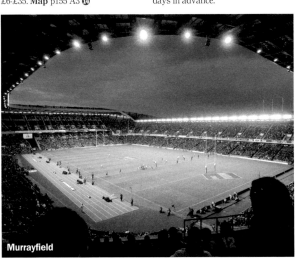

Murrayfield

EDINBURGH BY AREA

Glasgow

The rain falls on Glasgow two days out of three, the clouds rolling in from the low-pressure systems of the North Atlantic to hang over the Clyde valley. But Glasgow remains undaunted. The town – or 'toon', as the locals have it – has absorbed every shock and adapted to every change without breaking stride. If plagues, fires, cholera epidemics, the boom and bust of colonial trade and the collapse of local industry haven't spoiled the general mood, then a few drops of water will never bring it down.

The wealth generated by the town's once-dominant place in the world of trade and commerce transformed the semi-rural medieval city into one of the most elegant urban centres in Scotland. It's a small but perfectly formed arrangement of decorative stone canyons: laid out in an easily negotiable grid akin to that found in a modern American city, but definitively Victorian.

The heart of Glasgow is George Square, a former swamp first laid out in the late 18th century; it's benefited handsomely from a recent renovation and is now back to something like its best. The square's centrepiece is a soaring statue of Sir Walter Scott, not as grand as the tribute paid to him in Edinburgh's Princes Street Gardens but impressive all the same. Robert Burns, William Gladstone and Queen Victoria are commemorated in other statues around the square. The most notable building is the magnificent City Chambers to the east; opened by Queen Victoria in 1888, it's a potent reminder of

Botanic Gardens & Kibble Palace

Glasgow's former importance in the British Empire. The square hosts a year-round programme of public events, including the city's wildly rowdy Hogmanay celebrations.

Sights & museums

Botanic Gardens & Kibble Palace

730 Great Western Road (0141 276 1614/www.glasgow.gov.uk). Hillhead underground. **Open** *Palace* Apr-Oct 10am-6pm daily. Nov-Mar 10am-4.15pm daily. *Gardens* 7am-dusk daily. **Admission** free.

Glasgow's Botanic Gardens are dominated by the huge dome of Kibble Palace, a marvel of Victorian engineering that is currently being restored to its original glory. Look out, too, for the abandoned railway station, the extensive herb garden and, in summer, the gardens host Bard in the Botanics: an open-air Shakespeare performance festival.

Burrell Collection

Pollok Park, 2060 Pollokshaws Road (0141 287 2550/www.glasgow museums.com). Pollokshaws West rail, then 10min walk. **Open** 10am-5pm Mon-Thur, Sat; 11am-5pm Fri, Sun. **Admission** free.

When Sir William Burrell gave his prodigious collection of art and artefacts to the city of Glasgow in 1944, he stipulated that it must be kept at least 16 miles from the city centre to avoid it being covered in soot. Thankfully, Glasgow's air has improved since he died, and his estate agreed to it being exhibited fairly nearby in Pollok Park. The collection encompasses treasures from ancient Egypt, Greece and Rome, ceramics from various Chinese dynasties, and an assortment of European decorative arts, including rare tapestries and stained glass. It also boasts one of the finest collections of Impressionist and post-Impressionist paintings and drawings in the world. Try to come on a sunny day, when the reflected light in the interior glass-roofed courtyard is breathtaking.

Centre for Contemporary Arts (CCA)

350 Sauchiehall Street (0141 352 4900/www.cca-glasgow.com). Cowcaddens underground. **Open** *Centre* 11am-11pm Tue-Thur; 11am-midnight Fri, Sat. *Gallery* 11am-6pm Tue-Sat. **Admission** *Centre* free. *Gallery* prices vary.

Threatened with closure after recent financial problems, a chastened Centre for Contemporary Arts is quietly regaining its strength under its new administrators, the Scottish Arts Council. Part of the CCA's problem – and, simultaneously, the reason it's so essential – is that it has always spurned the populism of GOMA (see below) for more challenging work, in terms both of its exhibition programme and its choice of films. The imposing courtyard café, though known locally as 'the prison', is actually a quietly convivial spot, even

on a Saturday night; a raucous upstairs bar hosts DJs throughout the week.

Clydebuilt Maritime Museum

King's Inch Road, Braehead (0141 886 1013/www.scottishmaritimemuseum. org). Bus 23, 101. **Open** 10am-5.30pm Mon-Sat; 11am-5pm Sun. **Admission** £4.25; £2.50-£3 reductions.

One of the Scottish Maritime Museum's three sites (the others are at Dumbarton and Irvine), Clydebuilt tells the worthwhile, intertwined story of Glasgow and the Clyde, from trading to shipbuilding. Double the fun by taking the Clyde Waterbus from the city centre.

Gallery of Modern Art (GOMA)

Queen Street (0141 229 1996/ www.glasgowmuseums.com). Buchanan Street underground/Queen Street rail. **Open** 10am-5pm Mon-Wed, Sat; 10am-8pm Thur; 11am-5pm Fri, Sun. **Admission** free.

Burrell Collection

www.treesforcities.org
Trees for Cities
Charity registration number 1032154
Travelling creates so many lasting memories.
Make your trip mean something for years to come - not just for you but for the environment and for people living in deprived urban areas.
Anyone can offset their flights, but when you plant trees with Trees for Cities, you'll help create a green space for an urban community that really needs it.
To find out more visit www.treesforcities.org
Leave Your Mark
Create a green future for cities.

The traffic cone almost permanently attached to the equestrian statue of the Duke of Wellington gives a neat Glaswegian touch to the classical grandeur of GOMA. Since it was built in 1778, the Cunningham Mansion has been used as a townhouse for a local tobacco baron and offices for the Royal Bank of Scotland. Today, it's the second most visited contemporary art gallery in the UK outside London. The permanent collection contains significant works by Euan Uglow, Grayson Perry and Douglas Gordon; it's supplemented by a programme of first-class touring shows.

Glasgow Science Centre

50 Pacific Quay (0871 540 1000/ www.glasgowsciencecentre.org). Exhibition Centre rail. **Open** *Science Mall* 10am-5pm Tue-Sun. *IMAX film times vary.* **Admission** *Science Mall or IMAX £7.95; £5.95 reductions.*
This futuristic titanium and glass structure boasts three riotously stimulating floors of hands-on science and technology exhibits as part of the Science Mall. Since opening in 2001, it's become deservedly popular with kids and armchair scientists for its well-run displays and planetarium. The centre also houses an IMAX cinema. The Glasgow Tower, which rotates 360 degrees to reduce wind resistance, would give spectacular views over the city if it ever worked properly.

Hunterian Museum & Art Gallery

University of Glasgow, Hillhead Street (museum 0141 330 4221/ gallery 0141 330 5434/www.hunterian .gla.ac.uk). Hillhead underground. **Open** *Museum & Art Gallery* 9.30am-5pm Mon-Sat. *Mackintosh House* 9am-5pm Mon-Sat. **Admission** free. *Mackintosh House £3; free-£2 reductions (free after 2pm Wed).*
The Hunterian is divided into two distinct but equally fascinating parts. The museum, found amid the Gothic grandeur of the Gilbert Scott building, features dinosaurs, archaeological finds and an engaging hands-on display of Glasgow scientist Lord Kelvin's inventions and experiments. The art gallery across the road houses Scotland's largest print collection and a fine collection of paintings, including a room devoted to Whistler. The gallery leads on to the Mackintosh House; this recreates the architect's home in Southpark Avenue, where he lived from 1906 to 1914.

Kelvingrove Art Gallery & Museum

Argyle Street (0141 276 9599/ www.glasgowmuseums.com). Kelvinhall underground/Partick rail. **Open** 10am-5pm Mon-Thur, Sat; 11am-5pm Fri, Sun. **Admission** free.
Reopened in July 2006 after a massive refurbishment, the Kelvingrove is now Glasgow's must-see museum. Cleaned of a century of grime, the impressive atrium sparkles in the light that floods in through the windows. The ground-floor exhibitions cover every subject under the sun, from architecture to war; on the first floor, masterpieces by Dali, Rembrandt, Van Gogh and Botticelli add up to an embarrassment of riches.

Lighthouse

11 Mitchell Lane (0141 221 6362/www.thelighthouse.co.uk). Buchanan Street or St Enoch underground/Central Station rail. **Open** 10.30am-5pm Mon, Wed-Sat; 11am-5pm Tue; noon-5pm Sun. **Admission** £3; £1.50 reductions.
Tucked away down an alleyway off Buchanan Street, Mackintosh's Glasgow Herald building is now the hypermodern Centre for Architecture, Design & the City, and was central to Glasgow becoming UK City of Architecture and Design in 1999. Several years on, its evolving programme of exhibitions and events continues to make it an exciting part of Glasgow's cultural scene. The well-contextualised Mackintosh Interpretation Centre leads to a daunting helical staircase that offers those fit enough to climb it stunning views over the whole city.

Museum of Transport

1 Bunhouse Road, Kelvinhall (0141 287 2720/www.glasgowmuseums.com). Kelvinhall underground/Partick rail. **Open** 10am-5pm Mon-Thur, Sat; 11am-5pm Fri, Sun. **Admission** free.

The Clyde Room, where Glasgow's shipbuilding industry is celebrated and mourned, helps to make this one of Britain's more engaging transport museums. Every possible mode of transport is represented, but the highlight is the recreation of a fictional 1930s shopping street, complete with underground station and operational cinema.

People's Palace/ Winter Gardens

Glasgow Green (0141 271 2962/ www.glasgowmuseums.com). Bridgeton rail. **Open** 10am-5pm Mon-Thur, Sat; 11am-5pm Fri, Sun. **Admission** free.

Built in 1898, The red sandstone People's Palace originally served as a municipal and cultural centre for the city's working classes. It now houses a much-cherished exhibition that covers all aspects of Glaswegian life, but pays particular attention to the city's social and industrial history. The adjoining Winter Gardens is one of the most elegant Victorian glasshouses in Scotland. Just outside the People's Palace is the Doulton Fountain; built to celebrate

Queen Victoria's rule over the Commonwealth, it's the largest terracotta fountain in the world.

Pollok House

Pollok Park, 2060 Pollokshaws Road (0141 616 6410/www.nts.org.uk). Pollokshaws West rail, then 10min walk. **Open** 10am-5pm daily. **Admission** free-£8; free-£5 reductions.

This magnificent 18th-century mansion displays the Stirling Maxwell collection of Spanish and European paintings, including beautiful works by Goya, El Greco and Murillo. The highlight is William Blake's tempera painting of Chaucer's Canterbury pilgrims.

Scottish Football Museum

National Stadium, Hampden Park (0141 616 6139/www.scottish footballmuseum.org.uk). King's Park or Mount Florida rail. **Open** 10am-5pm Mon-Sat; 11am-5pm Sun. **Admission** *Museum* £6; free-£3 reductions. *Stadium tour* £6; free-£3 reductions.

This display of Scottish football history is comprehensive to the point of obsession, documenting all the players, kits and trophies since 1867. Pride of place is given to a life-size model of Archie Gemmill scoring his famous goal against Holland in the 1978 World Cup in Argentina.

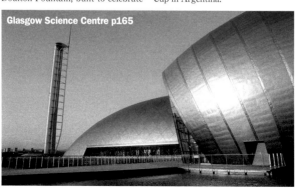

Glasgow Science Centre p165

Essentials

PRESTONFIELD

"So extravagant it's like walking onto the set of some
flamboyant costume drama."
Condé Nast Traveller

www.prestonfield.com